Deregulation, Innovation and Market Liberalization

Over the past 50 years the U.S. economy has experienced economic dynamism and technological change at a dizzying pace, driven substantially by innovation in digital communication technology. This dynamism has had limited effects in the electricity industry, and institutional change within the industry to adapt to these changes has been variable. Many states in the U.S. do not participate in open wholesale markets, and even more states have either no retail markets or have implemented such a restricted and politicized version of retail markets that potential retail market entrants still face substantial entry barriers. This book explores institutional design and regulatory policies in the U.S. electricity industry that can adapt to unknown and changing conditions produced by economic, social, and technological change.

Whereas the dominant regulatory paradigm has traditionally been centralized economic and physical control based on natural monopoly theory and power systems engineering, the ideas presented and synthesized by Kiesling compose a different paradigm – decentralized economic and physical coordination through contracts, transactions, price signals, and integrated intertemporal wholesale and retail markets. Digital communication technology, and its increasing pervasiveness and affordability, make this decentralized coordination possible. Kiesling argues that with decentralized coordination, distributed agents themselves control part of the system, and in aggregate their actions produce order. Technology makes this order feasible, but the institutions, the rules governing the interaction of agents in the system, contribute substantially to whether or not order can emerge from this decentralized coordination process.

This book will be of interest to students and researchers engaged with electricity regulation and deregulation in the U.S., as well as institutional economics and technological change in industry.

L. Lynne Kiesling is Senior Lecturer at the Department of Economics and Kellogg School of Management at Northwestern University.

Routledge studies in business organizations and networks

Deregulation, Innovation and Market Liberalization

Electricity regulation in a continually evolving environment

L. Lynne Kiesling

Routledge
Taylor & Francis Group

LONDON AND NEW YORK

First published 2009
by Routledge
2 Park Square, Milton Park, Abingdon, Oxon OX14 4RN

Simultaneously published in the USA and Canada
by Routledge
270 Madison Ave, New York, NY 10016

Routledge is an imprint of the Taylor & Francis Group, an informa business

© 2009 L. Lynne Kiesling

Typeset in Times by Wearset Ltd, Boldon, Tyne and Wear
Printed and bound in Great Britain by TJI Digital, Padstow, Cornwall

British Library Cataloguing in Publication Data
A catalogue record for this book is available from the British Library

Library of Congress Cataloging in Publication Data
A catalog record for this book has been requested

ISBN10: 0-415-77282-6 (hbk)
ISBN10: 0-203-89285-2 (ebk)

ISBN13: 978-0-415-77282-2 (hbk)
ISBN13: 978-0-203-89285-5 (ebk)

Contents

Acknowledgments

My gratitude is necessarily extensive, as many people have given of their time, money, and effort to make this project a reality. I have received constant support for my research activities from Northwestern University and the Economics Department, and financial support for this research from the International Foundation for Research in Experimental Economics and the Searle Fund for Policy Research at Northwestern University. In particular, the Searle Fund provided the resources that enabled me to take a research sabbatical to work on this book.

I am exceedingly grateful to my many colleagues, collaborators, and friends who have contributed to this project in various ways, from reading half-baked drafts of chapters to making me laugh when I needed to. The genesis of this book was a lunch with Deirdre McCloskey, during which she urged me to write it, and I appreciate her encouragement.

Among my colleagues and collaborators, I would particularly like to thank Jason Black, Federico Boffa, David Chassin, Jerry Ellig, Michael Giberson, Ray Gifford, Jean-Michel Glachant, Shane Greenstein, David Haddock, Dale Hatfield, P.J. Hill, Ben Hobbs, Steven Horwitz, Marija Ilic, Céline Jullien, Andrew Kleit, John Panzar, Mark Pennington, Rob Pratt, Evens Salies, Richard Sandor, Doug Sicker, Vernon Smith, Anthony Star, Carine Staropoli, Scott Stern, Kathy Tholin, Phil Weiser, Dean Williamson, Bart Wilson, Martin Zelder, and David Zetland for sharing their ideas with me and considering mine, and for helping me to refine the ideas that form this work. In particular, I thank the organizers of and participants in the "New Directions in the Study of Emergent and Spontaneous Orders" conference, sponsored by the Atlas Economic Research Foundation, in October 2007.

Part of my objective is to formulate a set of ideas for thinking differently about the problems of regulation in the presence of pervasive technological change, not in an "ivory tower" sense, but in a way that is informed deeply by real-world institutions and technologies. Doing that well requires asking a lot of questions and talking to a lot of regulators, regulatory staffers, and industry professionals, all of whom have been extremely patient and generous with me. In the regulatory community, I am especially grateful to Parviz Adib, Frank Bodine, Nora Mead Brownell, Bob Lieberman, Diane Munns, Dick O'Neill, Ken Schisler, Eric Schubert, Barry Smitherman, and Charlie Whitmore for sharing their insights and experiences with me. Industry experts who have helped me understand the regulated electricity industry and the entrepreneurial potential of new technology include Guy Braden, Tom Casten, Carrie Cullen-Hitt, Ahmad Faruqui, Roger Gale, Steve Hauser, John Howe, Ed Reid, Jeff Roark, Vicki Sandler, Dan Sharplin, and Jim Steffes. I am particularly indebted to Toby Considine, Ed Reid, Jeff Roark, and Charlie Whitmore for reading draft versions of several of the chapters.

I owe a special debt of gratitude to Stephen Littlechild and Pat Wood III, both for being extraordinarily generous in sharing their ideas and experiences with me and for providing evidence that forward-looking economic ideas and leadership can change regulatory policy. Before them, I did not believe it was possible to achieve what they have achieved. Their work has truly changed my thinking about electricity regulation.

These ideas have developed in conjunction with my service on the GridWise Architecture Council, which has informed my thinking substantially on the potential value of digital technology in the electric power network. I am grateful to all of my colleagues and fellow council members past and present, particularly Erich Gunther and Mia Paget, for their intellectual stimulation and cameraderie. I am especially grateful to Alison Silverstein for providing a role model for having the courage of my convictions.

A work like this is difficult without research assistants, and I have had several who have contributed substantially to this project in a variety of ways: Matthew Berland, Jose Guillermo Diaz, Kristle Kilijanczyk, Eric Leslie, Kristen Ounanian, Zahra Siddique, and Josh Unterman.

My friends have been very patient and supportive, particularly Peter Delmenico, Amy Derksen, Sharon Dudley, Nancy Lutz, Diane Owen, David Short, and Samantha Zyontz. I owe Samantha particular gratitude for her willingness to read chapter drafts and to indulge me in long brainstorming sessions. I am grateful to Stewart, Giovanni, Eugenio, Kellie, Nancy, Kim, Meg, and Michelle for bringing rhythm back into my life. Without all of this friendship this project would never actually have happened.

Beyond everyone else, I am grateful to my husband, Matthew Coffey, for his patience, understanding, humor, and emotional and intellectual support as I worked through the ideas contained here. Whether explaining Maxwell's equations and reactive power to me over a bottle of wine or bucking up my spirits when the project felt more like an albatross and less like a labor of love, his encouragement has been unwavering.

Another person who deserves special recognition is my father, David Kiesling, who passed away in September 2006, just as I was beginning the actual writing of this book. In addition to being my father he was a close friend and intellectual companion, who encouraged me ceaselessly in my intellectual pursuits and curiosity throughout his life. He kept up with energy news and always wanted to read and discuss what I wrote, either in formal articles or online at Knowledge Problem. Although he did not live to read this actual work, his spirit spurred me on in my work; I am sure he is happy that I discussed both Adam Smith and Frances Hutcheson in a book about twenty-first-century electricity policy.

1 Introduction

Introduction

This book addresses two interrelated topics – the electricity industry in the United States and institutional design. The investor-owned electricity industry is a $245 billion/year industry; it pervades our daily lives and makes our work, our leisure, and our standards of living possible. Few in the U.S. can imagine or desire a life without electricity.

The private firms in this industry have been regulated almost since the industry's inception. Intended to stand in for rivalrous competition in an industry with natural monopoly characteristics and to provide a more stable investment environment for firms, regulatory institutions have focused on cost recovery, *ex post* rate determination, and regulatory approval of "prudent" investments. These institutions have provided firms with a range of economic incentives, some of them perverse, but they have contributed to the vast electrification achieved in the twentieth century and the remarkable economic growth and increased living standards achieved during that time.

What these institutions do not do, though, is adapt well to unknown and changing conditions. Over the past 50 years we have experienced economic dynamism and technological change at a dizzying pace, driven largely by innovation in digital communication technology. The major institutional adaptations that have occurred in electricity regulation – federal legislative and regulatory changes to remove entry barriers to wholesale power markets – were prompted by innovations in electricity generation technology and transformed the industry, unleashing further economic value creation and institutional change. This institutional change is incomplete and ongoing, though. Many states in the U.S. do not participate in open wholesale markets, and even more states have either no retail markets or have implemented such a restricted and politicized version of retail markets that potential entrants still face substantial entry barriers. The California electricity crisis of 2000–2001 (Sweeney 2002) and the Enron scandal (McLean and Elkind 2003) reinforced the idea that institutional change in this industry is risky and fraught with danger. In many ways we have been in limbo ever since.

This limbo has substantial opportunity costs. By not reducing retail and wholesale market entry barriers, and by not rethinking regulatory institutions to enable them to adapt to technological change and not serve as a barrier to its deployment, we forego the benefits of retail choice, of competition, and of innovation. Even in a network infrastructure industry these foregone benefits can be sizeable, but the problem is that they occur in the future; they are benefits we will fail to create.[1] Thus they will take forms that are currently unknown; in the language of Bastiat's "What Is Seen And What Is Not Seen" (1848), future benefits from a change are unseen, while current benefits of the status quo are seen.

> In the economic sphere an act, a habit, an institution, a law produces not only one effect, but a series of effects. Of these effects, the first alone is immediate; it appears simultaneously with its cause; *it is seen*. The other effects emerge only subsequently; *they are not seen*; we are fortunate if we *foresee* them.

These unseen benefits are often less salient than the current benefits of the status quo, especially in an industry that is as heavily politicized as this one. Those who argue for the importance of those unseen benefits usually cannot specify the form or the magnitude of the benefits, so inertia and status quo institutions are more likely to persist, even when they are ill-suited to a new environment brought about by innovation and economic dynamism.

This book is a contribution to helping overcome this inertia by laying out and applying a set of ideas in economics and complexity science that are not typically applied to the analysis of electricity regulatory policy. These ideas – from new institutional economics, Austrian economics, and complexity science – come together to form an argument for thinking differently about the problems associated with electricity policy in the context of rapid and pervasive economic and technological change.

For the past century the dominant paradigm has been centralized economic and physical control based on natural monopoly theory and power systems engineering. The ideas presented and synthesized here compose a different paradigm – decentralized economic and physical coordination through contracts, transactions, price signals, and integrated intertemporal wholesale and retail markets. Digital communication technology, and its increasing pervasiveness and affordability, make this decentralized coordination possible. This decentralized coordination differs from the "distributed control" concept that power systems engineers often invoke; distributed control in that context means using distributed technology to enhance centralized control of a system. *Decentralized coordination* is a paradigm in which distributed agents themselves control part of the system, and in aggregate their actions produce order: emergent order.[2] Technology makes this order feasible, but the institutions, the rules governing the interaction of agents in the system, contribute substantially to whether or not order can emerge from this decentralized coordination process.

That is the sense in which this book is about institutional design. Given that digital technology is increasingly making decentralized coordination possible and possibly value-creating, what institutions are consistent with allowing that process to happen and with increasing the likelihood that decentralized coordination will result in emergent order? In many ways the existing regulatory institutions are not compatible with this decentralized coordination paradigm, and indeed stifle decentralized coordination, either intentionally or inadvertently. Yet technological change continues, reinforcing the mismatch between the possible value creation that innovation reveals and the actual value that will exist if institutions cannot adapt to technological change. This potential value is again Bastiat's unseen. One goal of this work is to make this unseen value more visible, and to do so in the context of institutional designs that are more likely to enable that value creation to occur.

Context and motivation

Regulatory policy is a function of the underlying cost structure in the industry and the physics of alternating current (AC) power flow. The physical supply chain in electricity has three parts: generation, transmission, and distribution. Generation generally involves using a fuel (or the potential energy stored behind a dam) to drive a turbine that generates electric power.[3] Transmission and distribution wires transport that power from the generator to end-use customers. For both engineering and economic purposes, transmission and distribution are the same, except that transmission occurs over longer distances and therefore requires higher voltage capability. The economic supply chain in electricity focuses more on the transactions among the different steps in the supply chain, and thus adds a retail component to the physical description of the supply chain.

The challenge in a complex system like electricity is coordinating the physical and economic requirements of the system (Outhred 2003). Physical and economic requirements must coordinate, but the need for centralized dispatch with regulatory oversight does not necessitate centralized market design with regulatory oversight.

The year 2007 marked the anniversary of a century of formal state-level economic regulation of the electricity industry in the United States. Since the inception of the electricity industry in the 1880s, regulation has been an important determinant of outcomes for both producers and consumers. Initially the concern was twofold: ensuring the safety of electricity delivery to customers and managing or reducing the tangled web of wires strung across urban streets by multiple competitors. By the early 1900s economic regulation was a formal part of the institutional environment, with the establishment of state regulatory commissions starting in 1907.

Despite some adaptive changes over the past decade (such as incentive regulation or performance-based ratemaking, to provide firms with incentives to reduce their costs), the regulatory institutions governing the electric industry remain the institutions that were devised in the early twentieth century to facilitate electrification and to prevent the exercise of market power by a vertically-integrated monopolist. Grounded in neoclassical natural monopoly theory, these institutions embody four principal components: control of entry, price fixing, prescription of quality and conditions of service, and the imposition of an obligation to serve (Kahn 1988, vol. I, p. 3). The hallmarks of such regulation continue to be price determination based on historic cost recovery, an obligation for the regulated firm to serve all customers who request service, and a legal entry barrier that excludes potential competitors from offering some or all of the services in the regulated firm's value chain.

The U.S. economy and society have grown and changed far beyond the imaginations of the Progressive reformers in 1907, yet the electricity industry and its regulatory institutions have not grown and changed apace. Furthermore, the electric industry is one of the most technologically backward industries in the modern economy. Although digital technology has existed for several decades that could update and streamline the operations of the electricity value chain and reduce transaction costs, the physical assets in use remain, like the regulatory institutions, relics of the first half of the twentieth century. This fact is paradoxical, given the vital role that electricity plays in powering the modern economy that has created these innovations. The regulatory institutions of the twentieth century contributed to the electricity industry's ability to power extensive, pervasive economic growth.

Economic growth and technological change have brought the electric industry and its regulation to a crossroads. Technological change from outside the industry has prompted changes in both regulatory institutions and business models, leading to the incremental disaggregation of the vertically-integrated firm in some regions of the U.S. and not in others. Simultaneously, increasing use of market transactions within this vertical value chain provides further strains on the existing institutional environment, both in the U.S. and in other countries as we see both incremental market liberalization in the U.S. and the European Union and privatization of industry in many other countries.

This book presents a framework for thinking differently about many of the issues that arise in the regulation of network infrastructure industries (those involving physical interconnection and some economies of scale) in the face of constant and pervasive change, particularly the intersection of regulation and technological change. Because of the economic context of the early twentieth century and the technology of the electricity industry's infrastructure at the time, the traditional neoclassical approach to regulation forged at that time focuses on static questions of resource allocation: how can we minimize deadweight loss in the provision of a service that is essentially a commodity, in which the underlying economic structure is one of natural monopoly?[4] With such a focus, the emphasis of analysis logically falls on cost minimization and cost recovery. Thus our regulatory institutions were built to meet this static objective.

The economic regulatory institutions established in the early twentieth century were premised on neoclassical natural monopoly theory. The argument seemed straightforward: the large capital costs required to enter the industry could constitute an entry barrier, and as generation turbines increased in size after the adoption of the alternating current standard, a firm's cost curves exhibited economies of scale (downward-sloping, long-run average costs) and sub-additivity (economies of scale over the relevant range of demand for a multi-product firm). Furthermore, many of these assets were not redeployable, so a large share of those fixed costs became sunk costs.

They were also built on particular technology foundations in place in the early twentieth century. At the time, digital technology to measure, monitor, and meter the real-time flow of the energy commodity over the wires did not exist, so the technology of the time dictated a bundling of the sales of energy with the transportation/rental of the wires to transmit and deliver the energy to the end-use customer with the highest feasible economic efficiency. Combine the effect of bundling and vertical integration with economies of scale in electricity generation and the costly duplication of the wires network, and the natural monopoly characteristics of the industry in the early twentieth century are apparent. These factors led both to the establishment of vertically integrated firms in the industry and to state-level economic regulation of government-granted monopolies.

The policy and cultural climate of the Progressive Era also contributed to the expansion of regulation as an alternative both to large firms with market power and to government ownership. For many (such as Theodore Roosevelt, for example), regulation could forestall the Progressive impetus toward government ownership, given their perception of the inevitability of economies of scale in virtually every industry. The other half of the Progressive movement tended to believe in Jeffersonian small companies. This policy environment transcended the electricity industry, but certainly included it. The culmination of these policy movements was the set of New Deal measures in the 1930s.

Three major problems are associated with natural monopoly theory. The first is that first-best regulation requires that the regulator knows the cost function, which is typically an unrealistic and unfeasible requirement. The regulator knows the expenditure of the firm, which needs not be identical to the cost function, even for the observed levels of output, due to regulation-induced incentives differing from cost minimization. Hence, the regulator does not possess knowledge of the cost structure comparable to the firm's, and that asymmetric information reduces efficiency, inducing at most a second-best outcome from regulation. Second, price regulation can distort investment incentives, since sufficient gains (in terms of value of the product or of costs) cannot be appropriated by the firm that would be subject to price regulation once investment occurs. A related problem arises in that the benefits of investment are very hard for the regulator to capture on behalf of customers, and investment costs are difficult to detect. Even incentive regulation, which is intended to improve traditional cost-of-service regulation, only addresses costs; it is silent on value creation for consumers through innovation and product differentiation. Hence, except for very special cases, regulation of investment is extremely imperfect, and therefore not easily implementable. Third, natural monopoly regulation forecloses entry by imposing a legal entry barrier. Thus as technology evolves, the appropriateness of the natural monopoly designation cannot be put to a market test. Furthermore, this lack of a market test undermines any potential disruptive innovation, so efficiency gains through technological change will be incremental and small.

These regulatory policies have enshrined the regulatory compact: in return for being granted a monopoly franchise with legal entry barriers, the regulated utility assumed an obligation to serve all customers in their service territory who desired service. The compensation received for this bargain is an estimated normal rate of return based on costs incurred to provide the energy and the service (i.e., the rate base). The costs (rate base) plus the return on those costs form the basis of the retail rate structure, which divides this "revenue requirement" among three customer classes (residential, commercial, industrial) to determine the retail price, or rate, that each type of customer will pay for the service.

As a consequence of the regulatory compact, utilities focus narrowly and conservatively on investments and business strategies that they can be sure regulators will include in their rate base; this approach reinforces the construction of the types of physical assets used over the last century – generation capacity, wires, and mechanical substations, for example. The cost recovery basis of the regulatory compact, coupled with *ex post* prudence review by regulators, has stifled utility incentives to explore and invest in other types of assets, including distributed digital technology that could enhance the resilience of the physical grid, reduce operating costs and increase the ability to identify faults proactively, and enable the development and sale of differentiated products and services to end-use consumers.

From the perspective of consumers, the regulatory compact was intended to protect consumers, particularly the residential consumers who are also voters. It has done so by creating a policy environment in which the sole value proposition that regulators recognize as being "in the public interest" is one of keeping prices (rates) low and stable. In other words, a consequence of the regulatory compact is that the concept of consumer benefit in the electricity industry is narrower than in any other industry. By regulatory fiat, consumers benefit only from low, stable rates. The regulatory compact rigidifies the definition of consumer benefit, despite the fact that in many other industries, technological change and economic growth have created consumer benefit through innovation, new products and services, and product differentiation. As long as the regulatory compact retains the idea that consumer benefit in this industry derives only from low, stable rates, it prevents electricity consumers from having access to potentially valuable new products and services associated with electricity consumption, because it stifles innovation.

Over the course of the twentieth century, though, society and the economy grew and changed, and technology changed. These changes have decreased the relevance of the neoclassical natural monopoly model, in this as in other industries that have deregulated over the past 30 years. The beneficial effects of these changes have undermined confidence in centralized (including government) control of economic activity.

Electricity generation no longer exhibits strong economies of scale, nor does it have any essential economies of scope with the other activities undertaken in the vertically-integrated firm.[5] Technological change in generation has driven a lot of that change, reinforced by institutional change (such as PURPA (1978) and the Energy Policy Act of 1992) that has enabled the separation of the generation portion of the vertically-integrated firm.

Dissatisfaction with the results of regulation, in combination with technological change in generation, has led to movement away from rate-of-return regulation. Structural and regulatory reform in the electricity industry has followed the same basic model as that used in other network industries such as natural gas. This process involves first separating structurally or functionally the natural monopoly activities from potentially competitive ones, then deregulating prices in competitive activities so that consumers may be able to choose among competing suppliers. Natural monopoly activities are unbundled from supply of competitive activities and there is nondiscriminatory access to essential network facilities with prices determined by new regulation mechanisms that are designed to control costs better than traditional rate-of-return regulation procedures (Joskow 1997, 1989). These considerations have created an impetus for restructuring and regulatory reforms in the electricity sector, particularly in states with that have experienced above-average retail rates over the past two decades.

Institutional reforms to improve the performance of the industry are more complex, and the effects of the restructuring that has occurred diverge from the theoretical expectations of a decade ago. The main issue involved in any such effort is how to expand decentralized competition in generation and in retail such that the operating and investment efficiencies associated with vertical and horizontal integration are preserved while the costs of the regulated monopoly are reduced. The electricity industry in the U.S. (prior to restructuring) was supplying electricity with high levels of reliability, investment in new capacity kept up with the growth in demand, system losses were low and electricity was provided universally. Restructuring of the electricity sector is likely to lead to more long-run cost savings than short-run cost savings, with short-run cost savings arising from more efficient use of existing plants. However, medium-term efficiency gains may be obtained due to improvements in the operating performance of the existing stock of generating facilities as well as improvements in labor productivity. Significant long-run investments in generating capacity, or equivalent demand reduction capacity, may result from restructuring, but this expectation has not yet been borne out in the past decade. Except for Texas, a state in which restructuring has been a success because of its synthesis of wholesale and retail competition, restructuring has not promoted investment. In particular, investment in transmission and in demand-side technologies has not been forthcoming.

Other, more distributed and pervasive changes have taken place to transform the economic structure of the industry and the society in which it operates. In particular, changes in digital communication technology have made our society more networked, more globally integrated, more information-rich, and consequently more wealthy. The economic growth of the twentieth century unleashed a vibrant, dynamic social–technological environment in which the pace of change is rapid and individuals are constantly adapting to continuous change in their daily lives.[6] In such an environment, the expected period over which sunk costs create value is much shorter than in a static environment; thus dynamism implies having to absorb obsolete sunk costs or not incurring them in the first place.

Digital technology has also contributed to bringing us more choice as consumers. We now take as given that we will have choices when making consumption decisions. Choice is almost ubiquitous in our society, except for some network infrastructure industries, including electric power.[7] When we consume electric power service we do not expect the same product differentiation, the same anticipation of the undiscovered desires of the consumer. Why not? Do we continue to believe that electric power service is merely the provision of a commodity that is an input into the consumption of other goods and services? If so, is that perception correct, or has technology changed the nature of the potential set of services surrounding electric power that firms can sell to consumers? Furthermore, if we consider service reliability, do we really believe that all consumers want to pay enough *never* to have an outage, but that they are willing to accept any amount of outage from weather?

Digital technology has also made it possible to measure, monitor, and meter the flow of the real-time energy commodity over the wires, making it possible for that transaction to be independent of the transportation/wires rental. Given our experience with other commodity markets over the past two centuries, independent markets for the electricity commodity could be competitive commodity markets, integrated through time with spot and forward markets to provide hedging and price insurance. Yet the regulatory institutions premised on early-twentieth-century technology and social organization govern the bundled energy-wires transaction, and limit the development of independent electricity commodity markets and transactions. This limitation provides an example of how institutional inertia can make consumers worse off, by stifling the evolution of markets in directions that could be beneficial.

These regulatory institutions persist to this day; they have evolved in some ways, but in scope and in procedure they are essentially the regulatory institutions designed in the early twentieth century to deal with the economic challenges arising from the economies of scale and sub-additivity of cost. The original social compact persists, and the obligation to serve is a significant driver in utility incentives and regulatory policy.

One problem with this institutional persistence is that these regulatory institutions are premised on a static theory of human and firm behavior, but in reality the environment in which these institutions operate is dynamic. Particularly in the past 50 years, with the advent of digital technology, the growth of economic activity as more transactions shift out of firms and into markets, globalization, and fundamental demographic and labor market changes, the environment in which the electricity industry operates is extremely dynamic and fluid. This observation is also true for consumers, who have become accustomed to having variety and choice in consumer products and services, to having substantial (some would say excessive) information available to them, and to being able to control much of their personal environment and many of their transactions. Whether as a producer or consumer (or both), our lives have become more transactional, and much of our activity has shifted from taking place within firms and families to taking place through transactions mediated by market processes. This shift has increased wealth and human welfare significantly.

Regulatory institutions are not adaptive and generally do not deal well with change, particularly the effects of technological change. They arose in and are conditioned on a specific social–technological context in the early twentieth century that no longer exists. The policy challenges and objectives present then (such as ubiquitous electrification and the imposition of control on monopoly profits) have receded and been reprioritized along with new policy challenges: providing incentives to innovate and adopt new technologies, providing the type of customer choice and decentralized decision-making capabilities that consumers experience in nearly all other aspects of their lives, managing the environmental consequences of electricity consumption, and the overarching objective of maintaining reliable service in the face of consistent, pervasive change.

Such static, legalistic regulatory institutions are a mismatch with the fluid, vibrant dynamism we find in other aspects of life. In some ways this mismatch is paradoxical, because electricity service, its reliability and its quality are extremely important to our striving and ability to achieve what we want to, as individuals and in aggregate, in this modern era of vibrant dynamism. Why have regulatory institutions not adapted to changes in the underlying, fundamental environment in which they operate?

In part the answer to that question is because institutional change is incremental and takes time. However, there are still cases in which institutional change in response to disruptive fundamental change (such as, for example, sudden transformative technological change) has been beneficial. Some examples include the interstate highway system, the Internet, and the GPS satellite network; none of these systems, though, arose under the auspices of a regulatory agency. Indeed, there would even be some benefit from having institutional change anticipate future technological and economic change, but such foresight is difficult if not impossible. Thus the objective should be to have regulatory institutions that are adaptable, that can adapt to unknown and changing conditions. Adaptability means shifting the focus of regulatory institutions from specific details (like rate case reviews and top-down proscriptive decision-making) toward transparent principles, rules, and frameworks. The increasingly transactional nature of life from the perspective of the consumer, as well as within the industry, suggests that there are substantial benefits from transactional shifting from within the firm to using market processes, and from the associated shift of regulatory institutions to a focus on enabling a healthy context for those transactions.

One frequent argument against a more transactive electricity industry is that "electricity is different," or the normative claim that as an infrastructure industry electricity should not "be subject to" the volatility inherent in a dynamic economy. Telecommunications is one industry that provides an example, albeit a complicated one, of an infrastructure industry in which technological dynamism and competition have created substantial consumer benefit (through both price changes and product differentiation) and firm profits. While the manifestation of dynamism and competition in electric power would not be the same as in telecom, the ability to unleash the benefits of such dynamism is still important to consider at a fundamental, conceptual level.

Electricity is truly different from other network industries in only one meaningful way: the physics of alternating current power flow, given how the existing system is built. Kirchoff's Law means that electrons follow the path of least resistance, which cannot be specified or determined in advance. Thus two important conditions hold: (1) the physical network is nonlinear in the sense that adding wire capacity or new generation can actually increase congestion, depending on where it is built relative to demand; and (2) it is physically impossible for transacting parties to write a complete contract that encompasses the energy transaction and the wires transaction, because they cannot specify a physical path to correspond to the contract path. These two implications suggest that the wires portion of the electricity value chain is likely to be the segment, and transportation the last transaction, to be liberalized. Technological change will eventually make such deregulation possible, as the direct interconnection of distributed generation among neighboring agents becomes more widespread and makes wires contestable.

The electricity industry does not exist in the institutional and technological vacuum that is the framework of neoclassical natural monopoly theory. Technological dynamism occurring outside of the industry increases the extent to which this industry is not a closed system operating in a vacuum. The innovations that make more market-based transactions and smaller-scale distributed production possible also have reinforced the extent to which the electric power network is indeed an open system, complete with physical and economic nonlinearities and feedback loops (both positive and negative). Looking at technological change and its actual and potential effects in the electric power network amplify the inapplicability of neoclassical assumptions, suggesting that the current regulatory institutions in operation are indeed maladaptive and obsolete.

Although a large and increasing literature exists on the relationship between market structure and innovation, it is largely silent on the bi-directional relationship between regulation and innovation. An older literature exists, following Averch and Johnson (1962), on the investment decisions regulated firms make, but this literature does not analyze incentives to innovate, incentives for the regulated firm to adopt innovations that occur outside of the industry, or incentives of regulators to incorporate innovation into their decision-making or the definition of public interest used in scoping their administrative missions.[8]

The synthesis of economic change and pervasive technological change has created many opportunities to change the way people buy and sell electric power service, but the conjunction of institutional inertia, special interests and status quo bias among firms, and consumer inertia has kept those changes from occurring, even when they would be value-creating. Indeed, most incumbents share an interest in stifling disruptive technologies and developing institutions that enforce fundamental stasis.

Economic and technological change have, however, enabled more differentiation in consumer preferences, more granularity and more individuality to be expressed more affordably via markets. These changes have also created the means by which firms could serve those preferences by offering differentiated products and services, different bundles of the energy commodity with other services than just transportation of the commodity to the point of use via wires. Technological change has enhanced the potential for entrepreneurship in this industry, both by applying technology to manage energy use and by re-bundling the electricity commodity sale with other goods and services that consumers might value. New technology has made radical change possible, and maybe even inevitable.

This conjunction of regulation and technological inertia is no coincidence, although little theory exists to help us understand the relationship between regulation and technological change systematically. An environment in which firm pricing is based on regulator-approved cost recovery, and in which regulators can reject costs that are deemed imprudent *ex post*, gives firms strong incentives to avoid investments in new technologies with unknown outcomes. The long timeframe over which utility assets are depreciated reinforces that incentive. Thus, for example, many utilities continue to use analog watt-hour meters that are over 50 years old, even though the two-way communication technology embedded in digital meters creates a host of possible value propositions, reduces the operating costs of monitoring customer use, and provides potentially valuable information on consumer decisions to firms. In many other industries such new technologies have been used to facilitate firm–consumer communication and the creation of new products and services, and their use has led to economic growth, profits for producers, and enhanced well-being for consumers.

One of the largest challenges facing the electric industry and policymakers today is the mismatch between regulatory and technological inertia within the industry and the vibrant, thriving economic and social dynamism that technological change has helped to create in nearly all other aspects of human society. Is it possible for regulatory institutions to be less inertial, to be more adaptive to unknown and changing conditions like innovation, changes in fuel costs, and changes in environmental policy?

This book explores possible answers to that question, focusing particularly on the retail portion of the electricity value chain. As a result of some of the political bargains and design choices made in the state-level restructuring that has occurred in the U.S. over the past decade, retail competition has been overlooked and understudied. Restructuring started from the perspective that liberalizing wholesale electricity markets would reduce costs and promote efficiency in the industry, even if retail consumers still largely did not have the opportunity to choose differentiated services from competing retailers. As former FERC Chairman Pat Wood III characterized it,

Our piecemeal restructuring has been like a caravan crossing a swiftly flowing river. Some horses [states] made it over to the other side, others got swept away by the strong current and the rest never even tried to cross.[9]

By emphasizing the importance of retail competition, and of market designs that enable consumers to communicate information about their preferences through the value chain and into generation and fuel choice decisions, this book is intended to explore retail electricity regulation and technology in greater detail.

This work starts from the premise that the fundamental economic problem is achieving coordination. This premise differs from the premise of resource allocation that is the basis of current regulatory theory and policy; it consequently leads to different policy implications and different institutional designs. This coordination framework is a complicated one, because an important part of the argument is that the environment in which this industry operates is not only complicated, but also complex. The distinction matters; a complex environment is one in which the elements composing it interact in ways that can generate aggregate outcomes that cannot be predicted in advance (i.e., non-deterministic outcomes). The neoclassical picture of this industry is one of geographically contiguous, vertically-integrated electric utilities, each serving customers in their geographic footprint with a basic (but high-quality), fairly undifferentiated service. The actors in this world – firms, regulators, and consumers – all contribute to the complicated environment because of the incentives presented to them through the existing regulatory compact, and their natural risk aversion and status quo bias that leads to inertia. One aspect of this complicated relationship is the public choice aspects of their interactions, and in particular the behavioral public choice aspects of the question are most pressing: what are the cognitive realities of consumers, firms, and regulators in this industry, and how does that manifest itself in actual outcomes? Think, for example, of how risk aversion and status quo bias induce regulated firms to lobby for the perpetuation of their regulated status, induce regulators to make conservative policy choices that do not involve innovative technology or market designs, and induce consumers (and their political representatives) to remove regulators from office if they do anything other than provide for low, stable electricity prices.

This environment has these three primary actors (consumers, firms, regulators), preexisting institutional initial conditions (formal and informal, legal and cultural), and technological and economic change from outside of the industry. The environment is complex because in aggregate it demonstrates an emergent pattern of behavior through the interaction of these elements that is difficult to predict simply by using a model based on linear logic.

What are the best institutional arrangements for enabling individuals to coordinate their economic choices and activities in such a distributed, complex environment, and in the face of pervasive technological change? In most situations the simple answer is the best: market processes aggregate and transmit information among decentralized, distributed agents, enabling them to make decisions in their own individual interest while still (inadvertently) communicating information about their decisions (and their underlying preferences and costs) that will enable other agents to make decisions in their own individual interests. This is the means through which the decentralized coordination of economic activity occurs. However, there are reasons to believe that such market processes do not function as well in network environments, and in particular in supply network environments, because of concerns about "free riding" and the incomplete nature of property rights in networks.[10] This work will deal with the problem of incomplete and uncertain property rights in electric power networks, and institutional designs to enable decentralized coordination in such an environment.

Plan of the work

The institutional and historical details emphasized in this work are specific to the U.S., although the U.S. experience can both gain from and provide insights to experiences in other countries. The origins and history of electric utility regulation in the U.S. are unique in the federal, layered nature of the regulatory institutions and the high degree of private ownership of firms in the industry. Chapter 2 addresses both the history of the industry and its regulation in the U.S. and the theoretical framework that has provided the foundation for electricity industry regulation.

Chapter 3 presents the decentralized coordination framework from which I analyze policy and regulatory institutional design questions in the electric power industry. This book synthesizes several different fields of analysis to provide a structural, although not formal, theoretical framework to use as a tool for understanding these interactions, and for informing and shaping regulatory policy and the institutions governing the electric industry. The principal idea informing this analysis is the importance of coordination as the fundamental economic problem. Moreover, coordination in a system of heterogeneous agents with diffuse private knowledge is best achieved in a decentralized manner, in an institutional context that creates economic value by encouraging those agents to take actions based on their private knowledge. These decentralized coordination ideas draw extensively on the body of coordination literature within Austrian economics.[11]

The themes in this work also draw on complexity science, or the study of *complex adaptive systems*.[12] Markets are complex adaptive systems that involve large numbers of distributed actors and rules, or institutions, governing their interactions. A complex adaptive system has a large number of diverse actors, or agents, that interact. These agents react to the actions of other agents and to changes in the environment. The agents are autonomous, so control and decision-making are decentralized and distributed in a complex adaptive system. Through their interactions, the agents in the system adapt to the changes that they themselves help to bring about through their independent decisions. This distributed learning and decision-making process leads to potentially unanticipated changes in the environment, but a principal defining characteristic of a complex adaptive system is that it is self-organizing, and that self-organization, or order, emerges from the interaction (i.e., is an emergent property).

Given that the fundamental economic problem is coordination, a logical question is how individual agents work together to achieve this coordination. Addressing that question brings new institutional economics into the synthesis, because one function that institutions serve is the coordination of agent behavior. New institutional economics (NIE) is an interdisciplinary study of the origins, effects, and evolution of institutions. Two core characteristics of NIE are relevant to analyzing regulatory institutions (Eggertsson 1990, pp. 5–6). First, NIE's *transactional and organizational analysis* involves explicit modeling of the rules and contracts governing exchange, and the organizational form that agents and transactions take in these exchanges. Neoclassical microeconomics assumes complete contracting and fully-defined property rights, and thus presumes no need to model these rules and contracts. However, NIE is concerned precisely with the rules, contracts, and organizational arrangements that agents devise when property rights cannot be fully defined, or when contracting is necessarily incomplete because agents cannot possess perfect (or even stochastic) foresight – in other words, when transaction costs are nonzero.

The remainder of the work is essays on specific institutional design topics in electricity policy. Chapter 4 explores retail competition, demand response, and the ability of digital end-use technology to make customers actively transactive. The combination of institutional design to allow retail competition and end-user technology makes decentralized coordination possible in this industry.

Chapter 5 analyzes the bundled retail energy/wires transaction and suggests unbundling them to allow retail competition and the value creation discussed in Chapter 4 to occur. Chapter 5 also proposes a competitive joint venture ownership structure for the wires network that could substitute for conventional rate-of-return regulation. This competitive joint venture involves competing retailers owning shares in the upstream wires network. This arrangement has beneficial properties because it harnesses the downstream rivalry of the retailers and does not allow any wires shareholder to block entry (which could occur via sale or the construction of new capacity).

Chapter 6 is the first of three chapters that explore the question of reliability. Defined both as short-term security of service and long-term resource adequacy, reliability is the predominant policy objective in electricity regulation. This chapter presents an institutional design for a double-sided wholesale market with active demand and integrated spot and forward markets. By intertemporally integrating retail and wholesale markets, this institutional design enables decentralized coordination.

Chapter 7 analyzes a reliability construct unique to electric power – formal capacity markets. Capacity markets exist in some organized wholesale markets to induce investments to promote long-term resource adequacy. This chapter contends that such artificial institutions do not facilitate long-term decentralized coordination, cost minimization, or adaptability and technological change.

Capacity markets are a poor substitute for the integrated double-sided markets discussed in Chapter 6.

Chapter 8 takes on the common assertion that electric power network reliability is a public good. Reliability is not a public good for several reasons; instead, reliability is actually a common-pool resource. The differences between a public good and a common-pool resource lead to different policy implications and institutional design. This chapter uses property rights literature and the idea of institutional design to "govern the commons" (Ostrom 1990), combined with technological change that decreases the public good aspects of reliability, to argue for the sale of different levels of reliability to heterogeneous customers as different products. Such product differentiation would contribute to decentralized coordination of reliability.

Chapter 9 concludes by recommending institutional design and regulatory policies that can adapt to unknown and changing conditions produced by economic, social, and technological change. Adaptive institutions emphasize and enforce transparent *ex ante* principles instead of dictating specific *ex post* outcomes. Such adaptive regulatory institutions would not discourage innovation or product differentiation, and consequently would facilitate the emergence of forward-looking, technology-enabled decentralized coordination in the electric power industry.

2 A brief history and theory of electric utility regulation in the United States

Introduction

The electricity industry is the last remaining industry to be regulated fully as a public utility. This regulation has four elements: control of entry, price fixing, prescription of quality and conditions of service, and the imposition of an obligation to serve (Kahn 1988, vol. I, p. 3). The regulated firm has typically been a vertically-integrated, private, investor-owned utility.

The traditional structure and regulatory environment in the electricity industry are due primarily to economies of scale and scope; thus the electricity industry has existed over the past century as a multi-product natural monopoly. The defining characteristic of natural monopoly is declining average costs over the relevant range of demand; this characteristic is known as economies of scale for a single-product firm and subadditivity of cost in a multi-product firm. The primary source of this characteristic is the high fixed cost required to build the infrastructure necessary to serve customers. Low marginal cost is not necessary for the existence of economies of scale, but empirically the combination of high fixed cost and low marginal cost has characterized large-scale central electricity generation since the early twentieth century.[1] In a system with high fixed costs and capital requirements, it is inefficient to have similar utilities providing similar services in similar regions, for instance two distribution companies delivering electricity within a city.

Throughout history, different agents have proposed regulation of public utilities, with very different interests and beliefs about the objectives of regulatory policy. The electric sector has seen many instances of this occurrence. For example, after the consolidation of the industry in the Chicago area in the early twentieth century, the consolidated firm's representatives argued for the necessity of regulating the industry to avoid costly infrastructure duplication (see Stoft 2002). At the same time, consumer advocates argued for the necessity of controlling market power abuse by the recently-consolidated electric monopoly. This example illustrates the kind of questions that the analysis of regulatory policy addresses from normative and positive perspectives.

This chapter provides an historical overview of the economic regulation of the electricity industry in the U.S. over the past century. It also describes the neoclassical natural monopoly model that has been the theoretical foundation of regulation over that century. The next section presents a brief exposition of the rationale for economic regulation, along with a brief overview of the history of the economic regulation of the electricity power industry in the U.S. in light of the principles presented. The section following that summarizes the theory of optimal regulation and the evolution of regulatory theory over the past two decades. This section is concerned with the normative point of view of regulation, and so the questions addressed are mainly two: (a) when should the society regulate an industry?, and (b) what should be the objective of the regulation?

A brief history of applied electricity policy in the United States

The electricity industry in the U.S.: an overview

The physical supply chain in electricity has three parts: generation, transmission, and distribution. Generation involves using a fuel to drive a turbine that generates electric power. Transmission and distribution wires transport that power from the generator to end-use customers. For both engineering and economic purposes, transmission and distribution are the same, except that transmission occurs over longer distances and therefore requires higher voltage capability. The economic value chain in electricity focuses more on the transactions among the different steps in the supply chain, and thus adds a retail and customer service component to the physical description of the supply chain.

Despite advances in technology, the generation of electricity remains fundamentally the same as it was a century ago: rotating a magnet inside a coil of wire. The actual rotation of the magnet can come from a variety of sources including the generation of steam, falling water, or expanding gas. There are three general types of generators: baseload, peaking, and load-following or cycling. The most expensive to build but most efficient ones are called baseload generators and cover the greater part of electricity demand. Peaking units, while cheapest to build, are the most expensive to run. These typically supply the electricity in excess of what the baseload generators supply. The load-following or cycling unit operates when demand is beyond what baseload generators supply, but not yet at the point where peaking units must be used. It falls between the two types of generators in terms of cost of construction and operation (Standard & Poor's 2006, p. 13).

Because storing electricity is prohibitively costly given existing technology, the network must have the capability to generate electricity and then to transport it in real time. Electricity is delivered to consumers through transmission lines and distribution facilities. Utility companies use high voltage power lines to transmit electricity over long distances; then transformers reduce the voltage as electricity passes from transmission lines to distribution lines before reaching the consumer (Standard & Poor's 2006, p. 13). The U.S. electricity transmission grid is composed of three large synchronized alternating current networks with

150 separate control areas superimposed on the three networks, where vertically integrated utilities or groups operate through power-pooling arrangements. There are also organized regional wholesale markets through which utilities buy and sell electricity among one another to reduce costs of supplying electricity to customers. These transactions are regulated by the Federal Energy Regulatory Commission (FERC).

Electricity markets consist of the sale and distribution of electricity to end users that include industrial, commercial, and household customers. In 2005, total revenue from sale of electricity by all private and public utilities to end-use customers totaled $245 billion. Electricity to households accounted for about 51 percent of total sales at $124.9 billion. The percentage of use by value in the U.S. can be described as follows: residential 51 percent, industrial 23.7 percent, commercial 22.9 percent, other (which is primarily transportation) 2.4 percent.[2] U.S. markets are actually forecasted to decelerate. The U.S. compound annual growth rate (CAGR) of 4.5 percent from 2001–2005 is expected to fall to 3.6 percent for the 2005–2010 period, driving U.S. market to a value of $292.7 billion by 2010; this figure is a 19.5 percent increase from 2005 revenues. U.S. markets grew 2.5 percent in 2005 to reach 3810.3 billion kilowatt hours (kWh). Over the five-year period from 2001–2005, the U.S. CAGR for volume consumed was 1.9 percent. The U.S. market volume is forecasted to reach 4166.5 billion kWh in 2010 for an increase of 9.3 percent since 2005. CAGR for this predicted market volume will be 1.8 percent for the period 2005–2010 (Datamonitor 2006, pp. 7–11).

Of over 3170 power utilities providing retail service in the United States, 239 are investor-owned utilities, 2009 are publicly owned utilities, 912 are consumer-owned cooperatives, and ten are Federal utilities. Despite being large in number – representing about 63 percent of all electric utilities in the U.S. – publicly-owned utilities serve a small part of overall demand, only about 10 percent of generating capabilities, 15 percent of retail sales, and 14 percent of total revenue. Cooperatives are typically found in rural areas where it has been determined to be uneconomical to transmit power from other regions. Faced with no service, consumers established cooperatives to provide power and electricity. These utilities make up 29 percent of all U.S. utilities and represent around 4 percent of generation capability. In addition, cooperatives make up around 9 percent of sales and revenue. Investor-owned utilities (IOU) make up a mere 8 percent of the total number of electric utilities, but supply 75 percent of the generating capacity and 75 percent of retail sales and revenue (EIA Overview).

In 2006, residential consumers accounted for 42.7 percent of the revenue for investor-owned utilities, commercial 38.3 percent, industrial 18.8 percent and 0.2 percent to other end users. Industrial customers are in a position to negotiate a lower price – cogeneration and relocation are options – and pay the lowest rates. Commercial and residential consumers are not in a similar position and thus pay a higher rate (Standard & Poor's 2006, pp. 13–14).

The United States accounts for 24.6 percent of global market value in electricity. Currently in the U.S., the major IOUs are American Electric Power, Southern Company, FPL Group, and Duke Energy Corp. Of the U.S. electricity market, American Electric Power holds the greatest market share at 5.7 percent, followed by Southern Company with 5.2 percent, FPL Group at 2.8 percent, and Duke Energy Corp. at 2.2 percent. Most of these firms have both regulated subsidiaries, where they serve customers in their native service territory, and unregulated subsidiaries selling the electricity they generate through organized wholesale markets and through long-term contracts. The remaining 84.1 percent of the market is accounted for by other firms; the fragmented market share reflects the regional service territory aspect of the regulated utility (Datamonitor 2006, pp. 12–13).

The technological and political origins of state regulation[3]

The electric industry's technical development as a natural monopoly can be traced back to the 19th century. The industry's technology at the time shaped two related factors that determined the scope and form of regulation – economies of scale in power generation and wires transportation, and the bundling of generation, the wires transportation rental, and the retail sale into a single retail transaction; that bundling arose from economies of scope.

When electric current flows through a wire, it creates a magnetic field around the wire. Measuring that magnetic field measures the current flow, the amount of energy being transported across the wire. At the commencement of state-level regulation in 1907, the only way to measure and record the flow was with a human being, an induction coil, and a pen and paper; no mechanical or digital flow-monitoring technology existed. Thus monitoring current flow was very labor intensive, and therefore prohibitively costly. Installing induction coils along a utility's transmission and distribution network would also mean incurring a high fixed cost, much of which would be sunk, in addition to the high variable costs of gathering and recording the data regarding the current flow.

Given that technology, entrepreneurs began selling electricity service in large cities. The origins of the electric power industry in Chicago illustrate the process by which regulation arose. Between the years of 1887 and 1893, 24 power companies were established in Chicago. The city leader granted service franchises to these companies, frequently with overlapping service territories, and they competed aggressively on price to win customers. That competition in overlapping territories led to the construction of multiple overlapping wires networks, some of which were abandoned when competition drove the market price below long-run average cost and led some companies to exit the industry.

With overlapping markets, the competition was high and investment was largely duplicative. Samuel Insull of the National Electric Light Association resolved this problem in 1898 by purchasing all power stations in the city, establishing a monopoly. The creation of a monopoly led fairly directly to government regulations on monopoly profits, and while some pushed for competitive pricing, Insull advocated profits above the competitive level to enable the regulated monopoly to invest in infrastructure so it could serve all customers on demand (Stoft 2002, p. 6; Hirsh 1999, p. 14). State regulation was preferable to the granting of municipal franchises that had occurred since the 1880s, because that process was seen as fraught with corruption (Hirsh 1999, Chapter 1; Jarrell 1978, pp. 273–274).

The economic regulation of the electric utility industry began in Wisconsin and New York in 1907. Arising from the Populist movement, utility regulation granting exclusive monopoly franchises with obligations to serve everyone in their geographic territory reflected a desire to constrain both corrupt municipal politicians and greedy businesses.

> The Wisconsin law (1) converts all existing utility franchises to "indetermi-nate franchises"; (2) requires a certificate of "convenience and necessity" for new public utilities; (3) authorizes the state commission to establish service standards, to fix rates…, and to investigate rates; and (4) empowers the commission to control the capitalization and issuance of securities by public utilities.
>
> (Jarrell 1978, p. 271)

The arguments concerning the dynamics leading to regulation generally fall into two categories: the public interest theory of regulation and the rent-seeking theory of regulation.

Under the public interest perspective, creating monopoly electric utilities and regulating the rates of return they earned minimized the deadweight loss associ-ated with monopoly, while at the same time eliminating the competition that drove market prices below long-run average cost under free entry. This argu-ment is based on natural monopoly theory, in which the cost structure of the firms in the industry relative to the size of the market would ultimately lead to having a single firm operate in that market: "[t]he central premise of this theory is that the state acts in the public interest. That is, the state assumes the norm-ative role prescribed it by welfare economics" (Jarrell 1978, p. 272). The legal-ity of such regulation relies on the precedent established in *Munn* v. *Illinois* (1887), in which the judge found that the state could regulate private economic activity when such regulation was deemed "in the public interest" (Hirsh 1999, p. 18).

Under the rent-seeking theory of regulation, the interaction among the inter-ests of regulators and the various other parties affected by the regulations shapes the regulatory outcome. Stigler (1971) is a standard reference in this literature, arguing that regulation benefits politically powerful interest groups.[4] This model suggests that the demand for regulation could arise from the regulated industry itself, and that the repeated nature of the relationship between regulator and reg-ulated increases the probability of regulatory capture by the regulated industry. Not only did utility executives view state regulation as less onerous and more bearable than municipal franchise regulation (Hirsh 1999, p. 22), they also quickly realized that state regulation would enhance their ability to raise financial capital and fund construction (Hirsh 1999, p. 34; Hausman and Neufeld 2002).

Jarrell (1978) tests the public-interest and rent-seeking hypotheses for the period during which most U.S. states followed Wisconsin's model and adopted state utility regulation. He analyzed the process by which state PUCs were established, starting with the argument that the public-interest theory and the rent-seeking theory have different empirical implications. Public-interest theory suggests that prices and profits would fall in newly-regulated states because their monopolies were now controlled, while rent-seeking theory suggests that prices and profits would rise because regulation successfully circumvented pre-existing competition. Jarrell finds that the data support the argument that utilities welcomed, and even encouraged, the development of state-level economic regulation, rather than the public-interest theory that is more often used to explain the formation of regulation: "[t]aken together, the evidence on price, output, and profit seems more consistent with the hypothesis that state regulation was in greatest demand, and thus was established earliest, in states with more competitive markets for electricity" (Jarrell 1978, p. 289).

Utilities welcomed state regulation because in its absence their competition was vigorous, and they successfully argued that such active competition prevented them from investing in their service (Jarrell 1978). Other states followed Wisconsin's lead over the next three decades, by which time most states in the U.S. treated electricity as a utility regulated in the public interest, granting it a local service monopoly and barring entry into the provision of the bundled energy generation/wires transportation/retail sales service.

These policies were based on an important technical feature of electricity networks in the early 20th century: the technology did not exist to separate and meter the movement of energy across transmission and distribution wires. Thus by technical necessity, all sales of energy and wires were bundled.

Federal regulatory policy and the split jurisdiction

In 1920 the federal government began regulating the industry through the Federal Power Act, with the original objective of licensing hydroelectric power plants while still allowing for waterway navigation. The focus of this legislation was navigation, not the economic regulation of interstate commerce in electric power. It received substantial amendments in the 1930s, when Congress granted the Federal Power Commission (the forerunner of today's Federal Energy Regulatory Commission) regulatory jurisdiction over the pricing of interstate power transmission. Electric utility regulation remained primarily a state-level function until 1935, with the passage of the Public Utility Holding Company Act of 1935 (PUHCA).

PUHCA regulated the ownership structure of IOUs, after holding company acquisition of many local utilities led to some financial abuses (Bosselman *et al.* 2000, p. 716).

The Public Utility Holding Company Act, enacted in 1935, was aimed at breaking up the unconstrained and excessively large trusts that then controlled the Nation's electric and gas distribution networks.... Under PUHCA, the SEC was charged with the administration of the Act and the regulation of the holding companies. One of the most important features of the Act was that the SEC was given the power to break up the massive interstate holding companies by requiring them to divest their holdings until each became a single consolidated system serving a circumscribed geographic area. Another feature of the law permitted holding companies to engage only in business that was essential and appropriate for the operation of a single integrated utility. This latter restriction practically eliminated the participation of nonutilities in wholesale electric power sales.

(EIA 2000, Chapter 4)

Another piece of federal legislation, the Federal Power Act of 1935 (Title II of PUHCA), reinforced the federal support of state-level regulation of vertically-integrated utilities as natural monopolies. The Federal Power Act focused on regulation of interstate (bundled) power sales to ensure that they occurred at "just and reasonable prices." These acts were consistent with other New Deal legislation designed to control the effects of business decisions on consumers. By the end of the 1930s, a federal policy of national electrification had crystallized, and construction of plants, wires, and substations to meet that objective commenced.

The technological limitations on the economic generation and delivery of power in its early decades fed into the state-level regulation of the industry, and the federal legislation of the 1930s supported the energy-wires bundling and reinforced the split regulation jurisdiction between state and federal. To this day, states have jurisdiction over retail and intrastate operations of utilities with service territories in their borders, while the federal government has interstate jurisdiction over wholesale transaction. In both cases the jurisdiction remains over the bundled energy-wires transactions, although the Energy Policy Act of 1992 did amend PUHCA to allow for increased wholesale sales from non-utility generators.

The two decades from the 1940s to the 1960s saw massive investment to meet the policy of national electrification, induced by the regulated rate of return that utilities earned on those investments. By the late 1960s, though, investment slowed and so did the operating efficiency of new generation, which hit a plateau of approximately 33 percent in the early 1960s (Hirsh 1999, Figure 3.1, p. 57). By this time, though, the industry had largely achieved the federal policy objective of national electrification.

Around the same time, technological change outside of the industry started to change the ability to monitor current flow and meter actual consumption more precisely. By the 1950s, paper tape and then magnetic tape could record the magnetic field measurements and the current flow, eliminating the need for real-time human data recording. This dramatic change technically enables the unbundling of the wires transportation transaction from the retail sale, meaning that the existence of separate markets then became possible where it was not before.

Although possible, though, they were not yet economical technologies. These tapes were cumbersome and the data were not always easy to interpret and use. Furthermore, the large scale and cost of computing in the 1950s and 1960s made the metering of specific current flows both low priority and costly. Thus although this technological change made the existence of separate markets feasible, the costs of the technology were still high relative to the benefits. The invention of analog-to-digital converters, and the increasing power and decreasing scale and cost of semiconductors, reduced those costs and made current flow monitoring less expensive and easier to accomplish. The information technology revolution of the past two decades has decreased the transaction costs that hindered the formation of separate energy commodity markets in electricity.

The other technology that plays a role in this dynamic is the end-use meter. The typical watthour meter that most utilities use certainly predates the increased power and sophistication of semiconductor technologies, and it also predates the development of tape recording technologies in the 1950s. The core of the watthour meter technology became standard in the 1890s with the development of the induction-motor watthour meter that could measure electricity use on alternating current (AC) systems (Dahle 2003). The utility uses this meter to measure the amount of energy that a consumer uses, but the meter is not sophisticated enough to provide time-specific information about current flow, even though semiconductor technologies make such metering feasible and inexpensive. To this day, the watthour meter still requires a meter reader, adding substantially to the variable costs of its use. Utilities have a large installed base of end-use meters in homes, offices, and businesses, and the total energy use information from these meters is used to determine the utility's "revenue requirement," or the amount of revenue they are allowed to keep to ensure that they earn the regulated rate of return.

During the 1960s utilities also began constructing nuclear power plants, seen as clean and low-cost generation once the plant was built. During the 1970s, however, nuclear power plant capital expenditures escalated because of expanding construction times associated with complicated, idiosyncratic nuclear plant construction (Hirsh 1999, p. 173). Utilities borrowed to fund these expenses, and by the inflationary period of the early 1980s, interest payments on those debts became prohibitive and politically unpopular, as costs were passed on to consumers (Hirsh 1999, p. 174). California and Illinois experienced particularly high construction costs and debt levels, and some Northeast states also saw these high costs flow through to higher retail rates to end-use customers.

Institutional change: regulatory restructuring, 1978–2007

Large, centralized generators integrated with transmission and distribution systems have been able to realize significantly lower operating costs than smaller generators for most of the past century. Nonetheless, several factors have facilitated the shift to a more competitive market over the years. First, technological advances have led to more efficient gas-fired generators – compared to coal-fired generators – and high-voltage transmission lines providing transport of electricity over greater distances consequently give consumers more choices in power suppliers. Second, increases in retail electricity prices to residential and industrial consumers have led government officials to reconsider the traditional regulatory system. Finally, as a result of the Public Utilities Regulatory Policies Act of 1978 (PURPA), the rise of generators using renewable energy sources showed that there were reliable sources of power other than large-scale central generation owned by a vertically-integrated firm.

The 1970s saw rising fuel prices and increasing attention to environmental concerns, including air and water quality concerns associated with fossil fuel use. Combined with nuclear cost overruns, these issues created pressures for increased competition in the electricity industry. PURPA, passed in 1978 as part of President Carter's National Energy Plan, forced the competition issue with respect to electricity generation. In addition to provisions encouraging energy efficiency, Section 210 of PURPA authorized FERC to require utilities to purchase power from "qualifying facilities" (QFs), which were either small generation facilities using non-conventional fuels or cogeneration facilities using conventional fuels that recycled their waste heat (Bosselman *et al.* 2000, p. 718; Hirsh 1999, p. 87). The consequences of PURPA were largely unintended, both negative (long-term QF contracts at high prices, for example, in California) and positive (breaking the entry barrier in generation).[5]

At the same time, combined cycle gas turbine (CCGT) generation technology developed outside of the industry, and some aspects of PURPA decreased the economies of scale in power generation. An exogenous technological change thus changed both the economics of generation and the economics of the vertically-integrated firm; it was no longer the case that the only profit-maximizing organizational structure in the industry was the vertically-integrated firm with large-scale central generation.

The next meaningful institutional change at the federal level was the Energy Policy Act of 1992, which dramatically expanded competitive incentives and dynamics and created the potential for wholesale electricity markets. EPAct 1992 acknowledged PURPA's unintended consequences and liberalized wholesale trade of the electricity commodity at the federal level. Heretofore, utilities only traded to meet emergency needs, which meant that few high-voltage interconnections existed among service territories. This legislative change led to nascent wholesale markets, especially in areas like the mid-Atlantic region and New England, which had pre-existing power pool operations platforms to facilitate those emergency trades.

Economic theory suggests that such liberalization would lead to competition, which would lead to lower electricity commodity prices, leading to lower retail rates as those lower prices were passed through to consumers. This prospect was particularly appealing in states with cost overruns from nuclear plant construction and expensive QF contracts under PURPA; thus the first states to pursue state-level restructuring were Pennsylvania, Illinois, Maine, Massachusetts, and California. Other states soon followed (including New York and Maryland); currently 20 states and the District of Columbia have passed restructuring legislation.

At the same time, FERC Order 888 (1996) required all transmission owners to construct an open-access, nondiscriminatory rate tariff describing the transmission rates that they would charge to all generators, regardless of whether that generator was affiliated with the transmission owner. This open-access transmission policy was put in place to facilitate the growth of wholesale power markets by reducing the ability of transmission owners to price transmission service differentially between their affiliated generators and competing generators.

A related transmission policy was the development of independent system operators (ISOs). The role of the ISO is to coordinate, control, and operate the electric power network in a particular region; the ISO does not own the assets of the network, but has operational responsibility for the short-term and long-term reliability of the network. As such they operate under strict regulatory guidelines with respect to network frequency and voltage conditions and reserve margins (the requirement to have more than sufficient resources available at any time to meet forecasted demand). As wholesale markets have grown beyond state borders, several ISOs have transitioned (with the encouragement of FERC) into being regional transmission organizations (RTOs). There are currently four ISOs in the U.S. that are contained entirely within a state's borders, and four RTOs.[6] ISOs and RTOs also operate the primary wholesale power markets in their region; these markets typically include a real-time spot (sometimes called balancing) market, a day-ahead market, and markets for ancillary services that support system reliability, such as spinning reserves.

Over half of the states in the United States have embarked on so-called deregulation initiatives, which retain a substantial dose of regulation, but of a different form from the traditional regulatory treatment of the vertically-integrated industry. Some states, like Texas and Pennsylvania, successfully used their restructuring to enable utilities and merchant generators to create value for consumers. Others, like California, encumbered their market design process with so many political constraints that needed investments in capacity were deterred and consumers suffered substantial harm. This patchwork of experiences, in combination with the discovery of abusive trading practices by Enron and other market participants, reduced the liquidity of wholesale markets and contributed to a debt crisis for energy companies.

In most states the restructuring legislation focused on some form of wholesale unbundling (either functional separation or structural divestiture). Retail competition was delayed as part of the political bargain to induce utilities to agree to the restructuring proposal. For example, Pennsylvania's retail rate caps phase out over ten years and have not yet been removed; Maryland's phased out over six years and expired in July 2006, and Illinois' rate caps phased out over ten years and expired in December 2006. Another part of the political bargain was the payment of stranded costs to utilities, to compensate them for costs they had borne and generation investments they had made in anticipation of rate recovery over the 30-plus years during which the assets depreciated. Utilities bargained for these stranded costs and received them in addition to any revenue they earned from selling generation facilities.

A series of bad experiences and events have caused the national move toward restructuring and competition to stall. The California electricity crisis of 2000–2001 brought home two very painful lessons about restructuring and institutional change: restructuring in a complex network industry is harder than neoclassical theory would predict, and institutions matter. In this case, the institutions are the market and regulatory institutions comprising the market design that is largely unnecessary in more organic market processes.

The most recent formal institutional change was the Energy Policy Act of 2005, passed by Congress in August 2005. The most sweeping energy legislation since the late 1970s, EPAct 2005 ranged from subsidies for clean coal technology R&D to changing Daylight Savings Time. Its electricity provisions included support for demand response and smart metering policies.

Principles of regulation in the U.S. electricity industry: an overview

From a normative point of view, regulation is associated with the existence of a natural monopoly, with the term "natural" related to the result that in these cases the efficient structure of the industry is a monopoly. Given this fact, a first motivation for regulation is to control excessive entry; without it we may observe inefficient duplication of costly infrastructure. On the other hand, it is well known that a monopoly would generate distortions not only on the price and quantity traded in the market, but also on quality (see Spence 1975). It also creates production inefficiencies (see literature on "abuse"), and can potentially affect related markets, which otherwise could be more competitive (through vertical relationships, joint costs, etc.). Therefore, another important motivation would be to control the market power of the monopolist and reduce these distortions, thereby achieving the lowest feasible long-run average cost. Almost by definition, competition law can hardly be useful in an industry characterized as a natural monopoly.

In particular, the theoretical definition of a natural monopoly is an industry in which the technology of production exhibits cost subadditivity. Subadditivity means that the average cost of producing a quantity in the relevant range of production is lower if it is done by only one firm than by two or more firms. A related condition, and easier to verify in practice, is the existence of economies of scale, or diminishing long-run average costs. As Joskow (2007) points out, economies of scale imply cost subadditivity, but the converse is not always true (we can have an industry with increasing average costs and subadditive costs). The existence of relatively large fixed costs generally implies the existence of economies of scale. Therefore, it is not surprising to find natural monopolies, at least in some segments of the electric industry, that require big investments.

Another important characteristic of the electric power industry is the presence of the denominated "sunk" costs. Sunk costs are investments made on assets that are not redeployable, whose value on alternative uses is low or negligible. For example, the investment in public works for building a distribution network, or the construction of transmission lines, are hard to redeploy in other uses and are therefore sunk costs. In both cases, the incurring firms could hardly use the investments in activities different than distribution and transmission of electricity, respectively. This feature is important because even with a natural monopoly, other economic mechanisms could be used to effectively reduce the distortions, like franchise bidding (see Williamson 1976) or the threat of potential competition (called "contestability" in Baumol *et al.* 1982). However, the sunk nature of costs in many segments of the market would render both franchise bidding and contestability ineffective. In the first case, where the firms repeatedly bid for the right to be the monopolist provider in the market, the mechanism could not be implemented because once the investment in infrastructure is completed, it cannot be reversed (Williamson 1976). In the second case, the potential competition would never induce an efficient pricing by the incumbent monopolist, given that no firm would be willing to enter a market if they expect to lose the investment made after exiting (Tirole 1988). In fact, as Joskow (2007) points out, "a case for price and entry regulation based on a natural monopoly rationale therefore requires both significant increasing returns *and* long-lived sunk costs that represent a significant fraction of total costs."

Finally, price regulation has also been justified on distributional grounds. In the absence of distributional concerns, a mechanism in which the regulator imposes a lump-sum transfer to the firm that is equivalent to the consumer's valuation of the service provided (along the lines proposed in Loeb and Magat 1979), would give the utility the incentive to price efficiently (equal to marginal cost). However, if the regulator cares about the distribution of surplus between the firm and consumers, that mechanism would not be optimal because the firm would appropriate the entire market surplus. As Armstrong and Sappington (2007) establish, an aversion to make transfers to the regulated firm would suffice to prevent the lump-sum transfer mechanism from being optimal.

Theories of optimal regulation: a survey

This section presents some of the principles that economic theory suggests should be reflected in designing regulatory institutions. This involves using stylized models of reality that isolate the problems that authorities face rather than analyzing them simultaneously in the complex reality of regulatory policy.

The first subsection addresses the question of how optimally to recover a fixed cost with a multiproduct firm, which cannot receive transfers from the regulatory authority. The second subsection presents the results on peak load pricing: how optimally to set the price of a firm whose capacity should meet the peak size of a demand which varies widely in short time, given that the product is not storable. Both subsections present the results of models in which the regulator knows everything about the demand and cost structure of the firms. The third subsection presents some results that relax this assumption. They suggest how to set prices optimally for a firm when the regulator does not know some features of its cost structure, so-called incentive or Bayesian regulation.

Ramsey–Boiteux pricing

A well-known result in economic theory is that in an efficient competitive equilibrium, prices equal marginal costs of production. This result means that the valuation of the marginal consumer (the consumer with the lower valuation of the good) should be the same as the cost of production of the last unit of output.[7] This condition leads to the maximization of total economic surplus, which is defined as the difference between all the consumers' valuations and the cost of production of all the units, as seen in Figure 2.1.

In Figure 2.1, the consumer gross surplus, or the valuation for all the units consumed in equilibrium is the area below the demand curve. The area A is the net consumer surplus, which discounts the expenditure made by the consumers to buy the equilibrium market quantity (price times quantity). Firms decide the quantity to supply at each price comparing to the cost of producing each unit of production, so that the supply curve measures the marginal cost of production. Therefore the area below it measures the total costs of production. After discounting these costs from the firms' total revenues we obtain the firms' net surplus, area B in the graph. At the market equilibrium, the price equals marginal costs and the total surplus, the addition of areas A and B, is maximized.

That result holds, however, under some assumptions that are not met in the case of a natural monopoly. One of the most important failures occurs when

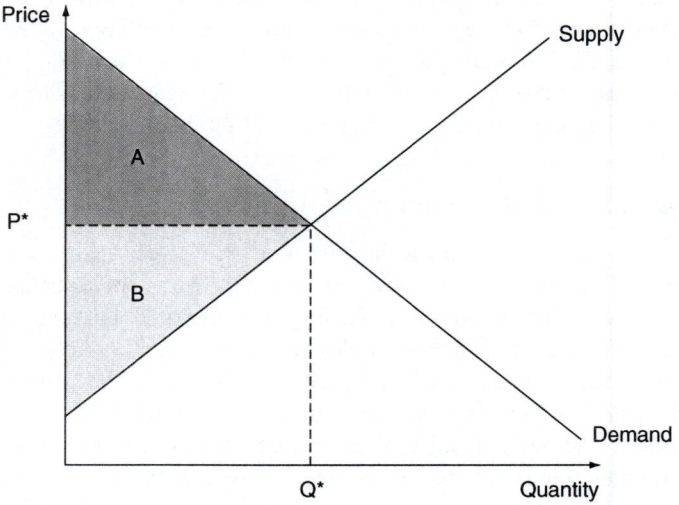

Figure 2.1 Graphical representation of efficient competitive equilibrium.

there is a high share of fixed costs. This could imply that marginal cost pricing is not enough to allow the firm to recover the fixed costs. When fixed costs are high, the average cost is dominated by the share of the average that corresponds to the fixed costs. Therefore, pricing at marginal cost, which is related to the relatively small share of the variable cost, would result in prices that fall below the average cost of production. At that point, the firm's profits are negative, and they cannot cover all of their fixed costs.

An extreme case occurs when marginal costs are constant for the entire range of production. In this setting, pricing at marginal cost would never allow recovery of any share of fixed costs. Although this is a theoretical exercise, it can still inform our understanding of scenarios in the electric industry that could look approximately equivalent. For example, imagine the case of a large hydroelectric generator serving a small market in a monopoly situation. The marginal cost of producing an additional unit (kWh) of energy is basically the same for all relevant levels of production (assume that the generator has enough capacity to serve the entire market demand), and is close to zero (equal only to the opportunity cost of the hydrological resource). In this case, pricing at such low level would never allow recovering the investment in building the central infrastructure, which can be significantly high. In the following graph, we have a cost function with constant marginal costs, and demand intersects the marginal cost curve at a price level under the average cost of production. Therefore, the average revenue per unit falls under the average cost of production.

Naturally, the optimal pricing formula should allow the firm to break even. Therefore, the problem for the regulator is to find the prices that maximize social surplus,[8] allowing the firm to recover all its costs;[9] in other words, allowing prices above marginal costs, as we have argued. But how should price vary from

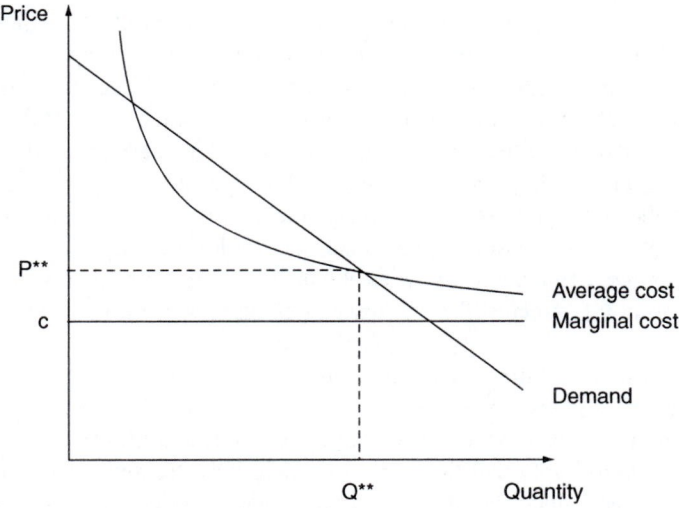

Figure 2.2 Graphical representation of a natural monopoly cost structure.

marginal cost? The problem is then one of allocating the allowed mark-ups (difference between prices and marginal costs) optimally across the products, so the firm makes zero profits. Boiteux (1956), building on the work of Ramsey (1927) on optimal taxation, solved this problem assuming that the regulator has complete information about demand and costs. Following the version presented by Laffont and Tirole (2000), assuming that the demands of the multiple products are independent, the optimal mark-up[10] formula reduces to:

$$\frac{p_k - c_k}{p_k} = \theta \cdot \frac{1}{\eta_k},$$

where p_k is the price of product k, c_k its marginal cost, θ is a positive constant less than one, and η_k is the own price elasticity of good k.[11] The formula states that the mark-up for each product should be inversely proportional to the own price demand elasticity. Therefore, goods with high demand elasticity should have a low mark-up, and the opposite for goods with low demand elasticity. This result is well known in economics and has a close resemblance to unregulated multiproduct monopoly pricing, in which the mark-ups are negatively related to the demand elasticities. However, in this case, the prices are lower than expected in an unregulated monopoly industry, given that the objective is maximizing the total surplus with the firm just breaking even.

The intuitive idea of the Ramsey pricing formula relates the mark-ups to the consumers' valuations of the good. A high demand elasticity (involving a high response of quantity demanded to variation in price) implies that consumers are relatively less willing to pay a price too distant from marginal costs. This high elasticity could be due to the existence of substitute goods, for example.[12] In this case, the Ramsey–Boiteux formula involves a low mark-up. On the other hand, if consumers are willing to pay a high price above marginal costs, the formula sets a high mark-up.

If we consider also the potential relations between the products *within* the firm's bundle of offers, the Ramsey–Boiteux formula grows complicated but still provides useful insights. More specifically, the products' relations in the bundle can be of substitution or complementarity between each other. If they are substitutes, the increase in the price of one good would increase the demand of the other good; and if they are complements, the opposite situation occurs.[13] Starting from the benchmark set by the independent demands case (summarized in the last equation, from two paragraphs above), the Ramsey–Boiteux formula with *interdependent* demands will now establish a mark-up for each product that takes into account the effect of the product's price on all other related products' demands.

For instance, take the simple case of a bundle consisting of only two products, which are substitutes between each other. Starting from the benchmark of the *independent* demands case, the Ramsey–Boiteux formula for *interdependent* demands now would imply that the mark-up should be increased. The intuition for this result is that, since the increase in the product's price would boost the demand for the other product in the bundle (which is substitute), it is therefore convenient to increase the mark-up above the level determined by the previous formula. Naturally, if the products would be complementary, then the result would be the opposite: the mark-up should decrease (in comparison with the benchmark) because raising the price of the product reduce the other product's demand.

As said before, when there are more than two products in the bundle of firm's offers, the mark-up of each product should consider the effect of its price on *all* the other products' demands. Therefore, the mark-up for each product would be different in comparison with the case of independent demands, by a measure determined by the overall degree of substitutability or complementarity of the product with the bundle of firms' offers.

From the previous discussion we can see that, according to the Ramsey–Boiteux formula, the efficient way to recover the fixed costs should be related to the demand elasticities for each of the multiple products. Considering the possibility of interdependent demands, the link with each good's cost of production is even weaker. Therefore it is easy to see that the straightforward application of the formula by regulators is out of the question, primarily for the heavy informational requirements: the regulator should know at each particular time all the demand elasticities and the complete cost structure of the firm.

Another important objection to Ramsey pricing is related to its distributional consequences. According to the Ramsey–Boiteux pricing formula (think of the independent demand case for simplicity), products with low demand elasticities should be charged the higher mark-ups. This would imply, for example, that for the provision of electricity distribution services residential consumers should be charged higher prices. Large commercial or industrial consumers can potentially resort to different technologies (less electric-intensive), or even try to supply their own energy requirements (with own generation, for example), so that arguably their demand elasticity should be higher in comparison to the case of the residential consumers. From a political economy point of view, the implementation of such schemes could naturally be problematic, and affect negatively the wealth distribution of the economy.

Despite the informational requirements mentioned, economic research has suggested practical approaches for its applicability. These are based on the hypothesized relation between the Ramsey–Boiteux formula and the unregulated multiproduct monopolistic pricing, mentioned above. Starting with Vogelsang and Finsinger (1979) there is a large literature devoted to dynamic mechanisms through which a virtually completely uninformed regulator can achieve prices close to the Ramsey–Boiteux benchmark, after a number of periods. The idea is to give some flexibility to the firm to set each of the product's prices, under a general cap for average prices.[14] Using its better knowledge of demand conditions, and constrained by the cap not to earn excessively high profits, the firm will gradually get closer to the Ramsey–Boiteux prices.[15]

The practical appeal of this mechanism is such that some researchers have argued it could also be applied to the regulation of access pricing.[16] Access pricing refers to setting the compensation of the provider of an essential facility (or input) to provide the final product. The classical example arises in telecommunications where the local network is an essential facility to provide the long distance service for example, but there are some examples in the electric industry also. The proposed global price cap would set a cap for an average of all the regulated prices, including the access price. According to the previous discussion, an appropriately designed cap should allow the convergence to the optimal Ramsey–Boiteux structure.

As can be seen from the previous discussion, the Vogelsang–Finsinger mechanism relies on setting an average price cap, under which the firm can have some discretion to fix prices. More concretely, the *price cap* in the usual policy regulatory discussion is a regulatory mechanism, which can embed the one described above. It consists of fixing an average price, not explicitly linked with the firm's realized costs, under which the firm can set the prices of each of its products.

Rate-of-return regulation is a different type of regulatory policy. In this kind of regulation, the regulator sets the prices for the firm, such that the realized rate of return (margin of realized revenues over some measure of realized costs) is under some pre-specified cap by the regulator. As we can see, under this alternative scheme, the firm is allowed less flexibility in price fixing, and the regulated prices are more responsive to the firm's realized costs. Cost-of-service regulation, the regulatory policy traditionally applied for the electric industry, is a form of rate-of-return regulation. Therefore, under such policy the possibility of using the Vogelsang–Finsinger mechanism and reaching Ramsey–Boiteux pricing is limited. A more specific discussion on this matter is carried on in later sections.

Peak load pricing

The electricity industry features the three elements that characterize the traditional peak load problem, as described in Braeutigam (1989) and Joskow (2007): demand varies widely in short time periods, capacity is fixed during these variations, and the product is not storable. Given this scenario, the regulator faces the problem of setting the appropriate level of capacity and the prices for each of the time periods during which production takes place, in the most efficient way (but the capacity is fixed at one level over all the time periods).

As Joskow (2007) points out, the (long run) marginal cost[17] of increasing supply during the peak hours includes the incremental costs of building and operating the additional capacity. On the other hand, during non-peak hours, to increase supply (given the fixed capacity in excess of the demand at these times) includes only the operating costs share. Therefore, the marginal cost can differ greatly between peak and non-peak hours, and consequently the appropriate price signals would also.

The peak load pricing problem has been long investigated, being the classical example the model presented in Steiner (1957), as described in Braeutigam (1989). As is intuitive from the previous discussion, the basic result in the Steiner model is that all the cost of the capacity should be recovered during the peak times. This result, however, depends critically on the technological characteristics of the firm, and the (implied) properties of its cost function. With different assumptions about these elements[18] the results are less extreme and imply recovering some share of the capacity costs on some non-peak periods. However, many of the properties of the optimal price setting are qualitatively similar across the different models, so it would help to state the simplified model of Steiner, to clarify the matter.

Assume that the relevant period of production (i.e., a month) is divided in multiple equally sized shorter periods (i.e., days or hours). Assume that to produce an arbitrary amount q_t of energy at time period t, it is necessary the following combination of input: $min\{x_t, k_t\}$. This technology of production exhibits *constant* returns to scale, and therefore we would be able to see that this problem is not necessarily linked to the existence of a natural monopoly. We can think of x_t as the variable input, and k_t as the capacity. Therefore, we may as well write $k_t = k$, given that the capacity will be fixed across all the periods in the model. Assume also that the unit cost of the variable input is b and of the capacity is β, so that the total cost of production during all the periods would be $\Sigma_t b.x_t + \beta.k$. Finally, the social benefit would be the sum of the consumer surplus of demanding q_t in each period. The maximization of the social benefit less the total cost of production yields that in non-peak periods the price of the product should be equal to b, and in peak periods it should be equal to $b + \beta$, as was discussed before.

If we add more general assumptions about the demand elasticities and a high enough fixed cost, as in Bailey and White (1974), the results can even be reversed, so that non-peak times could be higher than in peak periods. The result is analogous to the Ramsey–Boiteux result presented in the previous section, where the fixed cost is recovered according to the elasticities of demand in each market. Now the markets are defined by the demands of each time period, so that the fixed costs can be recovered at different time periods. Following the Ramsey–Boiteux formula we can see that the mark-up will be determined by the own-price and cross-price elasticities of demand.

Incentive regulation

As pointed out in the preceding sections, the models discussed thus far implicitly made the assumption of a perfectly-informed regulatory organization. This means that the regulator knows the details about the cost structure of the firm, and the industry demand. For example, to implement the Ramsey–Boiteux structure pricing described before, the regulator should use information about the marginal cost of each product, each demand's elasticity,[19] and the total fixed cost to be allocated. These informational requirements are large and unrealistic. It also seems natural to assume that probably the firm has a more precise knowledge of each of these elements and that it can use the information asymmetry to its own advantage. Thus even in a static neoclassical model, allowing theory to reflect these information constraints complicates the optimal configuration and actions of the regulator considerably.

The well-known contribution of Averch and Johnson (1967) proposed one of the first models that explored the potential distortions of having an uninformed regulator, in the context of traditional rate-of-return regulation. In this model, the regulator imposes (in a rather ad hoc way[20]) a rate of return bigger than the opportunity cost of capital, but lower than the monopolistic one. Given this constraint, the firm chooses the amounts of capital and labor factors to use to maximize its profits. The result of this model is that the firm will choose a higher than optimal amount of capital, given the market prices for labor and capital, due to the structure of the regulatory incentives such that the firm earns higher profits at the margin by employing more capital.

Joskow (2007) points out two features of this model that clarify this discussion about incentive regulation. First, the Averch–Johnson model does not speak to the decision-making process of the regulator,[21] and therefore does not give a thorough analysis of the incentives provided by the cost-of-service regulatory framework (which is how the rate-of-return regulation is implemented in practice). Second, the model does not generate X-inefficiency (the pure inefficiency), which is the major concern of regulatory policy, given that the firm is still on the efficiency frontier, with the only difference of having a capital–labor ratio that does not appropriately reflect the relative costs of each factor.

In the practical cost-of-service framework, the regulator usually takes into account some measure of the firm's costs that the firm will be allowed to recover over a number of periods.[22] Given that the firm is better informed than the regulator (about its behavior and cost structure), it has the incentive to use this advantage to influence those measures. For example, it can reduce the managerial effort in cost reduction, in order to signal a high level of production costs, and be allowed to make higher revenues. In consequence, a regulator may want to *respond* to that strategy by allowing, for example, the firm to make profits by not adjusting prices so often. This *regulatory lag* allows the firm to make profits through its effort in cost reduction, given that the prices are fixed for some period of time during which the firm is residual claimant of the all the benefits of cost reduction.[23] We can see from this discussion the two issues that the Averch–Johnson model does not examine: the strategic interaction between the regulator and the firm, where the asymmetric information plays a significant role; and the existence of "pure inefficiency" in cost reduction.

Economic theorists have developed a set of models that deal with those issues. They characterize the nature of asymmetric information as the regulator having an informational disadvantage regarding the firm's intrinsic characteristics and/or regarding the firm's actions.[24] In the models reviewed here, the first refers to the ability of the firm to produce at some particular marginal or fixed costs; the second refers to the effort the firm exerts in cost reduction.[25] Thus in these models the asymmetries of information revolve around cost determination. Even though the regulator can observe the realized costs, it cannot know whether it actually lies at the efficiency frontier (where there is no X-inefficiency), because (a) the actual ability of the firm to produce at low costs is unknown (henceforth denominated as "type"),[26] and (b) effort in cost reduction is not observable.[27]

The asymmetry regarding the firm's type[28] defines the problem of *adverse selection*. The asymmetry regarding the firm's actions to reduce costs defines the problem of *moral hazard*. The economic literature on mechanism design studies how to deal with both of those problems by designing optimal contracts to be offered by the regulator to the firm. The theoretical solution gives a framework for analyzing the real regulatory situations. However, to gain insight into those models, we follow Joskow (2007) and study first how the two polar cases of incentive regulation work to solve the asymmetric information problems described above. According to Joskow, the regulatory mechanism can be classified according to the power of the incentives it gives. The lowest-powered mechanism is fully responsive to the cost observations; the highest-powered one is not responsive at all, and has its revenue levels fixed *ex ante*. Naturally, between those two cases lie a continuum of alternative contracts with intermediate power, but the analysis of the two polar cases is illustrative.

A low-powered contract can solve the problem of adverse selection. Under this type of contract, basically the regulator rewards the firm for all the observed costs incurred. Given this, all possible firm types will have the same level of profit (revenue less costs), so all of them will participate and earn zero profits. However, the contract does not give incentives for cost reduction, so all firms will exert no effort. Under a high-powered contract, the opposite situation occurs. There the regulator set a fixed level of allowed revenues (equal to the efficient cost of the highest cost type firm, to ensure that all of the firm types has the incentive to participate), so that the firm is the residual claimant of all the cost-reduction benefits. In this case, the moral hazard problem is solved, given that all firms have the incentive to exert effort. However, the cost for the society is big, given that the revenue is fixed by the contract at the efficient cost of the *highest-cost* firm type.

More concretely, and following Joskow (2007) and Laffont and Tirole (1993), we can define the regulatory contract as allowing a level of revenues as a function of realized costs:

$$R = a + (1 - b)C$$

where R is the level of allowed revenues, C the realized firm's costs, and a and b are constants determined in the regulatory contract. The constant a reflects the fixed component of the contract (is independent of C), while the constant b is part of the component, $(1 - b)C$, that reflects the profit-sharing part of the contract.[29] The lowest-powered contract sets the constants a and b equal to zero, so that:

$$R = C$$

This contract can be related to rate-of-return regulation, where the rate of return is set exactly equal to the opportunity cost of capital, and so the economic profits are zero, for any level of effort exerted. Given this result, if effort is costly for the firm, then all firm types would exert low effort, as they are not going to be rewarded at all for exerting it. On the other hand, the highest powered contract sets b equal to one, and a equals the efficient cost level of cost of the highest cost type firm (following Joskow's notation, C^*):

$$R = C^*$$

This contract is related to the fixed-price contract, where the prices are set so that the firm makes revenues equal to C^*. Given that the firm can appropriate all of the benefits of cost reduction (the revenue is independent of its realized costs, C), it will exert a high effort. Therefore, $R - C^*$ will be positive in general (recall that C^* is the efficient cost level for the *highest* cost type firm), so that the firms will make positive profits under this scheme.

Schmalensee (1989) argues, using empirical simulations, that if one contract should be preferred from the class described above, the optimal (constrained, or second best) would be to select a and b within the intervals:[30]

$$0 < a < C^*$$

$$0 < b < 1$$

This result is consistent with the theoretical analysis of the model. The most prominent example is the one presented in Laffont and Tirole (1986). According to this paper, the optimal contract is to offer a menu of alternative pairs (a,b) from which the firm should pick a specific pair.[31] The intuition is similar to the one presented in the previous discussion. It is not optimal to set $b = 0$, because in this case firms have no incentive to exert effort. However, it is not optimal to set $b = 1$ either, because it will be too costly for the society to reward with C^* to the all the firm possible types. Instead, it is optimal to give only *some* (less than maximal, but positive) incentive to exert effort. As a consequence, in general we will not have a 100 percent efficiency cost level, but this will allow us to reduce the compensation to the firm, so that $a < C^*$. At the end, the regulator faces a trade-off between efficiency (maximal effort) and giving rents to the firm. And the best the regulator can do is to offer a *menu* of contracts, given that each possible firm type has a different ability to achieve cost reduction.

Some critiques of the natural monopoly model in practice

Our existing regulatory institutions and tools are built on the theoretical foundation of static, neoclassical microeconomic theory. This theoretical environment, with its focus on resource allocation as the primary economic problem and static efficiency as the primary welfare measure, provides a framework for enabling cost recovery of a monopoly's provision of a homogeneous product in a particular market with a fixed demand curve. The regulatory model falls within broader neoclassical microeconomic theory, and relies on its essential elements – stable preferences, the rational choice model of individual decision-making, and the importance and existence of equilibria (Eggertsson 1990, p. 5).

This model and the institutions built upon this model are based on the premise that the cost structure in this industry is that of a natural monopoly. Technological and economic dynamism have changed that cost structure, and have revealed that in electricity as in many other industries, focusing on value creation and on dynamic efficiency in addition to cost recovery and static efficiency become not only feasible, but important for continued well-being. This chapter presents a framework for analyzing regulatory institutions that takes into account technological and economic dynamism.

The static regulatory model was not created, and is not equipped, to help us analyze and create policy in the more dynamic technological and social environment of the twenty-first century. It is ill-suited to adapting to changes in environmental policy and our desires to change the balance of energy production and consumption with environmental quality. It also has not fostered innovative thinking with respect to ways of ensuring service for low-income consumers beyond policies that keep prices low and stable for all consumers. Most importantly, technological change has created the ability to unleash and harness the distributed knowledge embedded in the various agents who interact in the electric power network (which, for simplicity, we can classify here as firms, consumers, and regulators). This dynamic environment and set of issues requires that we think differently about the question of regulating a network industry in a dynamic, increasingly decentralized environment, and that we better understand the process of change in this industry and come up with a more dynamic model of individual choice and institutional change.

Dynamic models are tricky; they defy analytical closed-form solutions. Static models have the benefit of being analytically clean, with clear equilibrium policy prescriptions. In the static regulatory model, the objective function is to minimize deadweight loss, given a production function and a cost function, by setting the price the regulated monopolist can charge such that the regulated monopolist's expected economic profit is zero in equilibrium. As technology and society evolve over time, though, this model and these policy prescriptions are no longer appropriate, because the assumptions underlying the model are no longer (or never were) accurate. These assumptions include:

- cost structure: diminishing long-run average cost, economies of scale, subadditivity (for a multi-product firm);
- fixed demand, or demand increasing at a known, predictable rate and pattern;
- full information, particularly with respect to costs;
- fixed, constant technology;
- regulators that can, and do, fully implement the social optimum.

In this model with these assumptions, the outcome is a perennial equilibrium in which the firm earns zero economic profit, price equals long-run average cost, and deadweight loss is minimized.

By focusing on equilibria, such models fail to explain the process of equilibration. Furthermore, the assumptions of the static model laid out above do not hold in the electricity industry and regulatory policy.

Conclusion

The regulatory theory and history presented here provide a context for thinking about the relationship between regulatory institutions and economic and technological dynamism. In particular, these models suggest that existing cost-based regulatory institutions provide incentives to regulated firms that are not consistent with a more dynamic concept of social welfare, given the asymmetric information of regulators and the inability of cost-based institutions to adapt to economic and technological change.

Under regulation, utilities received exclusive franchises for specific service territories. This franchise generally carries with it an obligation to serve all present and future customers in the service territory at a reasonable price. The obligation to serve persists to this day as a fundamental characteristic of the monopoly franchise and has served to eliminate possible competition for utilities, including competition from new technologies for distributed generation or from retail energy service providers. Basing the rates that customers pay on cost recovery is one of the consequences of the obligation to serve (in combination with rate-of-return regulation). This focus on cost recovery in rates often provides an obstacle to the evolution of market-based retail electric pricing, because instead of considering the value created for customers it emphasizes only the cost of providing customers with a particular type and level of service.

3 A decentralized coordination framework for analyzing regulatory institutions

Introduction

The technological and economic history discussed in Chapter 2 help us understand the origins and persistence of the vertically-integrated regulatory and business model, and the application of natural monopoly theory in designing regulatory institutions. That discussion also highlights the changes that have reduced the natural monopoly model's relevance to the electric power industry. If this static model and its assumptions are inappropriate and a more dynamic regulatory model is required, what should that model look like? Following Beinhocker (2006), I categorize this model as one of "complexity economics." Complexity economics frames economic questions explicitly in terms of the dynamics of human action and interaction, over space and time. It also relies on economic coordination and productive/dynamic efficiency as welfare criteria, not on allocative/static efficiency, as discussed in Chapter 2. The coordination framework used in this analysis has the following defining ideas:

1   *Heterogeneous agents with diffuse private knowledge*;
2   The benefits of *decentralized coordination*;
3   The possibility of *emergent order*, both economic and physical, in electric power systems;
4   *Technological change* makes decentralized coordination and emergent order possible;
5   *Institutions* play a crucial role in enabling heterogeneous agents with diffuse, private knowledge to achieve decentralized coordination and emergent order; and
6   Institutions must have the *capacity to adapt* to unknown and changing conditions.

By these measures, our regulatory institutions are not evaluating the right criteria, implementing the right rules, or enabling aggregation of the distributed intelligence in the system in ways that lead to dynamic, adaptive efficiency. These regulatory institutions, based on neoclassical natural monopoly theory, are incompatible with this dynamic vision of technology-enabled decentralized coordination. The neoclassical natural monopoly framework is inherently static, focusing solely on equilibrium outcomes, and as a policy model it is now a failure. From natural gas to telecommunications, trucking to railroads, airlines to package delivery, the regulatory model has failed to deliver value to consumers or to enable entrepreneurship and innovation to create new value (Winston 2000). It has also failed to do so in electric power.

This coordination framework does comprise important aspects of standard neoclassical theory, such as profit maximization, utility maximization, and value maximization as objectives of individual agents (and their aggregates, firms), and the assumptions of individual rationality and self-interest. Individual rationality and self-interest are important assumptions, although the specifics of rationality here differ from the stereotyped, calculating *homo economicus* that many people define as rational. The idea of individual rationality underlying this analysis is that individual agents possess limited future knowledge and develop rules of thumb and other heuristics to enable them to make what they perceive as optimal decisions in the face of inevitable ignorance and uncertainty; this idea draws heavily on Simon's concept of bounded rationality and Smith's concept of ecological rationality (Simon 1996; Smith 2007).

To admit for the kind of dynamic changes and foresight limitations that characterize the real environment in which regulatory institutions operate, the neoclassical assumption of full information, or even stochastic information (where a known probability distribution covers all possible states of nature), cannot apply here. Rejecting this assumption opens up an opportunity to incorporate aspects of Austrian economics, particularly with respect to knowledge and the diffuse and private nature of knowledge. One crucial insight from this body of ideas is that in a dynamic environment with heterogeneous agents possessing diffuse, private knowledge, the fundamental economic problem is not allocating scarce resources – it is coordination of the actions and decisions of these agents to maximum mutual benefit (Hayek 1945, 1948).

In developing this framework I am modifying the question substantially from the one raised in the traditional neoclassical analysis of a natural monopoly. This work starts from the premise that the fundamental economic problem is not allocation of given resources in the face of scarcity, but is instead the utilization of knowledge not given to anyone in its totality (Hayek 1945). Instead of framing the fundamental issue as one of *resource allocation*, I am explicitly, intentionally, framing it as one of *coordination*. Thinking about economic coordination instead of economic resource allocation changes the way you look at problems and possible solutions to them. The focus on resource allocation is static, requiring a given technology set and set of resources, and establishing the optimal price vector that will maximize surplus and minimize deadweight loss in the allocation of those resources given that technology. Economic coordination, however, encompasses that static resource allocation problem, because optimal resource allocation is a consequence of good coordination. It also is broad enough to capture dynamic efficiency issues like investment and technological change as problems of intertemporal coordination. The question of coordination also incorporates a more central role for institutions, the "rules of the game" that structure incentives and agent interactions. Institutions can affect whether coordination happens or not, and an entire field of economics, new institutional economics (NIE), focuses on the study of economic and social institutions.

Framing the fundamental economic question as coordination also highlights the importance of adaptation (Williamson 1985). The coordination framework explicitly recognizes that changes will occur in the underlying economic and technological environment that are beyond the control of any individual agent (even a policymaker), and that part of individual decision-making and the ensuing economic activity is individual adaptation to those changes, given their private knowledge and institutional context. Adaptation changes the underlying environment, using market processes to transmit and aggregate information about economic choices. Thus the economic environment is complex; distributed agents adapt to their environment, changing the environment and the resulting emergent order in the process.

The electric power system comprises heterogeneous agents with diffuse private knowledge

The explicit recognition and treatment of heterogeneous agents with distributed, private intelligence is the foundation of this coordination framework. An agent is simply an autonomous entity that can make a decision and can take an action. The interaction of these heterogeneous agents within an institutional context determines their individual and aggregate outcomes. In general, one can model n agents, each of whom has his or her own private knowledge, and analyze how the agents act and interact under particular institutions, or sets of rules.

Existing regulatory institutions assume away the substantial heterogeneity of individual agents in the electric power system. Consider the environment in which these regulatory institutions developed and that they helped to bring about – one large, vertically-integrated firm supplying a standard, bundled service to all customers in a geographic region. In this monopoly environment the concept of supplier heterogeneity is alien. On the demand side, individual customers are treated in aggregate as "load," and the only heterogeneity recognized is the crude division of customers into residential, commercial, and industrial classes for rate determination purposes. This failure to acknowledge agent heterogeneity in the rate structure accounts for the extreme price inelasticity of demand that has historically held in the industry.

Despite its absence in existing regulatory institutions, agent heterogeneity abounds, and can have dramatic effects on both economic and physical outcomes. Not only are agents heterogeneous with respect to their roles (buyer, seller, regulator), but even within those roles they have diverse preferences, different cost functions, different business models – different objective functions in general, and different endowments and abilities to achieve those objectives in various ways. Depending on the market and regulatory institutions, these effects will differ. For example, charging a single fixed price to all consumers all the time creates different consumption patterns and system outcomes, including higher peak consumption, than allowing customers to choose time-varying rates.

Agents in the electric power system also have different structures. Agents can be individuals, partnerships, firms of varying sizes and constitutions, regulatory agencies, and so on. Agent heterogeneity means that value creation margins exist beyond the simple gains from trade that arise from the different motives of buyers and sellers. Heterogeneity within consumers can imply that different consumers will behave differently in a given situation. Furthermore, these behavioral differences can create negative feedback that leads to process convergence (i.e., equilibrium). Diminishing marginal returns for consumers and increasing marginal costs for producers are examples from economics of such negative feedback leading to convergence. Heterogeneity can also be beneficial with respect to positive feedback; for example, the case of early technology adopters allows for a positive feedback learning process. Their early adoption and communication about their experience with the new technology can induce others to adopt. Technology also makes agent heterogeneity possible that was not heretofore feasible. Embedded end-use digital communication technology combined with distributed generation on the premises of a home (and the ability to distribute power from the home over distribution wires) makes it possible for residential customers to be producer agents or consumer agents, depending on the situation, the information available to them, and the incentives facing them through their contracts with other agents.

This idea embodies the fact that individual economic agents are heterogeneous in terms of their preferences, resource endowments, roles, structures, information, and ability to acquire information. Moreover, they all have private knowledge about these dimensions of their characters. Private knowledge means that only the individual knows his/her true preferences or state with respect to a particular issue. Only I know my true preferences for consuming an additional kilowatt-hour of electricity at a given place at a given time. Similarly for firms, only the firm knows its true marginal cost and total cost for producing its good or service.[1]

This coordination model starts with buyers and sellers each striving to meet their individual, subjective objectives (such as profit maximization, utility maximization, happiness, wealth, sustainability, power); however, individuals all possess incomplete information. The incompleteness of information in this model has precise characteristics that go beyond the concept of asymmetric information as used in principal-agent models. Here information is incomplete on four dimensions:

- with respect to the preferences of others (i.e., asymmetric information);
- with respect to the set of known available value opportunities (i.e., information that one can acquire by incurring a search cost);
- with respect to the future (i.e., incomplete foresight); and
- with respect to possibly available value opportunities.

This last category is what Kirzner (1997) calls sheer ignorance. Sheer ignorance is unknown, and thus when an individual discovers a new value opportunity, there is necessarily an element of surprise in the discovery. Discovery on the part of both buyers and sellers increases mutual awareness of opportunities that were previously unknown; that awareness creates new entrepreneurial and profit opportunities that can benefit both buyers and sellers. Take the example of Apple's iPhone. The heretofore unseen opportunity was the value consumers would place on having a multi-function, touch-screen, portable communication device that was elegantly designed. Apple executives suspected that such value existed, due to their experience selling their other products and services, but they had to take the commercial risk to learn what value truly existed. On the demand side, consumers often do not know or cannot articulate their preferences until faced with having to make an actual decision (Hayek 1948, 1978). In the case of the iPhone this meant being able to weigh its features relative to rival offers, and to evaluate that tradeoff for themselves. In this sense dynamic intertemporal competition is a discovery process for both buyers and sellers.

Furthermore, knowledge is not only private; it can also be tacit. When agents make choices, including social interaction choices like market exchange, they are not always conscious of all of the information and knowledge that they bring to bear in making these choices. Tacit knowledge is knowledge that you do not know that you know, that you act on daily without thinking consciously about it. It is also knowledge people possess about how to do something, but that they never consciously learned (Polanyi 1969, 1983). This tacit knowledge feeds into the heuristics agents use to make choices in our many, interacting complex social and economic environments.

In the presence of these knowledge constraints, market processes enable these agents to achieve their plans mutually, and in the process of doing so market processes generate and aggregate information that reduces uncertainty and ignorance; it also enables agents to adapt by revising their plans and actions. Following Hayek (1945), here I take diffuse, private, and tacit knowledge as given, and focus on the role of economic, legal, and social institutions in aggregating that diffuse knowledge. To use Hayek's canonical example, the price system parsimoniously communicates dispersed, private information on buyer values and seller costs, and the price system exists within a context of formal and informal rules governing individual behavior in markets.

Why does it matter that the electric power system comprises heterogeneous agents with diffuse private knowledge? Put another way, what are the costs associated with regulatory institutions that are not designed with heterogeneous agents with diffuse private knowledge in mind? The costs of natural monopoly's blindness to agent heterogeneous agents with imperfect knowledge are the same as those enumerated in Hayek's (1944) critique of central planning and in the socialist calculation debate. Centralized control fails to maximize surplus creation because it cannot replicate the degree of information aggregation that occurs through decentralized coordination. The primary reason why centralized control cannot do so is because knowledge is diffuse, private, and often tacit.

Centralized control also relies on collective action decision-making processes, like politics, that encourage rent-seeking, which can generate outcomes that are both inefficient and inequitable (Olson 1965).

In electricity, the top-down determination of rates based on costs and centralized physical control fall prey to these critiques because neither process can access or take into account diffuse private knowledge. Furthermore, the fact that many decisions are made through political processes means that some agents – those with political power – can find ways to incorporate their knowledge and their preferences into the process and outcome. However, many cannot, and those who can engage in rent-seeking to increase the probability of their desired outcome actually happening. Thus centralized control can generate inefficient and inequitable outcomes in electric power.

Decentralized coordination has benefits relative to centralized control

Decentralized coordination and diffuse private knowledge

An important implication of these ideas for this coordination framework, and for the analysis of regulatory institutions, is the feasibility, or indeed even the optimality, of *decentralized coordination*. Given diverse agents with diffuse private knowledge, surplus max (producer and consumer surplus, welfare, well-being) is most likely to be achieved through decentralized coordination. It enables the discovery of, expression of, and communication of diffuse private knowledge through agent interactions in the system. Coordination results in equilibration tendencies and the formation of focal points to help agents coordinate (Schelling 1978).

Individual agents responding to price signals through competitive activity in markets provide an example of decentralized coordination of individual plans and actions; the benefits that arise from decentralized coordination are seen in the gains from trade, or welfare creation, that occurs through mutually beneficial exchange. Note also the similarity of this idea of decentralized coordination to the ideas of emergent order and self-organization emanating from complexity science (discussed further in the next section).

Decentralized coordination, market processes, and the dynamics of competition is a fundamental set of ideas that Austrian economics contributes to this synthesis.[2] Neoclassical economics, grounded in more static models, focus on equilibrium outcomes. Current regulatory institutions reflect neoclassical natural monopoly theory, with the attempt to use regulation as a "substitute for competition" in the effort to achieve the long-run competitive equilibrium outcome at which output price equals long-run average cost and the regulated monopoly earns zero economic profit.

Faced with incomplete information in the four dimensions described above, individual agents undertake activities to meet their objectives constrained by their budgets, their information, their ability to acquire information, and their sheer ignorance. At a very simple level, market processes are as effective as they are at creating new value in the face of these constraints because the process of exchange harnesses the beneficial tensions between buyers and sellers of goods, services, and ideas. Adam Smith articulated this beneficial tension as one in which buyers and sellers each have to recognize the self-interest of the other party if they are going to achieve a mutually beneficial exchange:

> In civilized society he stands at all times in need of the cooperation and assistance of great multitudes, while his whole life is scarce sufficient to gain the friendship of a few persons.... But man has almost constant occasion for the help of his brethren, and it is in vain for him to expect it from their benevolence only. He will be more likely to prevail if he can interest their self-love in his favour, and show them that it is for their own advantage to do for him what he requires of them. Whoever offers to another a bargain of any kind, proposes to do this. Give me that which I want, and you shall have this which you want, is the meaning of every such offer; and it is in this manner that we obtain from one another the far greater part of those good offices which we stand in need of. It is not from the benevolence of the butcher, the brewer, or the baker, that we expect our dinner, but from their regard to their own interest. We address ourselves, not to their humanity but to their self-love, and never talk to them of our own necessities but of their advantages.
>
> (Smith 1976 (1776), Book I, Chapter II, paragraph 2, p. 26)

This tension between buyer and seller, each with their subjective objectives that require exchange in order to be satisfied, is at the core of the equilibration process. Thus even though the focus here is on equilibration processes instead of equilibrium outcomes, this tension means that the process is stationary in the sense that it does drive toward equilibrium, even if it never gets there. This characteristic allows for an economy in persistent disequilibrium that is still stable in the sense that it has convergence properties. The information flow from transactions produces a convergent process that permits a stable market in most conditions without being locked into one (arbitrary) equilibrium state.

As mentioned previously, Austrian economics also contributes deep analysis of the nature of information and knowledge to this synthesis. The information context in which economic activity occurs is neither characterized by perfect (albeit probabilistic) knowledge, nor by radical ignorance. In a world of perfect knowledge, market processes to coordinate among the decisions of distributed agents are unnecessary; in a world of radical ignorance and irreducible uncertainty, such coordination is impossible. Real economic environments have knowledge gaps, and some knowledge cannot be had with any probability, but one important reason why market processes are so effective at coordinating decentralized decisions is that they induce agents to create, discover, and communicate such knowledge as is knowable. This fundamental idea bounds the nature of market information away from either perfect information known by all or complete ignorance, because the first would not require markets and the second would make markets unrealizable.

Kirzner (1992) characterizes gaps in coordination as profit opportunities for all types of agents, not just producers/firms, and argues that the equilibrating tendencies in market processes are the result of entrepreneurs looking for, discovering, and grasping profit opportunities (1992, p. 19). Entrepreneurs are both buyers and sellers who use information gaps to make profit, and by doing so move the market toward equilibrium. Importantly, agents act on *ex ante* perception and on their expectations of future outcomes, both of which can be incorrect *ex post*. Thus agents can make errors, but errors are only errors *ex post*. Such errors can lead to positive feedback and can be dis-equilibrating, leading to divergence instead of convergence, but that many heterogeneous agents are simultaneously striving to grasp profit opportunities mitigates against that divergence. Again here note the value of enabling the simultaneous actions of distributed, heterogeneous agents acting on their private information. Although these simultaneous, distributed actions can be dis-equilibrating, they more often lead to decentralized coordination, new value creation, and convergence to some, albeit moving, focal point due to the heterogeneity of their interests and actions.

How does this decentralized coordination occur? In market processes, it occurs through prices (Hayek 1945). Prices allow for the decentralized coordination of plans among distributed, heterogeneous agents with private knowledge. Price signals act as coordination mechanisms in two distinct ways (Kirzner 1992, pp. 144–146). First, in a market in equilibrium, the equilibrium price signals to individual agents what their decisions should be. In particular, price signals to lower-value consumers and higher-cost producers that they are low value and high cost, respectively. This mechanism is how prices coordinate decisions and plans. Second, in a market in disequilibrium, price signals communicate information that results in agents making systematic changes to their bids and offers; these changes themselves enhance the degree of coordination via feedback mechanisms.[3] Price signals are an information flow that may lead agents to revise their decisions, resulting in a higher degree of coordination of plans.

Combining Hayek's argument about how price signals induce individual behavior changes and lead to improved coordination with his argument that competition is a discovery procedure (1978) leads to a broader insight about the communicative and coordinating role of price signals. They communicate more than just existing knowledge; price signals also facilitate the discovery of new knowledge. This potential to discover and exploit new knowledge is a substantial driver of what Kirzner calls entrepreneurial behavior on the part of agents. For example, consumers seeing higher prices than they are willing to pay for a good will seek substitutes, learning in the process about new products, or about their preferences over products that they had not before considered; for producers, the potential to discover and exploit new knowledge drives decisions about product differentiation and market entry. Price signals communicate not only existing knowledge, but also expectations about new knowledge. Prices can signal both the current value and the expected future value of a good, which permits buyers and sellers to coordinate their future (production, consumption, innovation, substitution) behavior.

These ideas are relevant to regulatory institutions and institutional change in electric power because decentralized coordination through market processes offer forward-looking coordination of future behavior that is not available to central planners. Markets offer agents of all types incentives to make profitable discoveries. Central planning, and regulation as it is currently practiced, do not. Regulatory institutions are based on equilibrium models that do not incorporate or allow for perceiving opportunities and making discoveries.

Regulators, policymakers, utility executives, and regulatory economists have not heretofore thought of the regulatory policy challenge in the context of coordination of economic plans and actions. They tend not to think of disequilibrium prices as signals indicating to agents that they should change their plans, even though that is precisely what they are.

The concept of planning is central to this analysis. All human agents plan, taking as given a deliberate objective (or set of objectives) and the set of resources available to implement the plan. The individual's planning problem, ignorance of the true circumstances relevant to that individual's situation, is a basic knowledge problem in the sense discussed previously. This problem is not simply ameliorated through iterative additional planning, though. If that were true, then planning would simply be a problem of the supply of knowledge, easily solved by (potentially costly) search. The problem is not the supply of knowledge; the problem is not being able to articulate, define, or anticipate all of the types and pieces of knowledge to implement a plan. The real knowledge problem is that only by engaging in market processes does some of that learning take place that improves coordination, reduces uncertainty, and enables individuals to refine their plans.

Regulatory institutions face a much more complex challenge, because they must incorporate the plans of individual agents. Hayek's more specific point about the dispersed knowledge problem and planning builds on this idea and applies to regulatory institutions. Applying this individual knowledge problem insight at the social level, Hayek argued that the social knowledge problem has exponentially more dimensions than the individual knowledge problem, due to the requirement for that social plan to integrate with and incorporate the private plans of individual agents. Unknown ignorance is at the core of the basic knowledge problem, and the diffuse and private nature of knowledge exacerbates that problem with central, social planning. Central planners, including regulators, can be unaware of how ignorant they are with respect to the true circumstances in which they try to enact their social plan (Kirzner 1992, p. 158).[4]

Regulation is a form of central planning, and is therefore prone to the dispersed knowledge problem. How can the regulator overcome both unknown ignorance and the diffuse, private knowledge of agents to achieve a good (let alone "the optimal") plan?[5] Regulatory institutions are most effective when they incorporate the knowledge of a maximum number of participants into the regulatory plan. The most parsimonious way to do this is to enable decentralized coordination through market processes.

The dispersed knowledge problem shrinks via the competitive market process. This coordination and resolution of some of the dispersed knowledge problem is one of the most valuable aspects of market processes – markets are value-creating not because of their static allocative efficiency effects, but because of their dynamic information generating effects. Through the information-generation process and its effects on the individual plans and actions of agents, market processes provide decentralized coordination. By focusing on attempting to replicate "competitive outcomes" instead of enabling such information generation, regulatory institutions miss most of the action when they are used to stand in for markets.

Prices do convey information parsimoniously to all relevant agents, but the more important and effective role that prices and market processes play is that they alert agents to profit opportunities. The lure of potential profit can induce agents to modify their plans. When central planners and regulators circumvent this process, they simultaneously stifle the processes by which agents in markets overcome the knowledge problem and put themselves in situations in which they face it directly. Centralization impedes the market discovery process.

Note, however, that this point is particularly challenging in electric power, both because of the physics of AC power flow, and its necessary centralized control of the physical power flow, and because of the history and embedded culture of centralized economic control and regulation in the industry. The physical requirement for real-time balancing of power flow constrains the system away from purely decentralized coordination; this balancing requirement, though, is compatible with decentralized coordination in other aspects of the system, in ways that will be explored further in subsequent chapters.

Equilibration processes instead of equilibrium outcomes

Unlike the traditional neoclassical ideas that form the foundation of regulatory policy, an emphasis on coordination in the presence of distributed knowledge necessitates a focus on the equilibration process instead of on equilibrium outcomes. Complexity economics focuses more on the nature of individual interactions, characteristics of the process by which interactions may (or may not) converge to stable equilibria, and how the rules governing these interactions shape behavior and ultimate outcomes.[6]

This focus on interactions, dynamics, and the influence of rules intersects with the complexity science literature on positive and negative feedback loops and convergent processes (Erdi 2007). Focusing on the process of interaction, and the various positive and negative feedback effects that influence the convergence of that process, recasts the idea of equilibrium as a moving target in a dynamic world of continuous change. In such a world, even if equilibrium happens it is ephemeral, while the equilibration process is the more enduring object of analysis and policy. If there are enough negative feedback effects, a process can be convergent and stable, even if it never actually converges to a steady state, fixed-point equilibrium.

Why is the focus on equilibration instead of equilibrium relevant to regulatory institutions? We can think of the role of institutions in this feedback context, because institutions can embed either positive or negative feedback; if they embed positive feedback of a process that turns negative, that leads to worse outcomes than if the rules can adapt to changes in the environment and the process of interactions. Rules, or institutions, shape agent interactions, and regulation is one example. In electricity regulation, many institutions are focused on achieving specific outcomes (minimize deadweight loss, a "fair" profit to the regulated firm, low and stable prices to residential consumers, etc.). Regulation has chosen a specific outcome, but we cannot know if there are other, better outcomes because we have not permitted the decentralized market processes that enable agents to try to find them. This outcome focus of policy precludes us from designing institutions that instead focus on processes without driving the system to predetermined outcomes. Policies that focus on process instead of outcome are more likely to be able to take advantage of the heterogeneous and distributed knowledge in the entire system.

Real markets and systems are in constant change, making allocative regulation effective only in periods of stasis. While equilibrium models are somewhat relevant to understanding real-world markets and formulating policy with respect to them, the extreme model of frictionless, instantaneous convergence to equilibrium is irrelevant to many situations, and is thus not a good model of real economic systems. Market processes do exhibit tendencies toward equilibrium as agents make decisions and take actions that fill in the inevitable knowledge gaps. The reality of an environment/system in constant change, though, means that equilibria are generally moving targets, and in fact that actions of agents to coordinate and to reduce uncertainty can simultaneously contribute to the convergence properties of market processes and lead equilibration toward a different equilibrium from the previous one. That is the nature of learning and adaptation as embodied in the conception of the market process used in this framework.

This body of ideas is relevant to analyzing regulatory institutions because the existing regulatory institutions in the electricity industry enshrine the imposition of central control, grounded in natural monopoly theory. In so doing they circumvent the kind of decentralized coordination that unleashes and aggregates diffuse private knowledge and creates new economic value in the process.

Emergent order, both economic and physical, is possible

The idea of decentralized coordination laid out above implies that the interaction of heterogeneous agents with diffuse private knowledge will result in beneficial outcomes – in general, the coordination of private plans leading to increased surplus (consumer surplus and producer surplus), value creation, growth, happiness. In other words, for decentralized coordination to be a good thing, agent interaction has to generate good outcomes, as opposed to coordinating their behavior around negative or destructive focal points. This beneficial trait is one concept used here to characterize emergent self-organization, or emergent order.[7]

What does it mean for a system to have emergent order? Emergence in general simply means that a larger-scale pattern emerges out of the interaction of the smaller-scale decisions and actions of the agents. Emergence contrasts with imposition of a pattern in a top-down or command-and-control sense; the pattern arises out of the interaction of the decentralized agents acting with distributed control (e.g., self-control in response to individual incentives). The most interesting cases of emergence are cases of emergent order, when the larger-scale pattern that emerges is one of coordination of voluntary activity.[8] In markets, for example, exchange between buyers and sellers at market-clearing prices over time is an example of emergent order; the identities of the buyers and sellers, the nature of the goods exchanged, and the market-clearing prices all can change over time, yet exchange persists.

Another important trait of an emergent order is stability. Stability as used here is not certainty, inflexibility, fixity, or anything implying constant or unchanging outcomes. Stability here is better understood as fluid adaptation to change. In complex systems the interaction of agents means that conditions and outcomes are changing all the time. As agents change their behavior to adapt, they themselves change conditions and outcomes; these changes in response to changes are examples of feedback effects. Feedback effects can be either constructive or destructive, leading toward stability or instability. All complex systems have feedback effects, but the material questions are their magnitudes and their stabilization properties. For example, my decision not to buy butter if I observe a price increase produces a feedback effect – a reduction in the quantity of butter demanded – that is small and does not destabilize the global butter market. But if many agents also choose not to purchase butter at the current price, the price will fall. The butter market will only destabilize if no agents will buy butter at any price that butter producers are willing to accept.

The most important trait of emergent order for the purposes of this work is the emergent, unplanned nature of the resulting system. An emergent order does not adhere to the particulars of a specific outcome determined in advance; it literally emerges from agents' interactions. Thus the possible outcomes are numerous – multiple specific equilibria exist – but each outcome can be considered ordered if it has the adaptive stability property described above. The precise outcomes in an emergent order cannot be known in advance.

Imposed or planned orders, on the other hand, generally serve the objective of achieving a predetermined outcome or set of outcomes. Traditional utility regulation is an example of an imposed order, with the joint objectives of enabling universal access to the service, determining the (theoretically economically efficient) profit of the regulated firm, and using the rate structure to determine the split of net benefits among residential, commercial, and industrial customers. An example of an imposed order is a planned economy in which a political authority determines what sellers produce, and may even determine the prices at which exchange will occur. The twentieth-century economic history of the Soviet Union, in contrast with more market-oriented economies, provide a high-level example of the idea that emergent order and imposed order can yield dramatically different outcomes.

The idea of planned order even arises in institutional design to promote competition through privatization or deregulation. Drawing on Hayek's (1948, 1976) extensive treatment of the difference between "competitive order" and "ordered competition," Burton (1997) contrasts competitive order and ordered competition in his analysis of the implementation of privatization and regulation in the British telecommunications industry. A competitive order is emergent: it "arises spontaneously, not from government or regulatory intervention; or, to put it another way, it is the result of human interaction and economic evolution but not of some top-down attempt to engineer an order according to particular precepts" (1997, p. 173). In contrast, ordered competition "involves massive and detailed regulatory management of the industry's internal structure; the rule of the competitive game; the enforced structure of 'taxes' and 'subsidies' that has to be transferred between industry participants; and the segments in which enterprises are allowed, and not allowed, to enter" (1997, p. 174).

This dichotomy between unplanned and planned order, between competitive order and ordered competition, becomes important but blurred when confronting the actual institutional design and change process, taking into account the various pragmatic, cultural, and political dimensions of such change. In reality in restructuring in network industries, the process of moving from regulation to a competitive order usually does not happen smoothly, or may get diverted into ordered competition and not happen at all. Ginsburg (2006) analyzes an example of this phenomenon in the legal rules governing the competition of local exchange carriers in the U.S. telecommunications industry following the Telecommunications Deregulation Act of 1996. These rules, specifying the economic arrangements by which competing local exchange carriers had to have access to the local physical infrastructure of the incumbent, created what he called "synthetic competition," as opposed to facilitating the more organic emergence of a competitive order.

Technological change makes decentralized coordination possible

This decentralized coordination and the resulting emergent order are possible where they were not before in the electricity industry because of technological change. The analog electro-mechanical technology that has formed the core of the electricity infrastructure for a century necessitated central control – service reliability and network stability would not exist without central control. Distributed digital technology now makes decentralized coordination possible, and can lead to reliability and to reduced infrastructure costs. But the central control of the analog mechanical era persists.

The burgeoning "smart grid" technologies illustrate this point. Imagine an electric power network capable of connecting the agents in the system using digital communication technology.[9] These agents can enter into contracts and transact in ways they could not before, enabled by communication technology. If these agents have distributed generation, they can transact and interconnect within the network more readily because of digital technology. The technology also makes it possible for such an agent to be either a buyer or a seller, depending on price signals and market conditions. Wires owners can use digital remote sensing and fault location devices to identify and correct line problems before they result in an outage (this capability is at the core of the "self-healing grid" concept). The visibility and transparency that digital technology provides also increases the ways that we can ensure reliability. Devices with digital automation of dynamic reactive power mean that we could have a wholesale market for reactive power as an ancillary service, instead of just relying on dumb analog capacitors to inject reactive power statically, at fixed intervals in fixed locations.

Most importantly, digital end-use devices and metering technologies enable retailers to offer a range of differentiated products and services to customers. These services can range from time-differentiated dynamic pricing contracts to contracts for different levels of service quality and reliability; they could also bundle these services together, or bundle them with complementary services like home security, home entertainment, building systems automation, and so on. Digital metering and end-use devices also give the retailer more visibility into the behavior and consumption patterns of consumers, enabling them to devise new products and services to attract customers. This visibility also brings operational benefits, allowing firms to optimize their maintenance and investment decisions.

Such digital technology makes decentralized coordination more possible because it reduces transaction costs. Transaction costs are the costs associated with the consummation of a transaction; examples include having to perform a title search to sell property or having third-party legal review of contracts. Transaction costs abound in real-world exchange, and when they are too high they can prevent exchange that would otherwise be mutually beneficial.

Neoclassical microeconomics assumes costless exchange and full information, but economic interactions and environments are full of transaction costs that make these assumptions invalid. The existence, magnitude, nature, and incidence of transaction costs affect whether exchange can happen at all, the net gains from exchange, and the form that exchange takes.[10] Understanding, modeling, and analyzing transaction costs is a crucial aspect of applying NIE research to regulatory policy because when it is costly to transact, institutions matter (North 1990, p. 12).

One of the most important connections among technology, regulation, and decentralized coordination is the effect that technological change can have on economies of scope. Joskow (1997) argued that even if economies of scale in electricity generation lessened due to technological change, economies of scope can still provide an economic justification for continued natural monopoly regulation. Focusing on the upstream transactions, he argued that the economies of scope between generation and transmission are difficult to replicate in a decentralized environment. However, digital communication technology reduces and changes transaction costs. These transaction costs both create the economies of scope and determine the transactional boundary of the firm (Coase 1937; Klein *et al.* 1978). As they change, the optimal organizational form, firm structure, contractual decisions, and regulatory institutions change as well.

This argument about economies of scope also applies to the bundling of the wires distribution transaction with the retail sale of electricity and other services. Technological change has reduced transaction costs and reduced the economies of scope between distribution and retail. Chapter 6 picks up this theme in more detail.

The size, nature, and incidence of these transaction costs are not etched in stone, but instead can change over time. As transaction costs change, so do the firm and market boundaries. Two primary factors influencing transaction costs are the institutional structure in which the market is embedded, and the nature and rate of technological change occurring in the environment in which the market is embedded. The dramatic technological change of the past 40 years has reduced transaction costs in the electricity industry in ways that make market-based transactions (and therefore decentralized coordination) more possible than before, and the costs of implementing digital technologies continue to decrease. However, achieving the benefits of technology-enabled decentralized coordination requires focusing on institutions and institutional change.

To make decentralized coordination happen in reality, institutions matter

Achieving decentralized coordination in complex human systems requires institutions. Institutions are the "rules of the game" (North 1990, p. 6), the "incentive structure of economies" (North 2005, p. vii), the rules that structure the actionable situations in which agents interact. Ostrom gives a broad definition of institutions:

> Institutions are the prescriptions that humans use to organize all forms of repetitive and structured interactions including those within families, neighborhoods, markets, firms, sports leagues, churches, private associations, and governments at all scales. Individuals interacting within rule-structured situations face choices regarding the actions and strategies they take, leading to consequences for themselves and for others.
>
> (Ostrom 2005, p. 3)

This definition encompasses both formal and informal rules in a variety of contexts, addressing a range of different challenges that arise in social interaction. Such rules include property rights and use rights; they govern contracts, and they shape the extent to which agents organize transactions through firms or through market processes.

Institutions affect the coordination of diffuse private knowledge. Take the simple example of a financial market for a commodity. Suppose the market rules say that sellers submit (price, quantity) offers – how many units they are willing to sell and the price at which they are willing to sell – and buyers then choose how many units to buy. This institution, or set of rules, will lead to different outcomes, convergence paths, and strategies than, say, a double-sided market where buyers and sellers submit bids and offers simultaneously. The latter institution taps into diffuse knowledge more deeply because it elicits bids from buyers that the other institution does not. Similarly, retail price regulation elicits only information on how much electricity different consumers are willing to consume at that price (and analog meters do not enable the firm to gather that information in anything even approximating real time!).

Institutions or rules enable agents to form expectations, which is crucial for any form of non-simultaneous, inter-temporal exchange. We form expectations of the potential benefits and costs of our actions, of the behavior of others, of the ability to get a benefit in the future if we incur a cost now, and so on. Therefore, institutions help us create focal points, or Schelling points, that facilitate our attempts to coordination individual actions and plans (Schelling 1978).

Among other things, the ability to form expectations is important for investment and future planning. Agents are more likely to be willing to invest (i.e., incur current costs that are likely to bring higher future benefits) if they can form reliable expectations about the realization of those future benefits. Institutions that enable simultaneous, mutual expectation formation reduce (but cannot eliminate) the costs of uncertainty inherent in investment and future planning.

In general, such expectation formation is crucial for the ability of agents to form contracts. Contracts are agreements between agents over the performance of certain actions over time, the payments in return for such performance, and the costs of non-performance. The existence of rules that facilitate this expectation formation for future events reduces the transaction costs associated with inter-temporal exchange.

With respect to economic decision-making and the role of regulation in a context of economic and technological dynamism, the most important institutions are those concerning property rights. Property rights are the rights to use, modify, alter, or dispose of a particular resource. A property right is a bundle of rights, and it can be defined and enforced either formally through legal institutions, or informally through norms and customs. Although such rights are valuable, property rights definition and enforcement are costly. For that reason property rights often are not codified unless benefits of doing so are high enough to outweigh those costs (Haddock and Kiesling 2003).

Property rights are important for institutional design in the electric power industry for several reasons. Property rights are fundamental prerequisites for exchange and trade, and therefore are important for realizing the theoretical benefits of competitive electricity markets. As such, property right definition and enforcement provide incentives consistent with static and dynamic efficiency. The property rights concepts are also applicable to regulatory uncertainty; too much uncertainty about the definition and enforcement of property rights is one way of thinking about regulatory uncertainty, because regulatory decisions change property rights. In some important ways, though, defining property rights in the electric power system is impossible, given existing technology. For example, the physical features of AC power flow discussed in Chapter 1 imply that property rights over specific units of electricity cannot be fully defined.

In fact, in most environments, communities, and markets, property rights are never fully defined.[11] Most resources that we use, produce, consume, and trade are common-pool resources to some degree (Haddock and Kiesling 2003). Even a private house has dimensions on which it is a commons, whether in relation to neighboring houses or within the house itself. Most commons in the world, from college campuses to individual homes to parks, are governed by webs of formal and informal rules and norms establishing appropriate behavior. In the presence of transaction costs, the optimal institutional structure could well be a commons framework with rules and norms, preferably rules defined and enforced in a common law/jury trial deterrent framework as opposed to a regulatory, top-down framework.

Ostrom (1990) essentially placed goods on a spectrum from total open access to entirely exclusive property rights, whereby goods could fall along the line between the two poles. Thus, goods can be understood as a blend of open access and excludable property based on their physical characteristics and the organizing structures of their surrounding societies. With Ostrom we depart from a binary framework for understanding common-pool resources to continuum of property rights definitions of different degrees of completeness.

Given the pervasiveness of incomplete property rights, even in commercial transactions, how are we able to engage in so much mutually beneficial exchange? We achieve it through the design of institutions to govern the commons (Ostrom 1990, 2005). These institutions can specify use rights, means for enforcing those use rights, and penalties for violating those rights. Again, defining and enforcing use rights is costly, but institutional design to do so happens when its benefits are high enough, and the institutional form varies depending on the environment and context.

Another important aspect of this governance is contracting. Contracting is a means of defining property rights and use rights in market transactions, but it too is necessarily incomplete because of economic dynamism and incomplete foresight. However, contracts that are "complete enough" in their terms to allow exchange to occur, and that allow adaptation and renegotiation when unforeseeable change happens, are crucial institutions for decentralized coordination.

Another important dimension of institutions is enforcement of these rules. Rules with no threat of enforcement, either formal (legal sanction) or informal (social sanction), are less likely to influence actions, interactions, and outcomes. Enforcement is costly, but it creates benefits – by reducing transaction costs it increases exchange, leading to gains from trade, new value creation, and economic growth. One of the most pressing policy challenges in institutional design and change is arranging effective, low-cost institutional enforcement. Again, technological change can alter enforcement costs in the same way that it alters transaction costs.

An important difference between NIE and neoclassical microeconomics is that NIE takes into account that institutions are created, implemented, enforced, and destroyed within particular social and technological contexts. In other words, institutions are endogenous within broader social systems, as is technology (Mokyr 2002). This embeddedness is why history and culture affect institutional persistence and change.

Note that the language used above – created, implemented, enforced, destroyed – is consistent with very deliberate design of institutions. However, many of the most effective social institutions are, to quote Francis Hutcheson (1747), the result of "human action but not human design." This "spontaneous order" concept is a common link between Scottish Enlightenment thinkers such as Hutcheson, David Hume, and Adam Smith, and Austrian economists (Boettke 1998). However, it also connects NIE and complexity science with this intellectual tradition. It indicates not only that institutions structure the emergent outcomes of market processes, but also that the process of institutional creation and change can itself be a bottom-up, emergent process. Institutions can emerge from the repeated interactions of agents within a social and technological context, as opposed to being imposed on them in a top-down fashion. Such emergent institutions are frequently later codified in formal law; indeed, legal scholars often credit the resilience of the common law and its extensive beneficial consequences to its emergent order properties. One example of such bottom-up, emergent institution formation and enforcement is the system of irrigation use rights in the western U.S. (Bretsen and Hill 2007).

Thus institutions can emerge and be designed in a variety of ways, all of which are a function of the social–technological context of their formation. The origins of electric utility regulation in the 20th century are an example of this embedded institution formation process. The social context of private enterprise and origination of the industry, the Progressive era suspicion of large firms and faith in administrative regulation, the technological context of the generator and wires infrastructure and inability to monitor current flow at the time, the economic theory of natural monopoly, and the legal precedent from *Munn* v. *Illinois* of public interest and regulation to serve it, all shaped the design of state-level economic regulation in the early twentieth century.

Institutional adaptation to unknown and changing conditions

As economic dynamism and technological change happen, institutions should have the *adaptive capacity* that they neither ignore nor stifle change in the industry that incorporates economic and technological change. Adaptive capacity, or resilience in the face of change, with respect to human social systems is determined by

- The ability of institutions and networks to learn, and store knowledge and experience.
- Creative flexibility in decision-making and problem-solving.
- The existence of power structures that are responsive and consider the needs of all stakeholders (Gunderson and Holling 2001).

Resilience is a concept that is very similar to the well-known concept of evolutionary stability in evolutionary game theory. Resilience means high fitness in a dynamic sense, because it incorporates the ability of an agent or an institution to adapt to unknown and changing conditions and still perform well relative to others.

Resilience is not rigidity. Herein lies an important tension that has to be addressed when considering the design of adaptive regulatory institutions: one key characteristic of NIE is that institutional transparency reduces transaction costs, reduces monitoring and enforcement costs, and increases compliance and the degree of coordination of economic activity. Thus transparency contributes to the emergent self-organization property of human social systems. However, transparency often means having clearly-stated rules that do not change, which can imply some rigidity and might work against resilience. Managing that tension is one of the crucial challenges in institutional change.

Another complicating factor in institutional design is designing institutions in the face of pervasive change. In addition to his earlier, pioneering work in NIE, North (2005) adds a fundamental insight that is directly relevant to analyzing regulatory institutions – human action and individual decision-making necessarily take place in a non-ergodic world: "the world we live in is non-ergodic – a world of continuous novel change..." (North 2005, p. 16).[12] Innovation continually produces unanticipated changes in the underlying environment.

This insight about the non-ergodic nature of social–technological change leads to several implications. One methodological implication is the even-further reduced relevance of static neoclassical models for enabling us to understand dynamic processes involving economic growth, technological change, and institutional change. Another implication directly relevant to this work is that institutions, such as regulatory institutions, are created within a particular social–technological context, but that context is going to evolve in novel directions that have never before been encountered or even imagined. Unless institutions can adapt and co-evolve with their social–technological context, we run the risk of institutions becoming maladaptive.

Several avenues exist through which institutions can become maladaptive. One is natural human inertia and resistance to change, which can enhance predictability of outcomes for some time but may eventually leave institutions that are ill-suited to the new environment. Another related avenue is the ability of agents to use political processes to reinforce the status quo in which they benefit, out of a desire to avoid the innovations in their daily practices or business models that may be necessary for them to adapt to this new environment.

One of the fundamental general research questions in NIE is how exogenous changes in the environment can lead to changes in organizational form and/or changes in the institutional environment. North (2005) proposes a model in which the "world," or the underlying environment, changes (apparently exogenously, but not really, because of underlying feedback effects), leading to a change in beliefs; that new belief system leads to institutional change. He mentions, but does not analyze extensively, the process through which institutional change can lead to further changes. Figure 3.1 provides a visual representation of this hypothesis.

The analysis in this work falls directly in that context – at the margin, exogenous technological change can open up new transactional possibilities in electric power. These possibilities create new opportunities and new organizational forms that may be more profitable than the existing ones. In market processes, agents use realized profit as a selection criterion, causing organizational forms to evolve in response to exogenous change; note how similar this concept is to the Austrian concept of agents exploiting profit opportunities discussed previously. However, in electric power, regulatory institutions exist that constrain the ability of agents to apply this selection criterion and change organizational or transactional forms. Thus regulatory institutions affect the adaptation to and adoption of technological change, thereby also affecting how organization forms evolve with those changes. Moreover, by influencing technological change and its adoption, regulatory institutions affect transaction costs, and therefore affect our ability to achieve decentralized coordination.

Furthermore, regulatory institutions affect the incentives of agents by adding an element of political bargaining to the dynamic. Using realized profit as a selection criterion, but in the presence of a long-standing political process, agents may find that their realized profits are higher if they can persuade regulators and policymakers to maintain legal entry barriers and use political processes to stymie the evolution that would otherwise occur with the exogenous techno-

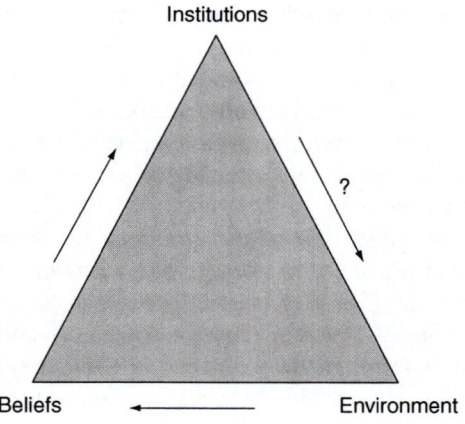

Figure 3.1 Theory of institutional change (source: North 2005).

logical change. Some stakeholders are more adept at that process, which distorts institutions and outcomes (Olson 1965).

If institutions are endogenously embedded in their social and technological contexts, then a logical question is what the process of institutional change looks like. If these three elements of a system co-evolve, what form does that process take? How does each element of the system affect the others? Clearly there will be direct and indirect effects – for example, technological change may produce institutional change directly, but it may also produce social change that itself produces institutional change. Both direct and indirect effects shape, induce, or stifle institutional change.

This discussion raises again the tension that lies at the foundation of this entire analysis. Institutions have to be flexible and able to adapt to unknown and changing conditions if they are to be effective in structuring behavior in changing environments. But they also have to provide transparency and some degree of consistency if they are to serve that objective and to create meaningful focal points for the coordination of behavior among heterogeneous agents with diffuse, private knowledge. This is the fundamental tension of institutional change – to be effective institutions have to be adaptive, but not so flexible that the incentive structure is as constantly in flux as the social–technological environment is. Well-designed institutions lend structure to the economic environment, but still retain a capacity for beneficial change.

Addressing this tension is critical for analyzing and changing regulatory institutions. Regulatory institutions change incrementally, and the time scales of change are slow, particularly when compared to the time scales of social and technological change in the past century. This mismatch is consistent with the observation that regulatory institutions are maladaptive, and that their definitions and the process for changing them does not enable them to adapt to unknown and changing conditions. However, the institutional change that has occurred in the past decade has created regulatory uncertainty in many instances, most notably in the returns to investment in high-voltage transmission infrastructure.

Achieving simultaneous institutional predictability and adaptability is a very hard problem. How do we achieve enough flexibility for adaptation while still fulfilling the crucial institutional role of structuring incentives and coordinating distributed knowledge in the face of uncertainty? This question, and its likely (albeit general) answer, is similar to North's observation with respect to the effect of strong central government on industrialization: "If you want to realize the potential of modern technology you cannot do with the state, but you cannot do without it either" (North 1984, p. 260).

One way to think about it may be to think of institutions as mechanisms that enable agents to pre-commit, but that also have clear and transparent adaptation rules. Such rules would make the triggers of the institutional change process more clear and thus reduce regulatory uncertainty. Depending on the adaptation rules chosen, this structure could create the institutional flexibility required to allow for institutional adaptation. Another way of thinking of this tension is that it is a natural tension inherent in focal points – establishing a focal point coordinates distributed knowledge and behavior, but its function as a focal point also means that changing from one to another can be slow and costly.[13]

How do we minimize this tension? By designing the institutions so they operate at a sufficiently general level that the agents operating under these institutions can themselves adapt to unknown and changing conditions. Yet this is one of the core tensions to explore in this work: how do you design institutions that are transparent, yet also themselves adaptable? The next few chapters delve into these questions in the context of specific regulatory institutional design.

Conclusion

The combination of agents with private knowledge and an institution governing their interactions and shaping their incentives will generate patterns of behavior and outcomes; these patterns can vary according to different initial conditions or different institutions, which enable us to learn how initial conditions and institutions affect behavior and outcomes. Importantly, complexity economics allows for agents to be diverse and heterogeneous. Too much of neoclassical economics and policy based upon it relies on representative agent models and assumptions of agent uniformity.[14]

All agents exist and interact in environments characterized by diffuse, private, and necessarily incomplete knowledge. In these environments, individuals undertake actions and make plans to maximize their objectives subject to their budget constraints, their information, their abilities to acquire information, and their unavoidable ignorance.

Achieving emergent order as opposed to imposed order is especially tricky in a vertically-integrated, regulated industry that is in transition due to economic and technological dynamism. Here, history and status quo inertia complicate that adaptation of agents and institutions to the economic and technological changes affecting their environments. For this reason, institutional change in such situations is rarely organic, and therefore typically requires more intentional institutional design to overcome the behavioral constraints that status-quo inertia presents. Thus in applying a complexity economics framework to institutional change in regulated network industries like electric power, it is important to remember that when talking about institutional change, such change is unlikely to be truly bottom-up and organic.

Technology and institutions are important determinants of achieving emergent order through decentralized coordination, but so is history. Complex systems that have many diverse agents with private knowledge, interacting given a particular institutional environment, may or may not succeed at coordinating their actions in a way that leads to order. The ability of a human system to achieve emergent order depends on a range of variables – the institutional structure, the traits of agents, technology, the potential gains available to agents (both pecuniary and non-pecuniary), and history. In particular, history matters because of inductive reasoning and its importance in human decision-making; induction contributes to our natural tendency to prefer the status quo, and to follow decision algorithms based on known, prior strategies and heuristics (Smith 2007). For these reasons, both initial conditions and path dependence, two crucial features of history, also matter a good deal in shaping whether a process will lead to emergent order or not.

In light of economic and technological dynamism, and particularly in light of how digital communication technology reduces transaction costs and increases the ability of a system to harness distributed intelligence and enable agents to interact in a more distributed, yet connected, way, it is important to analyze institutions and institutional change through the lens of complexity economics, asking questions such as

- How well do existing regulatory institutions adapt to unknown and changing conditions?
- Do existing regulatory institutions focus on creating a low-cost environment in which private parties can transact to mutual benefit?
- Do existing regulatory institutions take advantage of the benefits of distributed intelligence and facilitate decentralized coordination?
- Do existing regulatory institutions create an environment in which private parties can devise new approaches, technologies, markets, and transactions that can adapt to new policy challenges as they arise (such as environmental policy)?

This coordination framework suggests that increasing the transparency of information flows and the clarity of property rights institutions reduces transaction costs, leading to a higher probability of coordination and equilibration tendencies as individual agents take actions. These ideas also fall squarely in the realm of complexity science, which studies human, biological, chemical, and physical systems looking for, among other things, rules and contexts in which these systems are self-organizing and order is an emergent property.

One of the challenges of regulatory change is that it requires policymakers to trust and to act on the expectation that the decentralized coordination of the market will result in better outcomes. While we are awash in current and historical examples of such dynamism, there is no denying that we cannot guarantee the same for electricity. Of course our lack of clairvoyance is also exactly why we need to make the change. By so doing we are recognizing that we cannot anticipate the outcomes of decentralized coordination while we are in an institutional context and regulatory environment that asserts the potentially dangerous fallacy that it can predict and determine actual outcomes. Decentralized coordination using market processes, with its more diverse aggregation and discovery processes is better suited to address the issues of institutional design in a context of economic and technological dynamism.

4 Rethinking retail regulation
Enabling active demand and retail choice[1]

Introduction

Many of the assumptions underlying the traditional regulatory model are no longer correct. This chapter provides evidence supporting that claim with respect to the retail sale of electricity services to end-use consumers, and in particular their ability and willingness to respond to price signals. Technological change is the primary driver making the assumptions that consumers will respond false, although even without digital technology, customers can and do respond to dynamic pricing. The availability, and increasing cost-effectiveness, of digital technologies that enable consumers to monitor and control their own energy use and to see transparent price signals has made existing retail rate regulation obsolete. Instead, the policy recommendation that this analysis implies is that regulators should reduce entry barriers in retail markets and should allow for dynamic pricing and product differentiation, which are the keys to achieving decentralized coordination.

Electric loads follow patterns that vary over the day and the season. The daily variation is generally low (off-peak) demand overnight, a rise in demand in the morning to a shoulder period through the day, a high-demand period in the late afternoon and early evening (exacerbated by air conditioning on hot days), and a return to a lower, shoulder demand in the evening. In the absence of any price variation over the course of the day, this pattern repeats daily. The seasonal dimension depends on whether consumers in the area use electricity for heat or cooling, and the extremity of the climate variance.

The cost of generating and distributing electric power service to end-use customers varies over the day and across seasons. The fixed retail rates that customers have faced under retail regulation mean that the prices individual consumers pay bear little or no relation to the marginal cost of providing power in any given hour. Facing fixed prices, consumers have no incentive to change their consumption as the marginal cost of producing electricity changes. Furthermore, not all uses of power have the same economic value to the consumer, and those values differ and change over time. Fixed prices ignore any variation in these benefits to consumers across time. The consequences of this disconnect among cost, price, and consumption transcend inefficient energy consumption to include inappropriate investment in generation and transmission capacity.

Dynamic pricing provides price signals that reflect variations in the actual costs and benefits of providing electricity at different times of the day. Some of the more sophisticated forms of dynamic pricing harness the dramatic improvements in information technology of the past 20 years to communicate these price signals to consumers. These same technological developments also give consumers a tool for managing their energy use, in either manual or automated form. Currently, with almost all U.S. consumers paying average prices (even industrial and commercial consumers), consumers have little incentive to manage their consumption and shift it away from peak hours during the day. That inelastic demand leads to more capital investment in power plants and transmission and distribution facilities than would occur if consumers could make choices based on their preferences and in the face of dynamic pricing. The next section lays the theoretical foundation for the value of dynamic pricing coupled with enabling technology.

Without dynamic pricing, the power system will fail to deliver efficiency and value to consumers. The "one size fits all" of regulated and fixed rates is obsolete because of technological, institutional, regulatory, and cultural changes that have created a diversity of products and services that the electricity industry can profitably sell to consumers. Dynamic pricing is necessary to maximize the value of technological innovation and other market reforms that characterize the perfect power system; dynamic pricing also is, in and of itself, a valuable step in producing efficient and fair electricity markets.

The evidence of the past 20 years suggests that customers respond in a variety of ways and to a variety of degrees to dynamic pricing, even when they have only rudimentary-enabling technology. This chapter presents some of that evidence. While most existing programs and studies focus primarily on consumer behavior in the face of dynamic pricing, the focus is shifting to the question of the symbiosis of pricing and technology: with the enabling technology, do customers respond differently to dynamic pricing? In conjunction with dynamic pricing, the ability of customers to choose and to control their electricity consumption using digital technology is at the core of the pursuit of perfection in transforming the electric power network.

Several utilities have implemented some limited market-based pricing programs. Although small and exploratory, these have generated positive results that will be useful as more utilities move to market-based pricing. None of these programs implements true dynamic pricing, though; instead they are "demand response" programs that use time-of-day price changes to give customers incentives to shift load. They have typically been finite in duration and limited in the choices they present to customers. Nor do most of them explore the effects of digital enabling technology beyond simple interval meters. That said, these experiences do indicate how powerful price incentives can be for consumers, and how dynamic pricing contributes to a reliable, efficient electricity system. Price-responsive digital devices amplify those effects by lowering transaction costs; these devices enable consumers to automate their behavior and thus reduce the costs of participating actively in retail markets with dynamic pricing. A later section discusses the role of digital technology in reducing transaction costs that can limit consumer response to dynamic pricing, and the following section surveys the results of programs and field experiments for commercial and industrial customers (C&I) and for residential customers.

Dynamic pricing, product differentiation, and complementary technologies are the foundation of being able to achieve decentralized coordination in the electric power industry. They bring timely information to consumers and enable them to participate in retail market processes; they also enable retailers to discover and satisfy the heterogeneous preferences of consumers, all of whom have private knowledge that is unavailable to firms and regulators in the absence of such market processes. Institutions that facilitate this discovery through dynamic pricing and technology are crucial for achieving decentralized coordination. Thus retail restructuring that allows dynamic pricing and product differentiation, that does not stifle the adoption of digital technology, and that reduces retail entry barriers is necessary if this value-creating decentralized coordination is to happen.

Dynamic pricing and its effects

Defining dynamic pricing

In market processes, prices communicate valuable information about seller costs and buyer values. This information not only determines resource allocation in a static, snapshot sense; it also determines the levels and types of investments and innovations that occur. Those investments and innovations can change the nature and quality of the network as a whole, in part by changing the products and services available to consumers.

Competitive markets provide powerful incentives for all market participants to act in ways that benefit consumers. The incentives for innovation and efficiency that result from this process have been successful in powering our economy and have given American consumers a standard of living that is the envy of the world.

When evaluating fixed and dynamic pricing of electricity, economists use two concepts of efficiency – static efficiency and dynamic efficiency. Static efficiency measures the extent to which resources are allocated, produced, and consumed efficiently (that is, in ways that maximize total well-being or total surplus) in a short-run snapshot of the transaction. Dynamic efficiency measures the extent to which investment, innovation, and technological change occur that optimize resource allocation, production, and consumption over time. A static efficiency question is, given the existing resources in the electric power system, are those resources allocated in ways that maximize total surplus?[2] In contrast, dynamic efficiency evaluates changes in those resources through investment and technological change.

Static efficiency applies in the short run, which is defined as the period when capital assets are fixed. Competitive markets reward suppliers for maximizing output from existing facilities while at the same time deterring producers from operating uneconomic facilities. These markets also provide consumers with accurate signals of the true costs of producing the goods and services they are interested in buying, as well as providing a way for consumers to learn how their demand compares with that of other consumers in the market. These price signals permit consumers to take advantage of low-cost goods and services to the extent that they are available and to protect themselves from excessive prices by switching to other substitutes when market conditions cause any particular good or service to become uneconomic. This process is frequently referred to as "static" efficiency.

Dynamic efficiency is a long-run concept, when investments in new capital assets are possible. Competitive markets provide even greater incentives for dynamic efficiency, while also providing consumers with further protections from excessive prices. Unlike regulated distribution utilities, competitive suppliers face the very harsh reality that they will be forced out of business unless they can provide their customers with the goods and services they want at prices that are competitive with those offered by such suppliers' rivals. Thus, competition rewards businesses that excel at supplying customers with what they want at low cost, while punishing those that do not.

Most of the value creation that arises from retail competition comes from new investment and innovation to produce new products and services. As technology changes over time, robust retail competition is the means through which the product differentiation and cost-reduction benefits of these new technologies will be available for customers, and will simultaneously reflect and shape their preferences. Moreover, while competitive markets reward successful competitors with higher profits, those higher profits also provide other businesses with powerful incentives to invest their capital to compete with those successful competitors. Over time, this new entry tends to reduce prices and, hence, profits to normal levels, to the benefit of consumers generally.

Retail price regulation stifles the economic processes that lead to both static and dynamic efficiency. Keeping retail prices fixed truncates the information flow between wholesale and retail markets, and leads to inefficiency, price spikes, and price volatility. Fixed retail rates for electric power service mean that the prices individual consumers pay bear little or no relation to the marginal cost of providing power in any given hour. Moreover, because retail prices do not fluctuate, consumers are given no incentive to change their consumption as the marginal cost of producing electricity changes. This severing of incentives leads to inefficient energy consumption in the short run and also causes inappropriate investment in generation, transmission, and distribution capacity in the long run. It has also stifled the implementation of technologies that enable customers to make active consumption decisions, even though communication technologies have become ubiquitous, affordable, and user-friendly.

George and Faruqui (2002, p. 2) define dynamic pricing for electricity as "any electricity tariff that recognizes the inherent uncertainty in supply costs." Dynamic pricing can include time-of-use (TOU) rates, which are different prices in blocks over a day, based on expected wholesale prices, or real-time pricing (RTP) in which actual market prices are transmitted to consumers, generally in increments of an hour or less. A TOU rate typically applies predetermined prices to specific time periods by day and by season. RTP differs from TOU mainly because RTP exposes consumers to unexpected variations (positive and negative) due to demand conditions, weather, and other factors. In a sense, fixed retail rates and RTP are the endpoints of a continuum of how much price variability the consumer sees, and different types of TOU systems are points on that continuum. Thus RTP is but one example of dynamic pricing. Both RTP and TOU provide better price signals to customers than current regulated average prices do. They also enable companies to sell, and customers to purchase, electric power service as a differentiated product.

The benefits of dynamic pricing

The benefits of implementing dynamic pricing are extensive and widely agreed upon. Dynamic pricing makes the value and cost of their energy use transparent to consumers, and enables consumers to see when cost exceeds value. Dynamic pricing particularly benefits consumers whose consumption is flexible, but it does not harm the inflexible customer. Inflexible consumers pay averaged prices that reflect real costs, and dynamic pricing reduces the quantity of peak power demanded, which reduces equilibrium price in wholesale markets and thus reduces marginal cost to load-serving entities. When dynamic pricing reduces peak demand, it also reduces transmission and distribution losses, and therefore reduces transmission and distribution operating costs.

That flexibility and response to price signals leads to market power mitigation in wholesale power markets. Active retail demand disciplines the ability of suppliers to raise prices. Consequently, dynamic pricing leads to lower wholesale electricity prices, better capital utilization and load factors, reduced transmission and distribution losses, and reduced needs for additional generation and transmission investment. In this way dynamic pricing leads to long-term cost reductions relative to fixed, regulated rates. Dynamic pricing also promotes a more equitable distribution of those costs, because it prioritizes electricity consumption according to value and does a better job of reflecting the actual costs of service (Rassenti *et al.* 2003; Borenstein 2005).[3]

Increased reliability is one particularly valuable benefit of dynamic pricing (Hirst 2002b). Although reliability is traditionally treated as a supply issue, it is also a demand issue. Active demand response to price signals inherently acts to moderate strains on the entire system when that system's use is properly priced. The connection of dynamic pricing and demand response to transmission and distribution networks is the reduction of peak-period consumption. Customer load reduction can serve long-run reliability functions, by reducing the likelihood of transmission bottlenecks and insufficient generation. Reliability in the existing regulated model requires the utility to have (or have access to) sufficient generation capacity to satisfy *all* demand at *all* hours of the day – this high capital requirement is one consequence of the regulated, obligation to serve aspect of the government-granted monopoly franchise. The requirement to build to meet peak is expensive, but the failure to use dynamic pricing to reduce those peaks makes the capital requirement even higher.[4]

One of the most important benefits of dynamic pricing is its promotion of innovation. The transparency of price signals that better reflect actual costs gives consumers incentives to seek out novel products and services that better enable them to manage their own energy choices and make decisions that better meet their needs. This incentive induces entrepreneurs to invest their capital in providing products and services that consumers may choose. Competition for the business of active, engaged, empowered retail customers would drive innovation in end-use technologies, such as integrated home gateways that allow homeowners to manage their home theaters, stereos, appliances, and heating/cooling.

Another benefit of dynamic pricing is risk management (Hirst 2002a). Dynamic pricing exposes the information content of prices that is otherwise lost, an aspect of prices that frequently gets overlooked in political debates. Prices communicate valuable information about relative value and relative scarcity, and when buyers and sellers make consumption and production decisions based on those signals, they communicate further information about value and scarcity along the entire value chain, from end-use consumers to generators. This information transmission and aggregation process is at the core of the efficiency of outcomes generated through market processes. An important policy distinction arises between customers being *required* to see hourly prices, and customers having the *opportunity* to see hourly prices. Requiring real-time pricing would both contradict the idea of choice and expose some customers to more price risk than they might choose voluntarily.

One of the most pressing policy concerns in retail restructuring has been retail price volatility. However, concerns about retail price volatility are exaggerated, especially in an environment where suppliers are free to offer a menu of different pricing contracts to their consumers. One of the most valuable benefits of dynamic pricing, but also one of the most underappreciated and least understood, is its insurance aspects. Dynamic prices can provide two types of insurance: financial and physical. Financial insurance is protection against price volatility; physical insurance is protection against quantity volatility, or outage risk. From this point of view, the current regime has too much price insurance, although substantial disagreement exists about the optimal level of physical insurance.

As a wholesale commodity, electricity has volatile prices. The financial insurance benefit of dynamic pricing derives from this inherent volatility. The traditional fixed average rate for electricity has two components – the price of the electricity commodity itself, and the risk premium that consumers pay for being protected from volatile prices.[5] However, given that regulated rates are typically set to approximate long-run average cost, consumers do not always pay a full insurance premium for the extent that they are insured against price volatility, as a result of the political negotiations that result in the determination of the retail rate structure. Furthermore, in states that have pursued restructuring, the political bargain usually includes a fixed, discounted retail rate during a multi-year phase-out of price caps. Discounts on historic rates exacerbate the extent to which consumers do not pay a full insurance premium for the protection from price volatility that they enjoy.

Dynamic pricing would create an opportunity for consumers to choose how much of that price risk they are willing to bear, and how much they are willing to pay to avoid by trading it with some other party (such as a retailer). Although regulated rates have provided some form of financial insurance, they do not communicate the cost of insuring different types of consumers against different types of price risks. They simply fail to reflect the different degrees to which diverse consumers might choose to be insured. Customer heterogeneity means that customers have, among other things, different risk preferences, and different willingness to pay to avoid price risk. Dynamic prices allow the electricity commodity price and the financial insurance premium components of the price to be unbundled, and to be offered separately to customers. This unbundling would enable more efficient pricing of the financial risk, leading to better risk allocation.

Quantity volatility, and the associated outage risk, differs from price risk because it is a reliability of service issue that is not often connected with the idea of insurance. This physical insurance characteristic creates the opportunity for value in interruptible contracts, for example. Dynamic pricing enables some customers to shift load to off-peak (a form of physical insurance), which can benefit *all* consumers because it would reduce overall prices. Consumers who choose to use meters and face real-time dynamic pricing will provide their own financial insurance, or not, as they choose. But in so doing they may provide a physical spillover benefit to other consumers, by reducing overall peak usage and improving reliability for all, with less excess capacity, and therefore at lower average cost.[6]

Offering a menu of contracts that lets consumers choose contracts that match their risk preferences is an important form of product differentiation that highlights the role of market processes in aggregating the private knowledge of heterogeneous agents. Risk preferences are heterogeneous, even within the regulated customer classes, and averaged rates offer no way to discover, or satisfy, those different preferences, because all customers bear the same degree of price risk. Dynamic pricing enables retailers to discover and satisfy the preferences of heterogeneous agents with diffuse private knowledge; regulated rates do not. That discovery process is the fundamental foundation of economic value creation and consumer well-being.

Critics argue that the price risk considerations in offering a menu of different contracts are too complicated for many customers. Two important arguments address this concern. First, most customers, even residential, have experience buying automobile collision insurance, and many consumers have experience investing through financial markets. Consumers have experience in dealing with risk trade-offs, because they see this relationship in other contexts, like collision insurance, and different customers have different risk profiles and different risk preferences. Offering them alternatives that reflect those differences improves economic efficiency and resource allocation in the industry. For these reasons, if regulators allow customers to choose how much risk to manage and how much to pay to avoid risk, and how to manage those risks, consumers will themselves create physical insurance for the whole system. Similarly, customers have experience choosing mobile phone contracts and DVD subscription services (like Netflix), where they have to evaluate their uses of the service in ways that are very similar to evaluating price risk. Second, the network aspects of the system mean that even if only some large customers find it worthwhile to manage their financial risk, their choice to do so will benefit the system particip- ants more broadly, even those who do not choose to manage their own price risk through a TOU or RTP contract. Thus market-based pricing and product differentiation create relative price stability, even in the absence of regulated price caps.

Dynamic pricing can also contribute to improving environmental quality by enabling customers to shift demand away from peak periods with high prices, and/or by reducing their overall use. This economizing incentive is the source of the conservation benefits of market-based pricing. Conservation brought on by market-based pricing reduces energy costs and increases energy efficiency. This conservation typically takes two forms – curtailing consumption (reducing overall use) and shifting use to non-peak hours. Environmental benefits result from using more efficient generators, operating closer to the conditions for which they were designed, and reduced transmission and distribution losses.

The extent to which peak shifting induced by dynamic pricing reduces power plant emissions depends on the fuel mix of the generation portfolio between baseload and peak units, and how much additional pollution is produced during peak unit startup (Mansur and Holland 2008). For example, shifting price- responsive consumers from peak to off-peak means shifting from natural gas generation to coal generation in many regions, which may mean an increase in emissions. The question is complicated, though, because the operating efficiency of the coal-fired unit may be higher (i.e., it may have a higher heat rate), which means that it uses fewer BTUs of fuel to generate that power than the natural gas peak generation. Thus the static effect on emissions of price-responsive con- sumption smoothing is ambiguous.

The environmental benefits of dynamic pricing are much more evident in the effect that customer responses have on the investment decisions with respect to new generation and transmission capacity. The shift away from peak consump- tion reduces the required investment in generation capacity to satisfy peak period demand. Customers shifting and reducing demand would lead to less required investment and new plant and wires construction, which would also reduce long-run average cost by reducing capital costs. Furthermore, many of those assets are used during only a few peak hours each year, which means that building to meet peak requires using many physical and financial resources that sit idle much of the year. In addition to the cost saving from reducing the amount of idle peak capacity, reducing peak capacity creates environmental value by reducing required resource use to meet our electricity needs. Thus dynamic pricing would lead to both environmental benefits and reduced production costs from a dynamic efficiency perspective.

Technology's role in retail choice

Digital technologies are increasingly available that reduce the cost of sending prices to people and their devices. Gale *et al.* 2007 catalog a variety of end-user technologies, from price-responsive appliances to wireless home automation systems, that can communicate electricity price signals to consumers, keep data on their consumption, and be programmed to respond automatically to trigger prices that the consumer chooses based on his/her own preferences. Moreover, the two-way communication advanced metering infrastructure (AMI) that enables a retailer and consumer to have that data transparency is also proliferating, albeit slowly, and is declining in price.

Dynamic pricing and the digital technology that enables communication of price information are symbiotic. Dynamic pricing without enabling technology is meaningless; technology without economic signals to which to respond is extremely limited in its ability to coordinate buyers and sellers in a way that optimizes network quality and resource use.[7] The combination of dynamic pricing and enabling technology changes the value proposition to the consumer from "I flip the switch and the light comes on" to a more diverse and consumer-focused set of value-added services.

Such diverse value-added services empower consumers and enable them to control their electricity choices with more granularity and precision than the environment in which they think solely of the total amount of electricity they consume. Digital metering and end-user devices also decrease transaction costs between buyers and sellers, lowering barriers to exchange and to the formation of particular markets and products.

Whether it is a building control system that enables the consumer to see the amount of power used by each function performed in the building, or an appliance that can be automated to change its behavior based on changes in the retail price of electricity, these products and services provide customers with an opportunity to make better choices with more precision than ever before. In aggregate, these choices lead to better capacity utilization, better fuel resource utilization, and provide incentives for innovation to meet their needs and capture their imaginations. In this sense, technological innovation and dynamic retail electricity pricing are at the heart of decentralized coordination in the electric power network.

Customer response to dynamic pricing: evidence

Several studies have estimated the value of transforming the electric power network to incorporate more active demand and digital technology. A Government Accountability Office study reported estimates over the overall economic value of more active electricity demand and ability to respond to price signals ranging from \$4.5 billion to \$15 billion annually (GAO 2004, Table 1, Table 2).

In 2004 RAND performed an analysis of the benefits of the GridWise Initiative, a national initiative to modernize the electric power network using communication technology, building and appliance automation, market processes, and contracts. The GridWise Initiative emphasized the use of technology to communicate information, including price signals. Thus Rand's estimate of the benefits of GridWise provides evidence on the value of dynamic pricing and enabling technology. Projecting estimates forward to 2025, the Rand study compares a phased-in GridWise transition to the Energy Information Administration's Annual Energy Outlook projections over the same period. GridWise features modeled include peak load reduction due to dynamic pricing, capacity investment deferral for generation, transmission, and distribution, reduced operating expenses, improved power quality and reliability, and improved efficiency. They use ranges of estimates of these variables to arrive at aggregate discounted benefits from \$32 billion to \$132 billion. Their nominal estimate of the net present value of benefits over 20 years is \$81 billion (Walter *et al.* 2004, p. 28).

Commercial and industrial consumers

Utilities have been experimenting with dynamic pricing for large commercial and industrial customers for over 25 years. Larger customers are generally believed to be more willing and able to respond to price signals than smaller customers. In many, but not all, cases, larger customers have building controls and other installed technology networks that enable them to automate electricity price response behavior more readily and at less cost than smaller customers. Studies over the past 25 years demonstrate that this presumption is generally true, but that large customers do vary greatly with respect to their actual responses to dynamic pricing and to the enabling technology they possess and are willing to use to automate behavioral responses.

Studies of consumer behavior in the face of dynamic pricing use two different measures of response: price elasticity of demand (also called own-price elasticity or daily elasticity) and elasticity of substitution. Elasticity of substitution is the measure of response, which looks at the ratio of peak to off-peak quantity relative to the ratio of peak to off-peak price.

Early analyses of C&I response to price signals focused on a particular time-of-use structure called peak-load pricing. Peak-load pricing involves charging a higher price during a designated peak period and a lower price during the rest of the day, with both prices known in advance. Aigner and Hirshberg (1985) studied heterogeneous small and medium-sized commercial and industrial firms with peak-load pricing in Southern California. They find a "significant though small estimated elasticity of substitution of 0.4433" (p. 352). They also found that for the largest customers, their summer responses would have been sufficient to generate enough savings to offset more than the cost of the interval meter required to communicate the price signal to the customer. Note that this TOU rate structure does not even require an interval meter, as long as customers know the rate structure in advance.

Herriges *et al.* (1993) analyzed a time-of-use rate and a (revenue neutral) real-time rate experiment performed with Niagara Mohawk's large energy customers. Niagara Mohawk divided customers into a time-of-use group, a real-time group that received an hourly price, and a control group facing their current rate structure. Their analysis indicated that in peak hours the real-time price users reduced their consumption by 36 percent, while the control group only reduced their peak use by 5 percent. On the highest priced days, the real-time users decreased their energy use over the entire day, while the control group's use increased. These results provided early evidence that large users do respond to price signals and can both decrease energy demand and shift energy use to non-peak hours. Herriges *et al.* also found that responsiveness did vary, even among large users, but that the responses of a few large customers were sufficient to cut peak demand substantially. This result illustrates how nonlinear the system effects of dynamic pricing can be – small changes in individual behavior at the margin can have large effects on other variables like grid stability and wholesale energy prices. Also, these responses may be a lower bound, because the finite nature of these experiments implies that industrial customers would be unwilling to make major physical or operating changes in response to a short-term program.

More recently, Georgia Power's real-time pricing pilot program incorporates an innovation in designing retail pricing structures. Over 1600 customers with 5000 total megawatts (an average of 3.1 megawatts per customer) of peak demand participate (O'Sheasy, October 2002). Each participating customer has a right to consume the current load profile used in rate calculations for that customer, and any deviations from the load profile are priced with reference to a real-time price. Thus the customer can consume along the pattern that the utility expected when calculating the regulated rates, and that consumer would be no worse off. The consumer can also choose to deviate at the real-time price. This program uses load profiling to send the appropriate price signals to the consumer, at least for the energy portion of the bill. Monthly administration fees charged to customers range from $155 to $195 depending on plan and usage, to cover billing, administrative and communication costs. Customers also have access to an Internet website for the retrieval of price information.

Georgia Power has seen load reductions of 10–20 percent of peak demand for participating customers. Georgia Power has also observed that its commercial and industrial customers exhibit a wide range of price elasticities of demand when they can act on their preferences, even within two-digit SIC codes. These customers were able to shift demand away from peak hours, reduce overall demand, and smooth out both the prices and the aggregate load profile of Georgia Power's large users. Note that the Georgia Power program relies on creative use of the load profile as a baseline, and not necessarily on using technology to enable price signals and to automate responses to those signals.

Niagara Mohawk customers have had further opportunities to make retail choices involving dynamic pricing. In 1999, New York instituted retail competition and real-time pricing as the default retail option for large C&I customers (Goldman *et al.* 2004a). Thus large C&I customers could choose to purchase retail service from retailers other than the incumbent utility, and if they chose to stay with Niagara Mohawk, they would pay a real-time price for the energy component of their bill. Goldman *et al.* (2004a, 2004b, 2005) analyzed data for customers with peak demand larger than two megawatts that faced a real-time price, whether from the incumbent utility or from a competing retailer. On average, the customers responded to dynamic pricing with an elasticity of substitution ranging from –0.11 to –0.14. Although the reports do not provide much detail about the use of technology by the customers, customer survey responses indicate that although they may have building control technology installed, many of them do not use it to automate short-term response to price signals, but instead use it to manage their long-term energy use and budget (Goldman *et al.* 2005, p. 17).

Residential customers

Residential customers are generally believed to be less able to change their behavior in response to dynamic pricing, and to be less willing to do so. As with commercial and industrial customers, however, there is considerable heterogeneity within the residential customer class, a heterogeneity that technology and retail entrepreneurs could exploit to provide technologically-interested and early-adopter consumers with attractive, novel value propositions. Studies of residential response to dynamic pricing suggest that even without much enabling technology customers do respond to simple price signals; furthermore, when equipped with enabling technology that can include digital home gateways and/or smart, grid-friendly appliances, such technology produces even stronger responses to dynamic pricing.

Wisconsin was the pioneer in exploring the use of peak-load pricing to residential customers. Caves and Christensen (1980) and Caves *et al.* (1981) describe a residential peak-load pricing experiment in Wisconsin between 1976 and 1980. Different customers had different "slopes" or differences between off-peak and peak rates. Consumers did respond to peak-load pricing by shifting their use. Furthermore, the consumers whose behavior changed the most were those with air conditioners and those with electric water heaters. The price elasticity of demand of these consumers was higher in certain peak hours, and varied across the day, as measured by differences in elasticities of substitution. Caves *et al.* (1989) performed a similar analysis of Pacific Gas & Electric's TOU rate experiment, with similar results.

One brief episode during the California electricity crisis provides further evidence on the extent of customer demand response, even in the absence of advance price signals and enabling technology. By 2000 San Diego Gas & Electric (SDGE) had recovered its stranded costs and was released from the retail rate cap established by the California Public Utility Commission (CPUC). SDGE set its rates to end-use customers based on a five-week moving average of wholesale market prices. Between the summers of 1999 and 2000, average wholesale electricity prices increased four-fold, and retail rates doubled for most consumers (Bushnell & Mansur 2005, p. 494). Furthermore, consumers only saw the effects of the rate increase after the fact, when their bills arrived. Consumers complained, and complained enough to have rate regulation reimposed in September 2000, but they also conserved in response to price increases. Bushnell and Mansur (2005) estimated that the average price elasticity of demand during the three months before the reimposition of regulated rates was –0.068; a 100 percent increase in price led to a 6.8 percent decrease in consumption (Bushnell and Mansur 2005).[8] This event provides some evidence that, although demand for electric power is inelastic, it is indeed downward sloping, and customers can and do respond to price signals, even without communication technology or new end-use devices.

California Statewide Pricing Pilot, 2003–2004

California's electricity policy challenges, particularly the absence of active demand to discipline the pricing behavior of suppliers, led to the California Statewide Pricing Pilot (SPP). A joint project of the investor-owned utilities, the CPUC, and the California Energy Commission, the SPP tested different pricing structures and how customers responded to them during 18 months between July 2003 and December 2004. Some 2500 residential and small commercial or industrial customers faced different types of TOU price structures, some of which had a critical peak price (CPP). All participants faced at least a peak price and an off-peak price, except for one group that received only day-ahead critical period notification, but did not receive price signals. Prices varied seasonally, reflecting the higher cost (and higher value) of providing power during summer months. Participants received digital meters capable of receiving and communicating hourly price signals.

Residential SPP participants faced one of four pricing structures: CPP-F, CPP-V, TOU, and information only. CPP-F involved a fixed TOU structure on all weekdays, but on up to 15 days per year a critical peak price period could be called, for which participants would be notified 24 hours in advance, and the CPP price and length of critical peak were fixed. TOU participants faced the same price structure as the CPP-F households, except that they did not receive any CPP notifications. The CPP-V rate varied from the CPP-F rate in three ways: participants would receive notification of a critical period up to four hours in advance instead of 24 hours, the critical peak period they faced could vary from one to five hours, and they had supplemental enabling technology that they could use to manage their responses to price signals.

The SPP final report includes estimates of both the daily own-price elasticity of demand and the elasticity of substitution. For the CPP-F participants, the daily price elasticity in 2003 equaled –0.035, and the 2004 daily price elasticity was –0.054. The elasticity of substitution in 2003 equaled –0.09, and the 2004 elasticity of substitution was –0.086 (CRA 2005, p. 48). Average reductions in consumption were highest during the summer months (July, August, September), and the houses with central air conditioning had the largest absolute and percent reduction in consumption. Overall consumption did not decrease, so there was no conservation effect among these participants. Unfortunately, the TOU sample size was sufficiently small to limit any inferences that can be drawn from their behavior.

CPP-V participants had daily price elasticities ranging between –0.027 and –0.044, and elasticities of substitution between –0.077 and –0.111. However, the most important result from the CPP-V analysis is that the use of supplemental enabling technology amplified the impact (i.e., reduction of consumption in response to price signal) relative to that seen in the CPP-F sample. The impact of the group with enabling technology was more than double the average CPP-F impact (27 percent vs. 13 percent) (CRA 2005, p. 109). Furthermore, an econometric decomposition of the impact of the CPP-V decisions indicates that 60 percent of the impact was due to the use of the enabling technology, and 40 percent was due to other behavioral responses. This result is the crucial one for showing the potential that digital technology has for increasing the ease of automating decisions for residential customers, and thus for turning active demand into a network resource.

Information-only participants did not create significant reductions in use during critical hours. This result led the SPP analysts to conclude that demand response is unsustainable in the absence of the price signals inherent in dynamic pricing.

In 2004 the SPP participants had some instances of critical periods being called on multiple days (two or three) in a row. In these cases the repetition did not induce a statistically significant fatigue, or diminution in response to the dynamic pricing.

Gulf Power Good Cents Select, 2001–present

Gulf Power in Florida (a subsidiary of Southern Company) operates a residential demand response program, based on a combination of metering and control technology, customer service, and a TOU pricing structure. Note that this program exists within a vertically-integrated, regulated IOU operating in a state that has not passed any restructuring legislation. Gulf Power's Good Cents Select program uses a four-part TOU price structure, a programmable thermostat that allows customers to establish settings based on temperature and price, meter-reading technology, and load control technology for customers to shift load if they chose in response to price signals. Customers also pay a participation fee, which is one unusual feature of the Gulf Power program.

In 2001, 2300 residences participated in the Good Cents Select program. In that year Gulf Power achieved energy use reductions of 22 percent during high-price periods and 41 percent during critical (usually weather-related) periods. Furthermore, customer satisfaction is 96 percent, the highest satisfaction rating for any Gulf Power program in its history, notwithstanding the monthly partici-pation fee. Customers say that the $4.53 fee (which covers approximately 60 percent of program costs) is worth the energy management and automation benefits that they derive from participating in the program (Borenstein *et al.* (2002), Appendix B).

The Good Cents Select program is unique in its use of technology to provide residential customers with automation capabilities. Each home has a program-mable gateway/interface that, in addition to allowing thermostat programming, enables the customer to program up to four devices in the home to respond to price signals (GAO 2004, pp. 9, 42). When surveyed, part of the high customer satisfaction and willingness to pay a monthly participation fee arises from this ability to use technology to manage energy use in the home and increase the ease of making choices in the face of price signals.

ComEd/CNT Energy-Smart Pricing Plan, 2003–2005

The Energy-Smart Pricing Plan (ESPP) was an innovative three-year residential demand response program, a joint effort between the Center for Neighborhood Technology's Community Energy Cooperative and Commonwealth Edison. In its first year (2003), the program had 750 participants in a variety of neighbor-hoods and types of homes, from large single-family homes to multiple-unit buildings. In 2004 the program expanded to 1000 participants, and in 2005 the program had 1500 participants. It is the only large-scale program in the country that presents residential customers with hourly price signals. Commonwealth Edison provides the hourly prices, on a rate tariff approved by the Illinois Com-merce Commission.

The keys to the Energy-Smart Pricing Plan are simplicity and transparency in the transmission of information to residential customers. Participants receive a simple digital interval meter, and can either call a toll-free phone number or visit a website to see what the hourly prices will be on the following day. Further-more, if the next day's peak prices will exceed ten cents/kilowatt hour, cus-tomers receive a notification by phone, email, or fax. Customers will never pay a price above 50 cents/kWh, which the Community Energy Cooperative imple-mented by buying a financial hedge at 50 cents.

In 2003, the first year of the program, customers saved an average of 19.6 percent on their energy bills (Summit Blue 2004). They generally joined the program expecting to save $10/month on average, and were not disappointed. Surveys indicate that the participants found the price information timely, and that with this small inducement to save money on their energy bill by making small behavioral modifications, they actually became more aware of their energy use overall, not only in the approximately 30 hours last summer that had higher prices. They also said that their personal contributions toward reduced energy use and improving the environment by participating in this plan really mattered to them.

Although the summer of 2003 was mild in northern Illinois, the econometric analysis of the results showed a price elasticity of demand in those hours, at the margin, of -0.042. On average the residents on ESPP reduced their peak energy use by approximately 20 percent, a number similar to the reductions seen in other residential dynamic pricing programs. In 2004, another mild summer in northern Illinois, the price elasticity of demand was -0.08. As in 2003, the price elasticity of demand for multiple-family dwellings with no air conditioning was surprisingly high: -0.117 (Summit Blue 2005, p. 10).

Illinois saw a hot summer in 2005, with sustained periods of high electricity prices. Over the entire summer, the price elasticity of demand at the margin was -0.047. On the hottest day of the summer, July 15, total electricity consumption by the participants was 15 percent lower than the level of consumption predicted if the participants had not been receiving dynamic price signals.

The hot weather in 2005 also enabled examination of the effects of automated air conditioner cycling. Fifty-seven of the participants had automation switches added to their air conditioning in 2004 to enable price-triggered air conditioning cycling during high price notifications. The use of automated switches increased the price elasticity of demand for those customers to -0.069, an increase of 0.022 (46 percent) relative to the elasticity for the total participant pool. This result suggests that automation of control can amplify demand response and the various individual and system benefits that derive from it.

The GridWise Olympic Peninsula Demonstration Project

The projects discussed in the previous section show that residential customers can and do respond to dynamic pricing, and that enabling technologies increase the ability to respond and magnitude of the effects. The Olympic Peninsula GridWise Demonstration Project examined specifically the interaction of retail choice and enabling technologies (Hammerstrom *et al.* 2007).

The Olympic Peninsula GridWise Testbed Project is a demonstration project, led by the Pacific Northwest National Laboratory (PNNL), testing a residential network with highly distributed intelligence and market-based dynamic pricing. Washington's Olympic Peninsula is an area of great scenic beauty, with population centers concentrated on the northern edge. The peninsula's electricity distribution network is connected to the rest of the network through a single distribution substation. While the peninsula is experiencing economic growth and associated growth in electricity demand, the natural beauty of the area and other environmental concerns mean that the residents wanted to explore options other than building generation capacity on the peninsula or building additional transmission capacity.

Thus this project tested the combination of enabling technologies and market-based dynamic pricing to investigate the effects of dynamic pricing and enabling technology on utilization of existing capacity, deferral of capital investment, and the ability of distributed demand-side and supply-side resources to create system reliability. Two questions were of primary interest in this project: (1) what dynamic pricing contracts are attractive to consumers, and how does enabling technology affect that choice? (2) to what extent will consumers choose to automate energy use decisions?

One hundred and thirty broadband-enabled households with electric heating participated in the project, which lasted for the year April 2006–March 2007. Each household received a programmable controlling thermostat (PCT) with a visual user interface that allowed the consumer to program the thermostat for the home, and specifically to program it to respond to price signals if desired. Households also received water heaters equipped with a GridFriendly™ appliance (GFA) controller chip developed at PNNL that enables the water heater to receive price signals and be programmed to respond automatically to those price signals. Consumers could control the sensitivity of the water heater through the PCT settings.

These households also participated in a market field experiment involving dynamic pricing. While they continued to purchase energy from their local utility at a fixed, discounted price, they also received a cash account with a predetermined balance which was replenished quarterly. The energy use decisions they made would determine their overall bill, which was deducted from their cash account, and they were able to keep any difference as profit. The worst a household could do was a zero balance, so they were no worse off than if they had not participated in the experiment. At any time customers could log in to a secure website to see their current balance and how effective their energy use strategies were.

Upon signing up for the project the households received extensive information and education about the technologies available to them and the kinds of energy use strategies made possible by these technologies. They were then asked to choose a retail pricing contract from three options: a fixed-price contract (with an embedded price risk premium), a TOU contract with a variable CPP component that could be called in periods of tight capacity, or a RTP contract that would reflect a wholesale market-clearing price in five-minute intervals. The RTP was determined using a uniform price double auction, in which buyers (households and commercial) submit bids and sellers submit offers simultaneously. This project is the first instance in which a double auction retail market design has been tested in electric power.

The households ranked the contracts, and were then divided fairly evenly among the three types and a control group that received the enabling technologies and would have their energy use monitored, but did not participate in the dynamic pricing market experiment. All households received either their first or second choice; interestingly, over two-thirds of the households ranked RTP as their first choice. This result counters the received wisdom that residential customers want only reliable service at low, stable prices.

The results of the project have not yet been analyzed fully due to its recent completion, but some preliminary results are striking, based on a preliminary analysis of data from the first nine months of the program.

Preliminary Result 1: For the RTP group, peak consumption decreased by 15–17 percent relative to what the peak would have been in the absence of the dynamic pricing, even though their overall energy consumption increased by approximately 4 percent.

A 15–17 percent reduction is substantial, and is similar in magnitude to the reductions seen in the California SPP program and the Gulf Power program. The regression analysis reported in Table A1 in Appendix 4.1 suggests that, after controlling for price response, weather effects, and weekend days, the RTP group's overall energy consumption was 4 percent higher than the fixed price group's. This result, in combination with the load duration effect noted above, indicates that the overall effect of RTP dynamic pricing is to smooth consumption over time, not to decrease it. Further analysis of the data is required to explore the role of automation and the transmission of price signals to devices in this outcome.

Preliminary Result 2: The TOU group achieved both a large own-price elasticity of demand (–0.17) based on hourly data, and an overall energy reduction of approximately 20 percent relative to the fixed price group.

Table A2 of Appendix 4.1 reports the preliminary results of the econometric analysis of the TOU group hourly data for the first nine months of the program. The regression analysis suggests that, after controlling for price response, weather effects, and weekend days, the TOU group's overall energy consumption was 20 percent lower than the fixed-price group's. This result indicates that the TOU (with occasional critical peaks) pricing induced overall conservation, a result that is consistent with the results of the California SPP project.

Table A3 reports a time series estimation of the price elasticity of demand in the TOU group; the coefficient estimate is –0.17. The price elasticity estimate is calculated using an ARIMA model with a 1-, 4-, 8-, and 24-hour lag structure to control for natural autoregressive characteristics of energy use over the course of a day, as well as weather-related variables and weekend days. While consistent with the large conservation effect mentioned above, this price elasticity of demand estimate is high relative to those observed in other projects, and will require further analysis. One hypothesis to test is whether the automation capabilities of the technologies contributed to an increased price elasticity. The California SPP found a marginal conservation effect from the technology, but not a marginal price elasticity effect; however, their technology did not include as much ability to automate responses to price signals as the GridFriendly™ technologies employed in this project.

Preliminary Result 3: The fine-grained automation and price response capabilities in five-minute intervals change the nature of the RTP problem and its analysis.[9]

One of the useful features of the RTP market's double auction design is that we have data on the actual bids submitted by the devices in the households (and the two commercial consumers). Each of the 30 households on the RTP contract submitted bids to purchase electricity every five minutes for the entire year of the project. Thus these households participated in 105,120 market intervals, submitting bids in each. Their devices recorded the actual bids they submitted, which enables us to use these structural bids to calculate (not estimate) their price elasticity of demand in each five-minute period.

Using those actual bids, we calculated price elasticity relative to the market-clearing price, using the bids as the structural demand function. Thus, the demand elasticity is

$$\eta = \frac{Q_{clear}}{P_{clear}} \frac{P_{clear} - P_{bid}}{Q_{bid}}$$

Analyzing those structural price elasticities in five-minute increments reveals that they are not normally distributed. Rather, the price elasticity data follow a Pareto distribution, which is a power law distribution. Figure 4.1 shows a plot of the structural price elasticity data on the x-axis and the probability of that elasticity occurring in the data on the y-axis (both measured logarithmically). The asymptotically linear nature of the relationship seen in Figure 4.1 is consistent with data drawn from a power law distribution.

Exhibiting a power law distribution has two important implications for this analysis. First, when data exhibit a power law relationship they are scale-free or scale-invariant, which suggests that as more households have automation capabilities in response to price signals, the results we have observed in this project would not change meaningfully at different scales or market sizes. Another way to think of the scale-free characteristic is if the same project were run on

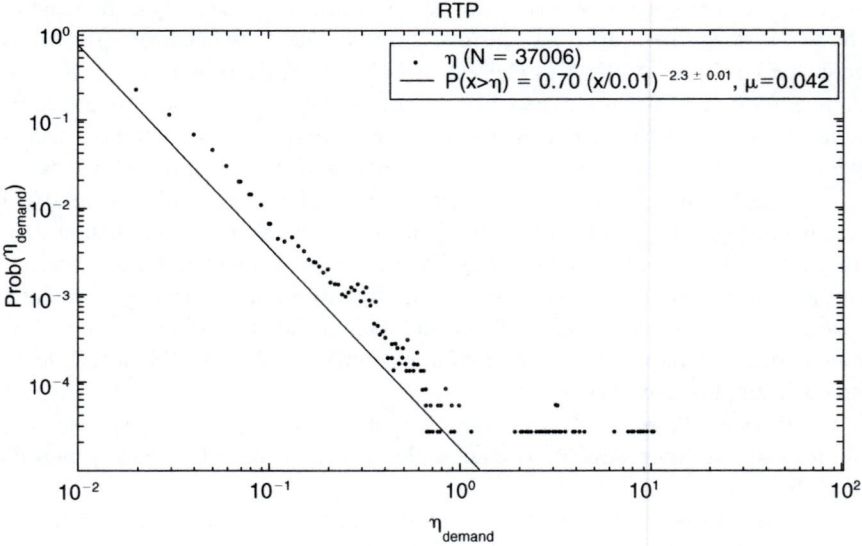

Figure 4.1 Structural price elasticity results for the complete RTP data set.

populations of different sizes, even dramatically different sizes, the pattern seen in the elasticity data would not change. Second, in complex systems a power law relationship indicates robustness and self-organization, and is thus consistent with the RTP double auction being an equilibrating process. In other words, in this system the combination of RTP and the digital technology led to emergent order and decentralized coordination.

These preliminary results suggest that the technological and institutional capacity to send prices to devices changes the nature of the network, its information content, and the choice set for individual behavior quite significantly.

Summary of results

Table 4.1 summarizes the own-price elasticity, elasticity of substitution, and impact/peak consumption reduction results in the projects discussed above. The range of results and the consistency of some degree of impact across the studies indicate that consumers (residential, commercial, and industrial) can and do respond to dynamic pricing, and that installed enabling technology creates the opportunity for them to amplify that response by automating their behavior.

These field experiments indicate that dynamic pricing does induce customers of different types and sizes to manage their own energy use in response to price signals. Even within traditional customer classes, consumers are heterogeneous, and dynamic pricing enables that heterogeneity of demand response to contribute to system reliability and to economizing on necessary infrastructure capital investment. Furthermore, enabling digital technology like building management systems, home gateways, and grid-friendly appliances amplify demand response, and work in conjunction with dynamic pricing to empower and inform consumers while contributing to system reliability and economic efficiency in the network as a whole.

Conclusion

The evidence presented here demonstrates that consumers of all types can and do respond to electricity price signals. Furthermore, consumers have responded to dynamic pricing with even the most rudimentary digital technology – a simple interval meter. Digital communication technologies contribute to and amplify that responsivity. Such responses benefit the individuals as well as creating system reliability benefits through deferred capital investment and reduced requirements for costly standby generation contracts in peak hours. Automation using digital technology and direct transmission of prices to devices avoids the requirement that the participants develop new habits, or remember to change the thermostat or turn off the water heater in the morning before they go to work. By so doing, digital technology reduces the transaction costs that could impede individual consumers and retail service providers from engaging in mutually beneficial exchange.

Evidence of the effect of enabling technology is largely impressionistic, because most studies and projects have focused on demonstrating customer

Table 4.1 Summary of elasticity and impact results

Location	Type of customer	Study	Year	Own-price elasticity	Elasticity of substitution	Reduction of peak consumption (%)
New York	C&I	Goldman et al.	2003		−0.14	
New York	C&I	Goldman et al.	2004		−0.11	
San Diego	Mix	Bushnell and Mansur (2001)	2000	−0.068		
CA CPP-F	Residential	CRA (2005)	2003	−0.035	−0.09	
CA CPP-F	Residential	CRA (2005)	2004	−0.054	−0.086	13 (average)
CA CPP-V	Residential w/technol.	CRA (2005)	2003–2004	−0.027 to	−0.077 to	27 (average)
CA CPP-V	C&I LT20	CRA (2005)	2003–2004	−0.044	−0.111	14.3
CA CPP-V	C&I GT20	CRA (2005)	2003–2004			13.8
Gulf Power	Residential	Borenstein et al. (2002)	2001			22 (high price sig) 41 (weather crit.)
Chicago ESPP	Residential	Summit Blue	2003	−0.042		
Chicago ESPP	Residential	Summit Blue	2004	−0.08		
Chicago ESPP	Residential	Summit Blue	2005	−0.047		
Chicago ESPP	Residential w/AC switch	Summit Blue	2005	−0.069		
Olympic Peninsula RTP	Residential	Preliminary results	2006			15–17 (average)
Olympic Peninsula TOU	Residential	Preliminary results	2006	−0.17		

response to price signals and not on the incremental effect of technology. In the cases discussed here (California Statewide Pricing Pilot, Center for Neighborhood ESPP, Gulf Power Good Cents Program, and the GridWise Olympic Peninsula project), studies have documented a substantial amplification of the demand response due specifically to the technology available to the consumer. Thus the evidence of consumer response to dynamic pricing presented here offers a lower bound on the type and magnitude of behavior we could expect from consumers empowered with the choice of more sophisticated technology. Moreover, the power law result from the GridWise Olympic Peninsula Project indicates that technology-enabled decentralized coordination is possible even at larger scales than just a pilot project.

One limitation of the programs and pilots that have taken place over the last two decades is their known, finite nature. If customers know that a program is finite, they may behave differently than they would if presented with open-ended retail options. Furthermore, the length of the program may not be sufficiently long to provide a payback to the customer for the change in behavior or for investment in new devices.

Retail electric choice puts more control in the hands of consumers and empowers them to make intelligent energy choices, including the choice to use digital technology to automate their behavior in response to dynamic pricing. Consumers could choose anything from a fixed price that incorporates an insurance premium to full real-time pricing, in which the customer bears the financial risk of price volatility, but could see electricity bills fall by shifting or reducing use.

The negative consequences of fixing retail rates have been hidden for decades by other aspects of regulation, such as the control of wholesale prices and excess supply in generation, but the problems arising from fixed retail rates have become more obvious in the era of restructuring. In particular, the liberalization of wholesale prices has disconnected the wholesale and retail markets, with unintended negative effects for customers and firms. The pursuit of perfection and the transformation of the electric power network requires reconnecting those markets through price signals, and one of the most effective means of accomplishing that goal is by harnessing the symbiotic relationship of dynamic pricing and enabling technology.

Despite these results, dynamic pricing and enabling technologies have proliferated slowly in the electricity industry. Proliferation requires a combination of formal and informal institutional change to overcome a variety of barriers; formal institutional change in the primary form of federal legislation is reducing some of these barriers, but it is an incremental process. The traditional rate structure, fixed by state regulation and slow to change, presents a substantial barrier. Predetermined load profiles inhibit market-based pricing by ignoring individual customer variation and the information that customers can communicate through choices in response to price signals. Furthermore, the persistence of standard offer service at a discounted rate (i.e., a rate that does not reflect the financial cost of insurance against price risk) stifles any incentive customers might have to pursue other pricing options.

The most important, yet also the most intangible and difficult to change, obstacle to dynamic pricing and enabling technologies is the set of incentives for inertia. The primary stakeholders in the industry – utilities, regulators, and customers – all have status quo bias. Incumbent utilities face incentives to maintain the regulated status quo to the extent possible, given the economic, technological, and demographic changes surrounding them; they have been successful at using the political process to achieve this objective. Customer inertia is deep because they have not had to think about their consumption of electricity and the price they pay for it; consumer advocates typically reinforce this bias by arguing for low, stable prices for highly reliable power as an entitlement. Regulators and customers explicitly value the stability and predictability that the vertically-integrated, historically supply-oriented and reliability-focused environment has created. But what is unseen and unaccounted for is the opportunity cost of such predictability – the foregone value creation in innovative services, empowerment of customers to manage their own energy use, and use of double-sided markets to enhance market efficiency and network reliability. Compare this unseen potential with the value creation in telecommunications, where even young adults can understand and adapt to cell phone pricing plans, and benefit from the stream of innovations in the industry.

Double-sided retail markets open up the potential for utilities to make more profit by selling less power, because they enable the dynamic pricing that can increase revenue on power sold in peak hours. But they have to see it as a viable business proposition, and regulators have to show leadership in enabling utilities to offer their customers a portfolio of contracts from which to choose, even those that include choosing to pay higher prices some of the time, or choosing to pay less for lower reliability or lower quality service.

Double-sided retail markets can also reduce the utility's costs in the long run. The level of peak demand determines investment in generation and transmission assets, and the more extensive active demand and double-sided markets become, the longer is the timeframe between costly and unpopular investments. Unfortunately, in the current regulatory environment based solely on cost recovery and profit as a rate of return on assets, neither the utility nor the regulator has sufficient incentives to pursue digital, demand-side technology and pricing innovations as the means for saving on future investment.

If policymakers and industry consider the possibility that utilities can offer different value propositions to their customers than just "juice coming through the wall," utilities can benefit from using market-based pricing as a tool for offering an attractive portfolio of service options to their customers. Creating value from this change, though, requires vision, and getting the transitions and the institutions right can be extremely difficult. Consumers will have to change how they think about buying electric service, and what that service is, exactly. For that change to occur, politicians and regulators will have to act on the leadership and vision that would allow consumers to take responsibility for their individual purchasing choices.

The potential for a highly distributed, decentralized network of devices automated to respond to price signals creates new policy and research questions. Do individuals automate sending prices to devices? If so, do they adjust settings, and if so, how? Does the combination of price effects and innovation increase total surplus, including consumer surplus? In aggregate, do these distributed actions create emergent order in the form of system reliability?

Answering these questions requires thinking about the diffuse and private nature of the knowledge embedded in the network, and the extent to which such a network becomes a complex adaptive system. The framework for thinking about the economic consequences of such a technology-enabled, knowledge-rich distributed system incorporates elements of complexity science, Austrian economics, and new institutional economics (NIE).

The synthesis of these approaches models the problem of prices to devices as one in which knowledge is distributed and necessarily incomplete (Hayek 1945; Kirzner 1997), the interaction of the decentralized agents acting with distributed control (e.g., self-control in response to individual incentives) can lead to emergent self-organization (Holland 1995, pp. 6–10), and the institutions (both formal and informal) governing the system matter greatly for shaping individual decisions and overall outcomes. The evidence presented here, particularly the preliminary evidence from the Olympic Peninsula GridWise Project, points to that synthesis as a model for understanding individual behavior in a world where prices to devices are possible and for thinking about the types of regulatory institutions that complement such a vision of the electricity industry.

Appendix 4.1

Preliminary Econometric Analysis of Olympic Peninsula GridWise Demonstration Project

Table A1 OLS regression to isolate marginal effect of being on the TOU and RTP contracts

. regress lnenergy lnprice saturday sunday weather wind humidity tou rtp, robust

Linear regression			Number of obs = 19687
			F(8, 19678) = 1093.94
			Prob > F = 0.0000
			R-squared = 0.3263
			Root MSE = .41488

lnenergy	Robust Coef.	Std. Err.	t	$P > |t|$	[95% Conf. Interval]	
lnprice	0.1448562	0.0083975	17.25	0.000	0.1283962	0.1613161
saturday	0.0187938	0.0086643	2.17	0.030	0.0018109	0.0357766
sunday	0.0756435	0.009022	8.38	0.000	0.0579597	0.0933273
weather	0.0335761	0.0004066	82.59	0.000	0.0327792	0.034373
wind	−0.0071104	0.0008578	−8.29	0.000	−0.0087917	−0.0054291
humidity	−0.006837	0.0002049	−33.37	0.000	−0.0072386	−0.0064354
tou	−0.2006103	0.0077279	−25.96	0.000	−0.2157575	−0.185463
rtp	0.0426333	0.009512	4.48	0.000	0.023989	0.0612776
_cons	3.351747	0.0415579	80.65	0.000	3.27029	3.433204

Table A2 AR regression, TOU group only, lag structure AR(1 4 8 24)

. arima lnenergy2 lnprice2 saturday sunday weather wind humidity, ar(1 4 8 24) robust
Number of gaps in sample: 1
(note: filtering over missing observations)
(setting optimization to BHHH)
Iteration 0:   log pseudolikelihood = 1149.2582
Iteration 1   log pseudolikelihood = 1773.7526
Iteration 2:   log pseudolikelihood = 1960.1353
Iteration 3:   log pseudolikelihood = 1978.8368
Iteration 4:   log pseudolikelihood = 1980.4968
(switching optimization to BFGS)
Iteration 5:   log pseudolikelihood = 1980.6704
Iteration 6:   log pseudolikelihood = 1980.6947
Iteration 7:   log pseudolikelihood = 1980.6951
Iteration 8:   log pseudolikelihood = 1980.6951
Iteration 9:   log pseudolikelihood = 1980.6951
ARIMA regression
Sample: 317744 to 324343, but with gaps
            Number of obs = 6598
            Wald chi2(10) = 50788.81
            Log pseudolikelihood = 1980.695 Prob > chi2 = 0.0000
            | Semi-robust

lnenergy2	Coef.	Std. Err.	z	$P > |z|$	[95%Conf. Interval]	
lnenergy2						
lnprice2	−0.1709742	0.0103838	−16.47	0.000	−0.191326	−0.1506224
saturday	−0.0004039	0.0093687	−0.04	0.966	−0.0187662	0.0179584
sunday	0.0102507	0.0096391	1.06	0.288	−0.0086416	0.0291431
weather	0.0167943	0.0011578	14.50	0.000	0.014525	0.0190637
wind	−0.0004381	0.000781	−0.56	0.575	−0.0019689	0.0010926
humidity	−0.000704	0.0003194	−2.20	0.027	−0.00133	−0.0000781
_cons	4.11171	0.0617684	66.57	0.000	3.990646	4.232774
	ARMA					
ar						
L1.	0.537301	0.0110945	48.43	0.000	0.5155563	0.5590458
L4.	−0.1252089	0.0064008	−19.56	0.000	−0.1377542	−0.1126636
L8.	0.0579915	0.0055723	10.41	0.000	0.0470699	0.0689131
L24.	0.4826831	0.0100405	48.07	0.000	0.4630041	0.5023621
/sigma	0.179013	0.0017466	102.49	0.000	0.1755897	0.1824363

5 Organizational form and the wires[1]

Introduction

Two of the most pervasive features of the retail sale of electric power service have been the bundling of the energy transaction with the wires transaction and the monopoly ownership of the physical infrastructure. Technological change has made it possible to change both of these features. Over the past century technological change has transformed the nature of the electricity value chain and its cost structure (Hirsh 1991). The vertically-integrated utility is no longer a natural monopoly, although the regulatory institutions premised on its being a natural monopoly persist. The only portion of the value chain that retains any natural monopoly characteristics (economies of scale and more efficient provision by a single firm) is the transportation function performed by the transmission and distribution wires. Despite that fact, the retail sales of the electricity commodity with the wires transportation service continue as a bundled transaction between individual customers and a single, regulated firm. Thus the electricity sale is still treated as a regulated transaction, even though the retail sale of the electricity commodity is technically competitive or contestable.

This chapter presents arguments for why enabling these changes could be valuable. Unbundling the energy and the wires transactions can enable competition in the retail provision/sale of electric power services. Retail markets are either competitive or contestable; wholesale markets for the energy commodity from generator to retailer are either competitive or contestable. Unbundling the retail transaction from the wires transaction would enable the dynamism inherent in market processes to create new value in those transactions while focusing regulatory enforcement on the wires transaction, until such time as distributed generation and technological change make the wires fully contestable.

As generation has become more competitive, and retail service is becoming increasingly competitive, the wires (transmission and distribution) become the sole remaining natural monopoly portion of the supply chain. Management and regulation of the wires is a current policy topic; while ownership of the wires remains concentrated in existing utilities, management and operational control of the transmission wires is vested in Regional Transmission Organizations (RTOs) or Independent System Operators (ISOs) in several regions in the U.S.

As more wholesale transactions cross those ownership boundaries, two concerns have arisen: monopoly pricing of wires access, and the incentives presented to transmission owners to invest in the wires infrastructure. The policy response in the U.S. to concerns about monopoly pricing has been to follow the lead of the telecommunications industry and implement transparent open access pricing, implemented by such federal rules as FERC Order 888. The perceived lack of investment in the wires infrastructure hit a crescendo in August 2003, when a large cascading blackout removed service for most of the Northeastern U.S. and parts of Canada. One estimate of the capital cost of keeping up with demand growth over the next 20 years is $384 billion (Walter *et al.* 2004, p. 10). Furthermore, this lack of investment has led to the aging of the wires network; the wires network remains an analog system, with the only true digital capability residing in control room operations and without any ability to perform digital monitoring or other network activities that use digital and communications technology.

Furthermore, technological change and increasingly embedded market networks have reduced the cost of having non-monopoly ownership of a single wires infrastructure – more so than a century ago, joint-venture ownership of the wires network is feasible, and can provide an alternative to natural monopoly cost-based regulation. This chapter presents a retail model in which the electricity and wires transactions are unbundled, and competing firms perform retail sales and marketing to end-use customers. This unbundling acknowledges that the wires, in this case the distribution wires, retain the single-infrastructure economies of scale consistent with natural monopoly. Moreover, the incentive, information, and innovation problems associated with rate-of-return regulation that were discussed in Chapter 2 raise the question of whether institutional alternatives to traditional regulation exist.

Importantly, the optimality of a single physical infrastructure does not imply the necessary monopoly ownership of that structure. In other words, one set of wires does not necessitate one owner. In particular, joint venture ownership is possible, and if structured properly, can undercut monopolization incentives facing the joint venture owners.

This chapter explores one such arrangement – a competitive joint venture – that allows for distributed ownership of the physical infrastructure. In this competitive joint venture (CJV), competing downstream retailers own shares in the physical assets of the wires distribution company, in proportion to the market shares they achieve in the retail sales of electricity service to end-use customers. This ownership rule provides the wires owners with a direct incentive to control costs and avoid monopoly pricing of the wires service, because such decisions would reduce their ability to compete downstream for retail customers. Thus CJV wires ownership can link the competitive retail sector with the wires sector, enabling us to exploit retail competition in the least competitive portion of the value chain. In this chapter we present a model that shows how such an institutional arrangement can generate superior outcomes relative to traditional regulation.

One important implication of this ownership structure is the change it implies for regulatory institutions. Over the past century regulatory institutions have struggled with the problem of asymmetric information and specific rate-base determination that accompanies cost-based, rate-of-return regulation. In the CJV model, though, the role of the regulator shifts from *ex ante* cost and rate determination to *ex post* validation and verification of the wires price charged to customers. This shift implies that instead of focusing on the unknowable specifics of distributed, private knowledge, the regulatory institutions focus on creating an environment in which agents (i.e., the retailers/CJV owners) interact in ways that induce them to reveal their diffuse, private knowledge through their actions and decisions. Thus the institutions shift from rate design to transparent information provision and contract enforcement.

As an example of institutional design, this CJV wires model embodies the decentralized coordination framework used in this book. The CJV model as a regulatory institution allows for flexible behavior within a transparent rules framework, and thus is consistent with the change and heterogeneity of agents and outcomes in dynamic systems. The retailer/CJV owner agents are themselves heterogeneous, with diffuse private knowledge, as are the consumers they serve and the regulators who implement the regulatory institutions. In this case, with shared ownership of a single physical infrastructure, institutions and institutional design matter a great deal for determining whether or not the wires market and the retail markets have equilibrating tendencies and can achieve emergent order.

This chapter describes the CJV model in some detail, and provides a survey of the various literatures that contribute to this institutional design question. In particular, the NIE literatures on joint-venture structure and use and on property rights and use rights over a common-poor resource inform this model and the ability of a CJV ownership structure to govern and regulate resource use and wires pricing in this context. The idea of joint-venture ownership of a single physical infrastructure arises from thinking about the wires network as a common-pool resource (CPR), and applying models from the extensive literature in new institutional economics (NIE) on the governance of CPRs and the management of ownership rights and use rights over CPRs. This chapter uses NIE literature about vertical integration, the transactional boundary of the firm, and CPR governance institutions to challenge the existing bundled structure of these transactions, as well as the perpetual monopoly franchise and cost-based regulation of that monopoly. The CJV ownership model and the implied regulatory institutions provide an illustration of how the complexity economics framework and thinking differently about the problem of a single physical infrastructure can lead to different approaches and institutional designs that are more adaptive and better suited to a distributed environment.

Unbundling the electricity and wires transactions

Since the beginning of commercial electric power in the 1880s, electricity has been sold to end-use customers as a bundled good – electricity and wires – through vertically integrated firms. It also has been regulated as a bundled good, both by regulatory fiat and, up to a point, by technological necessity. That regulation has largely taken place at the state level, starting with New York and Wisconsin in 1907 (Hirsh 1999, p. 21; Jarrell 1978, p. 270).

The separation of wires transactions from energy transactions was neither a business issue nor a policy issue, because of the limitations in the early technology that made measurement and recording of current flow prohibitively costly relative to its benefits. Then in 1935 the Federal Power Act bolstered the right of the states to regulate electric utilities, accepting exclusive service territory monopolies in return for the utility accepting a regulated rate of return on its assets and a mandatory obligation to serve all potential customers in the service territory, providing those customers with this bundled service.

By the 1950s, the separate physical measurement of electric current flowing down a wire without real-time human data recording became technologically feasible. This technological change created the possibility of unbundling energy and wires and creating separate markets for the exchange of each. The information technology changes of the 1980s and 1990s have built upon that feasibility and have made the development of separate energy and wires markets much more affordable through decreased transaction costs. Yet state-level regulation of energy and wires as a bundled service persists to this day.

Further technological change has increased the efficiency of small-scale electricity generation, creating contestability in electric energy markets. By 1992, the potential for competitive electricity commodity markets encouraged the passage of the Energy Policy Act. This legislation opened wholesale electricity markets, which are under the regulatory jurisdiction of the federal government instead of the states, to competition. Dynamic changes in the generation of power provide further technological arguments for the regulatory unbundling of energy from wires, yet to this day the regulation of energy and wires as a bundled good persists.

In the early twentieth century, technology affected both the regulatory environment and the transactional boundary of the firm. Absent regulatory lock-in and technological change could have changed the transactional boundary of the firm and allowed for the creation of new energy markets. Instead, interest pressures and inertia have combined to dilute or eliminate the realization of the potential for technological change to affect firm structure and market creation.

Although innovation and new technologies mean that bundling is no longer technically necessary and may not be welfare maximizing, our regulatory institutions are still tailored to an electricity network of bundled energy and wires sales. This institutional inertia and regulatory lock-in has contributed to the difficulties seen in the U.S., both with restructuring and with reliability. It provides an obstacle to the pursuit and discovery of other regulatory and business models that would benefit consumers while creating new business opportunities in the electricity industry.

Allowing for the legal and regulatory separation of energy commodity sales from the wires business is a crucial first step. Technologically, it is no longer necessary to impose the traditional regulatory assumption that energy must constitute a tie-in sale with the rental of the wires. Just as the rent you pay for a rental car is separate from your purchase of the energy required to operate it, so should your purchase of electrical energy be separate from the entity that charges you for using the wires. Reversing this retail regulatory lock-in would recognize the potential for and enhance the development of competitive electric energy markets.

Chapter 2 highlighted some of the early technological reasons for bundling and vertical integration, including the inability to meter current flow cost-effectively. What constitutes a firm and why is also very important for the analysis of the continued bundling of energy and wires; it also provides a theoretical foundation for analyzing a different model of wires ownership. In a benchmark competitive model, with full information and no incentive alignment problems, the existence of firms is entirely an artifact of the cost functions in the industry, of such associated issues as economies of scale and scope, and of the size of the relevant market. This approach undergirds the natural monopoly theory and the definition of subadditivity of costs that is the hallmark of electricity regulation.

Coase's "Nature of the Firm" (Coase 1937) and subsequent works in new institutional economics and agency theory recognize that this standard approach overlooks the incentive and governance reasons for having some transactions occur within firms and some occur in markets. Agency problems, the difficulty of writing complete contracts, and other transaction costs determine the transactional boundary of the firm, and when they change, the profit-maximizing firm's boundary should change to incorporate the new trade-off. The form and magnitude of the change in the firm's boundary is a function of the expected benefit and cost of rearranging how the transaction is realized, and also of the cost of bringing about the change (i.e., legal incorporation, contracting costs, merging different business cultures, etc.). As Coase and others have shown, the desire and ability to decrease transaction costs shapes vertical integration and contracting in a variety of industries (see, for example, Joskow 1988, 1991; Klein *et al.* 1978; Baker *et al.* 2002; Bajari and Tadelis 2001).

Furthermore, transaction costs determine whether or not markets exist at all for a particular transaction (Coase 1960). The standard example of the failure of markets to exist is pollution, most notably air pollution, because the cost of defining and enforcing the property rights that would enable markets for clean air to exist have been sufficiently high to prevent their arising to enable mutually beneficial exchange. However, technological change has changed the margin at which market existence is feasible and profitable. Improved emission-monitoring technologies have made trading emission permits possible, and researchers continue to work on nanotechnology fingerprints for individual polluters, which will further decrease the cost of defining and enforcing property rights. Thus technological change can decrease transaction costs, thereby both changing the transactional boundary of the firm and making markets feasible that were not before.

Transaction costs, the transactional boundary of the firm, and the feasibility of creating new markets forms the framework for understanding the potential for unbundling energy from wires. Electric utilities have always been vertically integrated, encompassing generation, transmission and distribution, and retail. Regulation of utilities based on natural monopoly theory ensued, and established an industry structure based on vertically integrated firms with large central generation and a single wire network.

This industry structure did not prevent technological change from occurring, but in fact the technological changes that had the potential to create energy markets – magnetic tape and analog-digital converter semiconductor technology – developed exogenously, and not with any specific design or intention for use in the electric industry. The large endogenous change has been the increasing efficiency of generation at smaller scales using combined-cycle gas turbine technology. These exogenous and endogenous technological changes have created the opportunity to change transaction costs in the industry, thereby creating opportunities to do two dynamic things: change the boundary of the firm in accordance with the change in transaction costs, and create new markets where they previously failed to exist because of transaction costs.

However, the industry structure is still a function of the regulatory environment, which has not been substantially updated since the 1930s. Technological change has created the potential for changing the transactional boundary of the firm and for market creation, but the regulatory environment's lack of a technological change feedback dynamic has eliminated the realization of that potential. Furthermore, the investment in metering technology that is a sunk cost, yet creates an information monopoly for the regulated utility, reinforces an inertial lock-in and reduces the likelihood of developing a technology feedback dynamic. Combining this technological path dependence with the incentives facing the regulators and regulated firms to perpetuate the status quo environment creates regulatory lock-in, and a potentially dynamically inefficient bundling of energy and wires transactions.

Three possible causes of this lack of regulatory adaptation to changing technology and changing market dynamics are:

- new technology adoption costs;
- interests of regulators in keeping bundled regulation of the energy/wires transactions;
- interests of utilities in keeping bundled regulation of the energy/wires transactions.

A standard argument for lags in adopting technological changes is the cost of that adoption. New technology adoption may involve fixed costs of acquiring new equipment, fixed costs of adapting the existing network to work with the new equipment, and variable costs for operating and maintaining the new equipment. Even before delving into the details of the costs of installing and operating new equipment, the argument is not persuasive given the large magnitude of cost decreases relative to performance that have been realized in the past two decades in information processing. In addition, much of the current flow-monitoring technology is installed along transmission and distribution lines to meet safety and reliability requirements, so the infrastructure is already in place to enable a fully unbundled retail energy market.

Regulators themselves might have an interest in retaining the status quo regulatory environment, for three reasons. First, the inertial tendency to maintain the status quo in the face of uncertainty cannot be overlooked as an important driver, particularly in the case of public utility regulation. Any change that might arguably threaten the reliability of electric service, and the ability of the regulators to believe that they retain control over this complex system, is likely to be met with hostility, or at least with great caution, due to risk aversion. Second, regulators may believe that retaining regulation of the bundled transactions is indeed in the public interest, largely because they may perceive unbundled electricity markets as they currently exist (i.e., at the wholesale level) insufficiently competitive to give customers meaningful choice. Finally, a rent-seeking perspective would suggest that regulators might perceive the unbundling and deregulation of the energy transaction as a reduction in their political and economic power, and that they might thus oppose such a move based on their individual interests.

Similarly, the incumbent regulated utilities might see the status quo regulatory structure as being in their interests, particularly if, as some analyses suggest, they have been successful in capturing the regulatory process (Hirsh 1999; Jarrell 1978). In addition to the capture aspect of potential benefit to the utilities, they could perceive a direct benefit from the legal prevention of competition in distribution, in retail, and in the metering that enables them to control the information flow that is crucial to the development of competing alternatives to regulated monopoly retail energy sales. This argument is consistent with Jarrell's analysis of the origins of regulation as being rooted in circumventing the competitive pressures that existed in the municipally regulated environment pre-1907. Even if utilities are not motivated by capture or the prevention of competition, they could also have inertial incentives – the regulated utility model is a known business model, and while regulation may limit the profit potential of the firm, it also limits its loss potential. Thus risk-averse utility executives may wish to retain this business model in the face of uncertainty.

These factors combine to make regulatory institutions slow to adapt to technological change and to changing market conditions. Regulatory agencies and commissions respond to the incentives facing them, in several ways. They are the product of direct legislative action, and as such operate in a very formal, law-driven, legalistic manner, with little room for flexibility or adaptation to changing and unknown circumstances.[2] These organizations operate under legislative remits within their states; these remits require the commissions to serve "in the public interest" in keeping with the precedent established in *Munn* v. *Illinois*. They thus strive to establish that they are applying the law in a manner in keeping with that remit. However, they may also have political incentives that incline them toward regulatory capture, and these incentives may have been present from the beginnings of utility regulation:

> Shrewd electric utility managers quickly found that legislatures had essentially abandoned their commissions, having given them limited resources with which to do their jobs. Utility executives had little trouble, then, in influencing the regulators and preventing them from impeding companies' plans to grow larger and more powerful. But the managers could never advocate the end of government oversight, because regulation legitimated natural monopoly status and provided numerous tangible advantages.
>
> (Hirsh 1999, p. 263)

This argument suggests what Jarrell (1978) found in his study of the motivations underlying regulation – the initial "public interest" argument for state regulation over municipal regulation-rested on the increased monitoring capabilities and the reduced probability of corruption at the state level, but in reality the budget constraints facing state agencies reduced their monitoring relative to the *ex ante* situation.

Technological change can decrease resource use, decrease costs, and increase consumer welfare through price decreases and through offering new products and services. It can also reduce the transaction costs that determine whether or not markets exist for particular transactions, as has been the case in the technological changes in energy.

This dynamic underlies much of the economic growth that has occurred for centuries (Mokyr 1990). Schumpeterian entrepreneurs, seeking out new profit opportunities through disruptive, discontinuous innovation, create growth through their willingness to bear risk; these efforts bring about new markets, new products, and new research and development (Heyes and Liston-Heyes 1998):

> The raw materials that we use have not changed, but as a result of trial and error, experimentation, refinement, and scientific investigation, the instructions that we follow for combining raw materials have become vastly more sophisticated. One hundred years ago, all we could do to get visual stimulation from iron oxide was to use it as a pigment. Now we put it on plastic tape and use it to make videocassette recordings.
>
> (Romer 1990, p. S72)

In fact, Romer's argument applies directly to the importance of technological change to growth in the electricity industry, although some of the cases of technological change that are relevant here (data recording and analog-digital converters/semiconductors) can be taken as exogenous, not endogenous. The development of the combined-cycle gas turbine generator was indeed an endogenous technological change, and did arise at least in part because of the regulatory change that occurred at the federal level, through PURPA in 1978 and the Energy Policy Act of 1992.

At the state level, regulation provides a barrier to the free entry of alternative energy providers to serve the energy needs of end-use customers; these energy providers would have the incentive to introduce demand response technologies –

metering, switching, and monitoring devices – designed to fit the preferences and budgets of customers, and enable them to take advantage of the low cost of off-peak energy.

One option for introducing unbundling that reduces these entry barriers is to allow several companies to bid for shares of the local utility. The winning bidders jointly share the distribution wires entity and its operating costs, under a competitively-ruled joint venture or cotenancy agreement, but they compete to supply the downstream retail customers their energy. This model has been used by the FERC to increase competition in gas pipelines networks, but it has not been tested in retail electricity markets.

A competitive joint venture wires ownership model

A description of a competitive joint venture

Consider a competitive joint venture (CJV) structure in which competing retailers own shares in the existing capacity of the distribution network. Each member's ownership share is determined by the distribution of market shares among the retailers in the downstream market.

Any member or subset of members can expand wires network capacity; the capacity use rights would belong to those members who funded the capacity expansion and would not be shared among all CJV participants. Furthermore, the CJV members cannot block an outsider from expanding network capacity (and thereby becoming a member of the CJV). Thus existing members cannot erect entry or expansion barriers. The CJV members share responsibility for network operations and management decisions and expenses.

With this model, Boffa and Kiesling (2008) propose and analyze the properties of a CJV possessing two important institutions: rules governing ownership structure, and rules governing the determination of the price of wires access. This framework thus suggests a regulatory institution that employs two instruments that are not standard in the mainstream regulation literature: the ownership structure of the CJV wires firm, and the decision-making procedure governing the firm. After setting the "rules of the game," the regulator does not intervene further, and the CJV partners face the task of autonomously establishing prices, quantity, and the level of investment.

In this CJV structure the retailer is both a customer and a shareholder in the wires company, because of its CJV ownership structure. This situation creates a potentially beneficial conflict of interests. On one hand, the firm would like the access price as low as possible as a wires service purchaser; on the other hand, as an owner, the firm prefers an high access price to gain more profit. Furthermore, the ownership share of the wires company is determined by the market share in the retail sector. The retailer is driven to lower its cost not only, as usual, to increase his share in the retail market, but also in order to increase his ownership stake in the wires company. Thus we have three driving forces of the prices beyond the standard ones. The retailer has an incentive to lower prices in order to gain a larger share in the distribution company. Also, he has an incentive to lower the access charges in his role of client of the distribution company. On the other hand, in his role of owner of the distribution company, he has an interest to increase the prices, in order to increase his profits. Furthermore, all of the retailers face these complex incentives, and interact both as competitors and as CJV partners. All retailers also face potential entry, and can choose to expand capacity. If that contestability effect is strong, it can undermine the ability of the CJV partners to act as a cartel.

In this institutional structure the regulator has three major tasks. It enforces the ownership structure of the distribution company. It guarantees the mechanism for defining the wires access charge. Finally, it guarantees that the prices the retailers commit to with the customers are indeed implemented. These tasks require the regulator to have less private and less *ex ante* information about firms' costs than the traditional natural monopoly. Thus this approach circumvents many of the problems that the Bayesian regulator literature addresses, as discussed in Chapter 2.

Boffa and Kiesling (2008) provide a theoretical model of this environment. In this model we find that the CJV rules lead to a (first-best) efficient outcome as a Nash equilibrium, in terms of the retail pricing and the wires access pricing for a given network capacity. This promising result will lead to further research and testing in more realistic experimental environments.

The NIE joint venture literature

At its core, the questions involved in ownership and governance of a single network infrastructure are questions of property rights. This section discusses research in new institutional economics (NIE) that is not usually associated with electricity policy, but which can inform the problems discussed above. Our analysis of the CJV as a regulatory institution for electric power distribution draws on several existing literatures.

The new institutional economics literature contributes a different dimension to analyses of traditional regulation and organizational alternatives to it. The NIE approach models the firm as more than a frictionless center of production and of transformation of inputs into outputs, with transaction costs both within the firm and the market shaping the optimal firm size and boundaries. The CJV structure analyzed here leverages the vertical nature of the electricity supply chain and the fact that some sectors within that supply chain can be competitive. In this sense the CJV is a contractual alternative to vertical integration in much the way that Klein *et al.* (1978) described in their analysis of the organizational substitutability of vertical integration and long-term contracting. Later work by Grossman and Hart (1986) and Hart and Moore (1998) elaborate on the tradeoff between vertical integration and contracting outside the firm and the effect of ownership on incentives.

The electric power network is not only part of a vertical supply chain; it is also a network comprising transaction-specific and site-specific assets. Wires networks also display two types of asset specificity – transaction specificity and site specificity – because each wire is currently used only to distribute electric power and can only physically be in one, fixed, place.[3] In many industries firms integrate vertically to internalize externalities and to avoid possible hold-up and opportunism problems that can arise from asset specificity (Williamson 1975). In such cases integration occurs within firms to economize on transaction and coordination costs, as opposed to occurring through bilateral contracting in markets (Coase 1937). In the case of electric power distribution, however, the risk of hold-up is mitigated by the presence of a large number of users, either the retailers when the distribution service is separated from the retail service, or the final end-use customers in the opposite case of bundling.

Hold-up problems in vertical supply chains in the presence of asset specificity were another focus in Klein *et al.* (1978), as well as Williamson (1975). The potential for a single infrastructure owner to hold up producers in the downstream industry in the chain is a salient one in electric power, both because of subadditive costs in the wires segment and because of asset specificity. We explore the extent to which a CJV structure can overcome such hold-up problems and opportunism while retaining the cost benefits of the network infrastructure.

Sampson (2004) explores the benefits of internal organization for controlling opportunism in a research equity joint venture context. Placing the joint venture in the continuum of governance institutions between market processes and hierarchy, she finds that the internal organization of a joint venture ownership structure can control opportunism and free riding through the use of both rules and information flow. Having a joint venture management board comprising representatives of all members facilitates monitoring, which reduces opportunism. It also provides an alternate dispute resolution venue, and one that may be less costly than courts given the reality of contract incompleteness. Sampson also finds that joint ventures enable members to respond to unanticipated conditions in ways that would not be possible if they were not acting in concert. Finally, she argues that the joint venture structure reduces transactions costs relative to a bilateral contract market mechanism, because the participants do not have to write as fully contingent a contract as they would if they were transacting through markets.

The CJV also provides a venue for dispute resolution among the wires owners, similar to that discussed in Sampson (2004) for research equity joint ventures, and in Williamson's (1985) invocation of hostages to create credible commitment. This means of contract enforcement may be less costly than the continued regulation of the bundled wires and energy transactions. Thus we conceptualize the CJV as a multilateral governance structure in which particular transactions occur, which incorporates the mutual reliance of the members (Williamson 1985, p. 528). Such a governance structure is likely to be more robust to costly and incomplete contracting and to unforeseen contingencies.

A related issue in applying these concepts in a network industry is access to the network. Carlton and Salop (1996) analyze the extent to which, and the conditions under which, network joint venture participants can exclude others from participating in the joint venture. With a network joint venture that provides an input that competing members use to produce output, members have an incentive to implement exclusionary rules to restrict access. Building on the earlier work of Carlton and Klamer (1983), Carlton and Salop argue that in some cases such exclusion can have beneficial efficiency consequences, while in others the exclusion is anti-competitive. Their joint venture model starts with an analysis of the negative and positive externalities that occur in networks; members have an incentive to free ride on the assets provided by other participants (as also seen in Sampson 2004), but each individual member cannot capture all of the surplus created through exclusionary access policies and the consequent possible output restriction. Within this context they analyze the efficiency trade-off in exclusionary access rules. Limiting membership (and hence access) can have both static and dynamic efficiency benefits through increased coordination to reduce the transaction costs that are common in interfirm coordination issues. Also, reduced free riding on the assets of other members can lead to optimal dynamic investment incentives. One cost of such limitation, though, can be reduced by downstream competition because the joint venture can facilitate price coordination; participants may also have more opportunities to raise rivals' costs. These access issues pose a fundamental challenge in determining the governance structure of a joint venture, particularly because the interplay of these opposing effects will differ from case to case. In such a context, and if a joint venture ownership structure is to provide a beneficial alternative to natural monopoly regulation, institutions matter a great deal.

Within the intersection of the property rights and NIE literatures, Eggertsson (2003) analyzes the differences between open access, common ownership, and corporate ownership. Open access implies that all people within the community have the right to use the good. Nobody can, however, exclude others from enjoying the good, nor can anybody alienate its rights to use the good. Management is either absent, in some forms of open access such as fields or a mountain, or exerted by the State. Common ownership, on the other hand, is a form of joint ownership between a group of insiders. Outsiders are excluded from enjoying the good. Bargaining for the right to manage has to be specified among insiders. With respect to corporate ownership, it displays the significant difference of inalienability of property rights. If we think of the CJV structure within Eggersston's context, it can be classified as a form of common ownership without a specified property right structure, with the consequence of not being able to specify who is managing the CJV or how incentives work. This line of research stems from Ostrom's (1990) seminal theoretical and field work on the use of governance institutions to avoid rent dissipation in situations with common ownership.[4]

Joint ventures in infrastructure industries and other contexts

The use of CJV structures in other industries with high fixed-cost infrastructure, such as oil and natural gas pipelines, informs this CJV model for the electric wires network. Gale (1994) considers a noncooperative joint venture of firms that associate in order to exploit the economies of scale of joint production, and the possibility of using unexploited capacity of their CJV partners. Gale finds that, under a use-or-lose clause, the CJV mechanism leads to efficiency because the use-or-lose clause induces cost revelation. His argument, common to all of the chapters described here, is that the CJV exploits the economies of scale of joint production, but each firm involved in it is independent, and independently sets the price. In Gale's model the operations and management of the CJV rest in an independent entity established by the CJV partners.

Alger and Toman (1990) model the creation of new markets to regulate natural gas pipelines. The structure they propose involved establishing a resale market for capacity use rights, which they argue would increase the efficiency of existing capacity allocation as well as the dynamic efficiency of capacity expansion. They report the results of experiments performed to test different designs of such a capacity market; the results suggest a computer-aided "smart market" that integrates pipeline owner pricing decisions, natural gas purchaser bids, and natural gas producer offers. A computer algorithm that maps onto the physical network uses all of that information to calculate all prices. In their conclusion, they suggest that "where markets are neither workably competitive nor capable of becoming so just by relaxing regulatory entry barriers, another option the FERC might pursue is to encourage the development of competitive joint ventures (CJVs)" (p. 276).

Rassenti *et al.* (1994) subsequently tested this CJV proposal experimentally for a natural gas network. Their results indicate that a computer-coordinated auction market mechanism can work to allocate resources with high efficiency in a network of commodity flows. Reliance on a computer algorithm implementation of a uniform price double auction to perform the centralized coordination and dispatch of flows enables the network to retain the benefits (and, in the case of electric power, the physical necessity) of central coordination while combining it with the competitive benefits of decentralized ownership. The natural gas network that they test enables several independent natural gas commodity retailers to exercise use rights to transport natural gas over a single pipeline network. By examining an integrated market for pipeline use rights, this research expands on the results described in Alger and Toman (1990), in which an integrated "smart market" outperformed other market institutions. The market institution tested here, a continuous real-time uniform double auction, provides transparent price information for both gas and transportation at each node in the network to all participants; not surprisingly, such an institution leads to rapid price convergence and robust trading to capture the internodal arbitrage opportunities. The treatment variable was the cotenancy of use rights on the pipeline network (versus a monopoly network link); an important feature of cotenancy in this analysis was the ability of agents to sell or lease their use rights to other agents without their fellow co-tenants blocking the transaction. In these experiments the cotenancy ownership structure increased overall efficiency, reduced pipeline prices paid by buyers, and increased prices received by natural gas sellers. Cotenancy ownership of the parts of the network that would otherwise be monopoly links reduced the expression of market power in the pricing of those links, which is the primary reason for the increase in overall efficiency.

Other economists have explored CJV ownership as a regulatory institution in other industries. Alger (1998) argues for using open ownership and competitive rules as opposed to Common Carriage for the New Zealand Natural Gas Pipeline Industry; this model involves open ownership so that anyone may purchase long-term rights to capacity at prices within regulatory constraints, owners must have undivided common interest in shared facilities, and it may be possible for owners to establish a total owned capacity which is artificially below physical capacity. Competitive rules would involve owners independently marketing services while paying regulated prices that just cover variable cost, a use it or lose it rule regarding available capacity and establishment of an operator who is independent of any user and who is charged to act neutrally with respect to all owners. These are the rules that may be applied generally for industries exhibiting networks where some activities are competitive and others natural monopolies; therefore they apply to the following industries (electricity, telecommunications, airlines, railways) as much as they apply to natural gas industries.

Doane and Spulber (1994) look at the effects of open access transportation on the organizational structure of natural gas in the 1980s. They find that open access integrated regional wellhead markets into a national competitive market for natural gas. They also find that introducing open access competitive buying and selling of gas at the wellhead removes any incentives for long-term contracts and other organizational arrangements between pipelines and producers. Lyon and Hackett (1993) and Mulherin (1986) also explore the effects of contracting and organizational form that have some joint venture characteristics.

Other industries in which CJV ownership is used to structure transactions include pharmaceutical research and development, computer memory chip production, and oil pipelines. In these industries CJVs serve to decrease costs while retaining economies of scale, using contracts to define use rights and to govern the sharing of benefits and of maintenance costs and investment.

Conclusion

Other than inertia and historical precedent, few reasons exist for the continued requirement of energy/wires bundling and vertical integration. Regulatory rules that prevent retail competition solidify this vertically integrated structure and preclude this unbundling from occurring in markets and environments in which it is feasible and beneficial. They also preclude the development of other wires ownership models that could provide a beneficial alternative to cost-based natural monopoly regulation.

Enabling retail competition could unleash dynamic innovation incentives to the mutual benefit of consumers and entrepreneurs. Unbundling the wires transaction and its regulation would allow that to happen while focusing regulatory policy on the sector of the value chain where it is still most relevant.

Viewing the historical development of the electric system in the U.S. from a new institutional economics perspective enables us to analyze the relationship among technological change, regulatory institutions, and the transactional boundaries of firms in the industry. Technological change changes the transaction costs that determine firm boundaries and whether or not separate markets for some goods can exist. As such, technological change affects the profit potential from the execution of some transactions through markets instead of within firms. But regulatory lock-in, due to the interplay of inertia and the interests of both regulators and the regulated incumbents, influences whether or not the benefits of those opportunities created through technological change are actually realized.

The legal formalism and lack of adaptability of existing regulatory institutions stifles the opportunities for external technological change to

- be undertaken (at the margin);
- reach consumers;
- provide the dynamic incentives for technological change within regulated incumbent utilities.

Thus less technological change is likely to arise, and what technological change has been undertaken has occurred in a heavily constrained environment.

Furthermore, unbundling and the potential for competitive retail creates the opportunity to think differently about the regulatory institutions themselves. If we think of the wires network as a common-pool resource and the policy challenge as one of governance institutions to optimize common-pool resource use, we admit for consideration joint-venture ownership of the wires network. This option can achieve first-best static efficiency, is likely to promote dynamic efficiency, and changes the role of the regulator in ways that remove some of the most problematic information and incentive challenges inherent in current cost-based, rate-determination regulation.

Specifically, we apply various literatures within new institutional economics to examine the specifics of governance, incentives, and performance of a CJV institution that integrates downstream competition and upstream use and control rights. The integration of the ownership rule and the price determination rule in the CJV enables us to address the type of agency problems and hold-up problems analyzed in the NIE literature. Furthermore, our institution's use of a downstream market share as a form of auction provides a practical way to handle problems of contract incompleteness that would invariably arise in such a complex set of transactions.

Despite a relatively limited hold-up risk, the case of electric power distribution is more complicated than many transactions in other industries. Its historic regulation as a transaction occurring within a vertically-integrated, government-granted monopoly means that our starting point is one in which the wires transportation transaction is already bundled with the sale of the energy commodity transported on the wires. This bundle comprises two potentially separable transactions: one for a transportation service, whose duplication is costly, and another for a good that can be (and often is, under other regulatory institutions in other countries) sold in markets through competing retailers. The poor performance of regulation of these bundled transactions in the face of dynamic change, both economic and technological, has led to over a decade of institutional and economic change in the United States. Network industries are increasingly unbundling as technologies, other industries, and customer preferences change. For example, in electric power both the generation and the retail marketing portions of the value chain have become workably competitive, while the physical transmission and distribution wires and network operation and coordination retain some natural monopoly characteristics. The regulated, vertically-integrated firm is disintegrating under these technological and economic pressures; the main concern is how to introduce competition, or mechanisms that approximate market institutions, while making sure that the benefits of network externalities and cost subadditivity are not lost. Another concern is the kind of regulatory and institutional structure that would work well for industries characterized by networks.

In the face of these concerns, we propose thinking differently about the problems of monopoly pricing and investment in such a highly-meshed network. We explore ownership structure as an alternative to traditional regulation of government-granted monopoly ownership. In particular, we consider a competitive joint venture (CJV) ownership structure, in which competing retailers are joint owners of the wires network. Their ownership shares are determined by their market shares in the retail electricity market, and their ownership shares buy them voting rights in decisions concerning wires access pricing and management decision-making over the existing assets. Furthermore, the competitive nature of the joint venture means that existing JV members cannot block either expansion or entry; if a coalition of JV members chooses to invest in capacity expansion, or an entrant chooses to build new capacity, the existing members cannot erect entry barriers to preclude such investment. Under a contestability model of entry, such an ownership structure should lead to optimal access pricing and capacity expansion/investment.

Any reform that separates the market for wires from the market for energy will be vigorously resisted by the local franchised monopoly. From the beginning of state regulation nearly 100 years ago, these monopolies have had the right to tie in the sale of energy with the rental of the wires network. This de facto right is jealously guarded and protected. Many regulators will also resist these changes because it means that energy prices will be regulated by competition, rather than by regulators applying average cost of service formulas.

6 Network reliability and short-term security

Decentralized coordination using demand as a resource[1]

Introduction

On August 14, 2003, a large blackout occurred in northeastern North America. Precipitated over three hours, this cascading failure affected 50 million people and caused $4–10 billion in economic losses in the U.S. (U.S.–Canada Power System Outage Task Force 2004, p. 1). As often happens with crisis events, it also caused extensive re-examination of decades of electricity reliability policy.

Post-event forensics focused on physical and engineering factors that affected security of supply on that day, including (much-ridiculed but important) tree trimming to reduce the probability of overloaded wires leading to an actual outage. Those forensics led to 46 policy recommendations, ranging from enacting mandatory reliability standards (which has been done) to more specific operational recommendations. Throughout the recommendations, though, and indeed throughout the whole report, the idea that sending timely price signals to consumers and enabling them to reduce their consumption was utterly and completely absent. The blackout report did not consider demand as a crucial resource for network reliability.

The Blackout Task Force recommendations did address demand-side issues in a small way. In two short paragraphs in a discussion of research needs, the report: (1) cites "demand response initiatives to slow or halt voltage collapse" as one aspect of research into ways to prevent cascading power outages; and (2) urges the "study of obstacles to the economic deployment of demand response capability and distributed generation."[2] In addition, with a little creativity, a role for demand response might be read into a few other recommendations. For the most part, however, the blackout report is about a supply failure and supply-side proposals. For most of the blackout report, end-use consumers are simply the "load," a passive burden that the supply side must simply bear and satisfy.

This forensic engineering focus on physical supply causes of such a massive cascading failure was not surprising, given the century-long supply orientation of the industry and its regulation, as described in Chapter 2. Such a focus, however, obscures the important underlying reality that the failure to reduce demand was even more of a root cause of the outage and its propagation than physical issues like tree trimming or time stamp synchronization across control areas. The inability to tap into decentralized coordination processes to reduce demand in a three-hour timeframe was the root cause of the blackout's magnitude.

The persistence of thinking physically and not economically about electric service reliability limits the imagination of both industry and regulators, and correspondingly limits the policy approaches they devise and the regulatory institutions they design to achieve the objective of reliable electric service. Thinking more in terms of transactions and contracts between agents with diffuse private knowledge in dynamic environments opens up a range of reliability policy tools beyond the typical command-and-control approach that characterizes the centralized control paradigm.

The North American Electric Reliability Council definition of reliability divides the concept into two separate concerns – "supply security" and "resource adequacy." Oren (2001) explains the two issues in this manner:

- *Supply security:* "the ability of the system to withstand sudden disturbances." This aspect concerns short-term operations and is addressed by ancillary services, which include: voltage support, congestion relief, regulation (AGC) capacity, spinning reserves, non-spinning reserves, replacement reserves.
- *Resource adequacy:* "the ability of the system to supply the aggregate electric power and energy requirements of the consumers at all times." This aspect concerns planning and investment and is addressed by planning reserves, installed capacity, operable capacity, or available capacity.

Oren observes, "Security and Adequacy are clearly related since it is easier to keep a system secure when there is ample excess generation capacity" (2001, p. 7). This chapter addresses security, while the next chapter discusses resource adequacy. For the purpose of this chapter, the term "reliability" means only security.

This chapter challenges that persistent supply focus by highlighting one specific aspect of reliability policy – the potential reliability benefits of thinking of demand as a resource, and of designing institutions that enable consumers (or the load-serving entities that purchase power in wholesale markets to serve them) to benefit by responding to price signals or other market transactions to provide active, engaged demand response. Digital technology contributes to expanding both the type of institutions that are possible and their granularity – digital technology both extends the set of possible dynamic demand-side agents and shrinks the timeframes over which such agents can respond to price signals.

In particular, this chapter presents a double-sided integrated wholesale and retail power market model that, in conjunction with the forms of retail contractual choice and end-user technology discussed in Chapter 4, would engage retail customer demand in ways that would enable dispatchable demand reduction for short-term supply security as well as incorporation of active, dynamic demand into capital planning and resource adequacy.[3] In this model, both buyers (load-serving entities (LSEs) buying on behalf of their customers) and sellers submit bids and offers in intertemporally-integrated spot and forward markets for a variety of products, such as electricity, spinning reserves, ancillary services, reactive power, or other new products that might develop as society, markets, and the industry evolve.

In this type of environment, with digital technology that enables agents to execute and quantify demand reductions (thereby making them dispatchable), agents can offer demand reductions as supply resources in all of these markets. Offering demand as a resource creates a transaction with a legally binding contract that requires the resource to reduce a given amount of demand, in return for which the resource owner is paid the market-clearing price in that market. Furthermore, this double-sided market design induces retail LSEs to incorporate active demand, dynamic pricing, retail choice, and enabling end-use digital technologies into their business models. Such strategies would reduce the demand being bid into the suite of wholesale markets, thereby contributing to lower prices in those markets as well as to reliability, security, and adequacy.

This double-sided market model embodies the decentralized coordination framework of this work in many ways. The suite of double-sided markets for a range of intertemporal electricity products allows for the expression and aggregation of diffuse private knowledge. If the market institutions and regulatory institutions are designed well, these markets will work in conjunction over time toward equilibration, the incorporation of newly-discovered knowledge when disruptive change occurs, and re-equilibration. As such, this market model is likely to lead to emergent order, in the form of reliability, from the interaction of many agents, as opposed to imposed order due to the decisions of control room operators and capacity planners. This emergent order is likely to be superior to (or at least as good as) the reliability in the imposed order, because the reliability in the emergent order captures all of the diffuse information about values, costs, and trade-offs that the agents reflect in their intertemporal bid and offer decisions.

The assumptions about reliability that are embedded in reliability policy include:

- Customers want as close to 100 percent reliable service as possible, regardless of the cost of providing that level of reliability;
- Reliability is a supply-side and engineering issue, and not a demand-side and economic issue; and
- Network reliability is a public good.

In this chapter I examine the second of those assumptions; Chapter 8 examines the other two assumptions and suggests policy options based on thinking differently about the public good aspects of network reliability. Technological change has made these assumptions more questionable than ever before. We do not have good information on how consumers perceive and evaluate the opportunity cost of reliability – what do their demand curves look like? What are they willing to trade off in return for more, or less, reliable service? The question has never been put to a market test, because reliability has always been dictated by regulatory fiat.

This chapter challenges the beliefs that reliability is only a supply-side engineering issue. Demand can be a reliability resource, even in many of the short timeframes needed to meet security considerations. Demand's ability to serve as a reliability resource is enhanced by technology and contractual and market institutions that enable demand-side resource to be paid for the value they help to create. However, demand's ability to serve as a reliability resource is dampened in the longer term by artificial quasi-markets for installed capacity, which will be discussed in Chapter 7.

Integrating retail and wholesale markets through price signals

Wholesale double auction market design

This model focuses on the crucial integration of wholesale and retail markets, and on the role that prices play in transmitting information across those markets and across time, via forward markets. Market institutions and prices provide platforms through which buyers can discover their preferences in the face of potentially ever-changing technology and service offerings from competing retail providers, taking into account other changes (like the personal computer) that can affect their demand for particular electric services; sellers can discover their opportunity costs, their comparative advantage, and the potential value of new business models and new technologies. The Independent System Operator (ISO) can play a crucial role in this nexus of institutions because of the perpetual need for system balancing and coordination; however, our model contrasts with the implementation of top-down demand-response programs at ISOs by articulating a vision of double-sided markets with active demand that enables decentralized coordination.

Simply put, a double-sided market is an institution that enables buyers and sellers to find each other and to consummate transactions for mutual benefit. Think, for example, of ebay, a market platform that simultaneously accommodates multiple supplier listings and buyer bids. Details of double-sided market designs can vary – in most retail transactions, for example, double-sided markets take the form of retailers posting prices for goods and potential buyers looking at those prices as "take it or leave it" offers. In financial markets, multiple buyers and sellers make simultaneous bids and offers, using a set of predetermined rules to govern the consummation of transactions.

This market institution is in direct contrast with the supply-oriented, single-sided market that is typical in electric power. In wholesale power markets we have become familiar with generators submitting offer curves, or a schedule of offers for different portions of their generation capacity, but without active bidding on the demand side it is still only a single-sided market. Figure 6.1

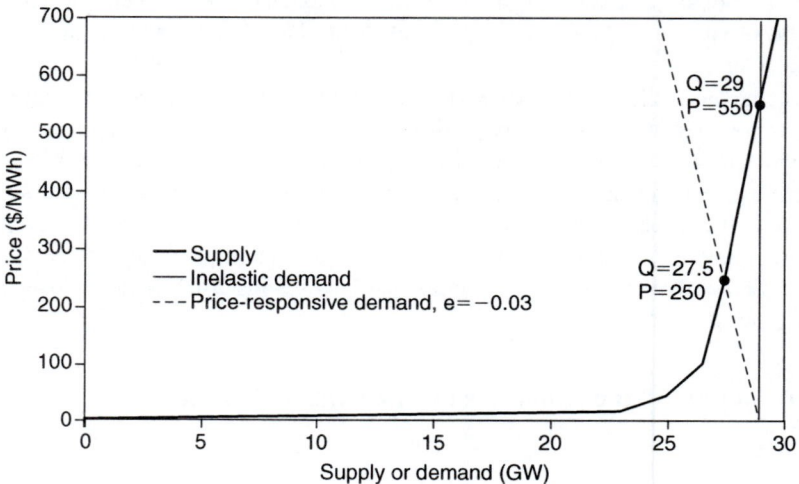

Figure 6.1 The price-reducing benefits of double-sided markets (source: Hirst and Kirby 2001, p. v).

shows how a single-sided market with passive, inelastic demand, tends to have higher prices than a market with active demand and supply – a double-sided market.

The double-sided market in this model is one in which economic agents on the supply side submit offers, economic agents on the demand side submit bids, and a computer algorithm coordinates the bids and offers to determine the market-clearing price and the amount sold. The most important detail in this model that is substantially missing from existing electricity markets is active demand. Active demand means customers in retail markets making bids, in which they essentially state a set of prices above which they do not wish to purchase any more power. Their load-serving entities (LSEs) take those active bids into the wholesale market, and bid on behalf of the bids their customers have submitted. Note the crucial difference here between active demand and LSEs bidding in the wholesale market on the basis of load shaping and average profiles. Active bidding communicates more precise information about the preferences of consumers into both retail and wholesale markets, integrating them and consequently leading to better decisions and more efficient resource allocation.

Consider a wholesale electric power market environment in which several integrated markets coexist. Real power (the actual energy flow) markets, both spot and forward, would enable buyers and sellers to transact over sales of electric power in the short run, in long-term contracts, and in financial instruments to hedge price risk. Reserve markets for reserve availability at various time intervals would also provide the necessary reliability of supply to ensure system balancing. Such reserve markets would range from ten-minute to day ahead, and could accommodate long-term contracts in which generators supply reserves in conjunction with real power sales for which they have entered into long-term contracts. Similarly, markets for ancillary services would enable buyers and sellers to transact over the provision of voltage support through reactive power or other services that complement the sale of real power. In other words, the market design would not restrict the creativity of market participants if they come up with a mutually beneficial transaction innovation in either real, reserve, or ancillary power markets.

In this set of integrated markets, the supply participants would not be restricted to generators providing power, but would also include demand reduction, voltage management, and load control technologies. Such technologies provide reduction that can be measured in megawatt-hour equivalents, and can thus be sold directly into real, reserve, and ancillary markets that are denominated in megawatt-hours. This portfolio of market platforms would be technology neutral, meaning that no particular way of providing a megawatt-hour equivalent would have an advantage bidding into these markets.

The demand side in this portfolio of markets would be the load-serving entities (LSEs). In some cases, such as states in which retail competition is healthy (such as Texas), LSEs may sell power on to retail service providers; however, in the current environment most LSEs engage in both the physical delivery to and the retail relationship with end users.

The spot market institution is a uniform-price, double-sided market. In a double-sided market, suppliers offer their capacity into the market in each period, and can change their offer curves each period. If they have entered into bilateral contracts then the capacity they have available to offer into the spot market is the difference between their total capacity and their contracted amount. The demand side in the double-sided market, the LSEs, submit purchase bids, which they can also change every period. A "smart market" computer algorithm ranks the offers from lowest to highest, ranks the bids from highest to lowest, and determines the market-clearing price as the point where the supply (offer) curve and the demand (bid) curve intersect. In a uniform-price market, all buyers pay the market-clearing price, even though all except the marginal buyer were willing to pay more, and all sellers receive the market-clearing price, even though all except the marginal seller were willing to accept less.

The forward markets, reserve markets, and ancillary markets could have similar designs, although market designs perform best when they are customized to local conditions and trading customs. It may also prove valuable to choose to run some markets together, in a combinatorial fashion. For example, the bid to purchase a megawatt-hour of real power for a given hour would have to occur in conjunction with a bid for a particular amount of reserves for that hour and a particular amount of reactive power supply to accompany the real power transaction. In addition, voltage control technologies and other innovations increase the feasibility of decentralized day-of reserve markets, so the market design should not rule out the development of such markets. Combinatorial and day-of reserve market designs are complicated and are the subject of further research.

In addition to the market institution, the legal institutions in which this market model operates matter a great deal. The LSEs on the demand side, either by contract with retail service providers or by their obligation to serve, should have the legal obligation to meet end-user demand. In a Coasian sense, this assignment of legal liability is a definition of property rights, which provides robust incentives and reduces the transaction costs that can hamper trade (Coase 1960). In the presence of transaction costs, the best place to put legal liability is on the least-cost avoider – which party is the one that can avoid harm to the other party most cheaply? In the sale of power from LSEs to end users, if reliability is a good that has value that LSEs provide to end users, the LSEs are the least-cost avoiders. The relevant property right that integrates the retail market with the wholesale market is the contractual right to a particular level of reliability.

This definition of property rights seems to contradict the legal reality that utilities do not guarantee service to customers. For this reason, the idea of legal liability for reliability resting with LSEs should accompany contracts that enable customers to purchase the quality of service that they desire. In other words, LSEs should be free to sell reliability as a differentiated product to customers with different preferences, through an instrument like reliability insurance. Technology increasingly enables us to privatize many aspects of reliability, opening up the opportunity to create value by selling reliability-differentiated electric power retail service.

While creating an environment in which participants can transact freely, these legal institutions impose commensurate obligations on market participants. On the demand side, LSEs must also treat the bids they make to buy in the wholesale market and financial and legal obligations. This legal rights assignment reduces the incentive facing LSEs to underschedule their bids, as seen in the Power Exchange market in California in the late 1990s. The suppliers face similar legal obligations to meet the terms of their transactions, implying legal liability if they fail to deliver as agreed to in a transaction. The ISO has a legal obligation to provide a transparent and technology-neutral market platform and operating environment for the facilitation of these transactions.

In this market model the ISO could serve two crucial roles: a market platform for each of several markets, and the system operations and coordination to maintain system balance. Bilateral contracting and the use of other market platforms should not be prohibited, as such a prohibition would essentially create a monopoly market platform in the ISO. This concern is most pressing for the transactions least associated with the ISO's real-time balancing operations, in other words, for the real power markets and day-ahead reserve markets. However, the ISO's system operation function requires ISO knowledge of transactions and commitments that will occur in the system, so the ISO should implement, and the participants should agree to, a scheduling reporting requirement that covers all bilateral and non-ISO transactions. This requirement would be implemented in a transparent manner but would have to protect the privacy of the participants, so the requirement should not be to reveal, for example, prices.

Implementing integrated double-sided markets could have several possible effects. The static efficiency, or resource allocation, benefits include transparent

price signals from end users through LSEs to wholesale market, increased efficiency by better aggregation of more information from both sellers' and buyers'
participation, and better discipline of the ability of suppliers to exercise market
power (Rassenti *et al.* 2003). The dynamic efficiency benefits could include the
application and development of new technologies, such as demand voltage
control, direct load control, thermal storage, building controls, and grid-friendly
appliance technologies.

Note that two additional valuable benefits arise in this model: capacity planning and forecasting through energy markets, and network/critical infrastructure
security. As discussed above, the double-sided market model promotes more
efficient capacity utilization, but it also provides a platform of spot and forward
energy markets through which capacity price signals would flow. In addition,
the distributed nature of customers and sellers, differential preferences over reliability, and the technology to perform controlled individual interruption
enhances critical infrastructure security while maintaining overall system
reliability.

Retail double auctions: the missing markets

Even a well-designed wholesale double auction market is like one hand clapping
unless retail markets exist. Consider a system in which *n* networked end-use
customers participate in a retail market in which they can choose from among *m*
rival retailers. These retailers offer differentiated products as described in
Chapter 4; customers choose among a menu of contracts. Some of these *n* consumers choose a real-time price (RTP) contract, with the energy cost portion of
the price they pay reflecting the real-time wholesale electricity price. Suppose
further that these customers have digital devices (such as a thermostat, and
appliances) that they can automate to be price-responsive – a consumer can
program the devices with his/her own preferences, with a demand function.

Customers with such choice and enabling technology can participate actively
in a retail double auction. In a retail double auction, end-use customers submit
bids reflecting their willingness to pay for the energy portion of their service,
and sellers (LSEs) simultaneously submit offers; on an RTP contract these offers
communicate the wholesale price.[4] Thus the retail double auction communicates
the preferences of RTP customers into the wholesale spot market, integrating the
two markets via the information transmitted through price signals and customer
choices.

The enabling digital technology plays a crucial role. Without it, a double
auction like this would be impossibly costly for most retail customers, very few
of whom would choose to spend their time monitoring price fluctuations and
adjusting their electricity use in response. Digital devices that can submit market
bids, receive price signals, and be programmed to change settings automatically
in response to those price signals reduce the costs of participating in such a
market. In other words, the technology reduces transaction costs that otherwise
would prevent mutually beneficial exchange from occurring. The technology

lowers the participation hurdle facing customers. It also shortens the timeframe in which transactions occur; when market participants have more ability to program and automate their choices, the double auction can take place on a more granular timeframe.

This model describes the retail double auction tested in the GridWise Olympic Peninsula project discussed in Chapter 4. In that project, the first to employ a retail double auction, individual households on an RTP contract submitted bids into a double auction market that cleared *every five minutes*. Without enabling technology such a market would be impossible, especially for residential customers.

Institutions that allow retail choice, and technology that enables customers to submit price bids and automate their responses to the ensuing price signals, make it possible for retail customers to transact in the most information-rich market institution – the double auction. As sellers in retail double auctions and buyers in wholesale markets (designed as double auctions, as described above), LSEs transmit the information that integrates wholesale and retail markets.

Technology-enabled decentralized coordination and reliability

The traditional model of achieving short-term security is top-down central coordination: reserve margins and ancillary services (and reliability must-run requirements in severely chronically constrained load pockets), and system operator responsibility for physical real-time balancing. The physical reality of power flow, combined with the lack of economical storage, means that centralized real-time physical balancing is still necessary, although innovation in storage technologies is likely to change that fact over time. However, the necessity of centralized real-time balancing does not imply that centralized coordination is required throughout all of the stages and timeframes leading up to the five-minute timeframe in which centralized coordination is essential. Outside of that timeframe, digital technology, market processes, and the ability to send prices to devices and automate end-user responses have created a new potential for *decentralized coordination*.

Without the combination of grid technology (such as remote sensor and phasor technology) and end-use digital technology, the network could not self-organize and achieve decentralized coordination, because the technology enables the distributed agents in the network to have intelligence and to act on their private knowledge, particularly in response either to changes in the network environment or to changes in prices. Historically the electric power network has not had this distributed intelligence capability, and thus has relied on centralized coordination based on centralized intelligence. Thus there exists historical path dependence in our centrally-coordinated institutions for reliability, and in the development of culture and beliefs that the centralized approach is the only appropriate one, particularly among system operators and regulators, who are justifiably risk averse with respect to the consequences of outages, both economically and politically. Therefore, we can only expect meaningful institutional change once evidence exists demonstrating the beneficial reliability effects of decentralized price-based and incentive-based coordination.

A blackout appears to be a supply failure, so the natural impulse is to look for supply-side solutions: more transmission lines, high-tech system monitoring, building power plants closer to population centers, better grid planning and testing procedures. But on the demand side of the market, consumers can help make the grid more reliable by becoming more engaged in the market. Consumer participation in markets enhances reliability because it harnesses downward-sloping demand and results in customers decreasing quantity demanded precisely in hours and at places in which the system is facing the highest strain. New technologies for metering and end-user voltage management are allowing the demand side to make more active contributions to managing reliability as well, as discussed previously.

Demand can be a resource for short-term security through two paths and two time scales: either through retail markets or through RTO programs, in day-ahead or day-of timeframes. Whether price-based or incentive-based, day-ahead forecast-based RTP can induce changes in consumption in a timeframe that operators can use in their real-time planning.

The shorter timeframe, day-of (typically hourly) RTP, can also help system operators avoid blackouts. Incentive-based retail or RTO contracts, such as curtailment or interruption contracts or direct load control, provide a valuable real-time resource to system operators. It is important to share some of the savings achieved through these contracts with consumers, so that they have incentives to participate. Furthermore, despite the skepticism reflected in the traditional beliefs and assumptions in the industry, price-based day-of RTP contracts can also empower demand to act as a reliability resource, and digital technology in combination with retail markets enhance the value to system operators of this distributed and potentially uncertain resource. Digital end-use technology that enables automated device response to price signals makes price-based demand response easier for consumers to achieve. Retail choice, and in particular demand aggregators, enables retailers to use enabling technology and their own risk-management business models to provide system operators and wholesale markets with dispatchable demand. This claim is also true a fortiori at the day-ahead time scale, but digital end-use technology combined with dynamic pricing and retail demand aggregation creates the ability to do so even in hour-ahead wholesale markets.

Another example of enabling consumers to contribute directly to reliability comes from efforts to turn demand response into a tool that transmission system operators can call on in their efforts to keep supply and demand constantly in balance. In this vein, responsive customer demand can be used as spinning reserves dispatched by the system operator to meet system reliability requirements. For example, a significant portion of the California Independent System Operator's spinning reserve requirement could be supplied from the California Department of Water Resources (CDWR) pumping load. Given the appropriate economic incentives, the CDWR could stop pumps for brief intervals to make small adjustments in response to specific short-term transmission system needs. Another approach would enable controllable air-conditioning units to be cycled off for brief periods when the system is stressed (Kirby and Kueck 2003).

Reducing peak use contributes to greater operational security, as fewer reserves are necessary to maintain reliability, and eases stress on adequacy planning, as the need for system expansion to support ever-greater system peak loads is diminished.[5] Both historical experience and laboratory experiments show that electricity customers do respond to price changes, and that both suppliers and customers can be better off from doing so.[6] This option does not currently exist for most customers in most places.

Conclusion

Demand is a potentially valuable short-term reliability resource, and the combination of digital end-use technology, dynamic pricing, and retail market models that allow demand aggregation allows us to tap that potential. Digital technology enhances the capability of demand to serve as a resource by reducing transaction costs that can prevent the network from being truly transactive, and therefore by creating the opportunity for decentralized coordination. To achieve that potential also requires institutional change: changes in regulations concerning retail pricing, entry, and business model, changes in regulations concerning system operations and the ability of demand to participate in short-term wholesale balancing markets, and changes in beliefs that prevent us from being open to the opportunities that these changes have created.

Healthy electricity markets are impossible without a demand side. Active retail demand transmits end-customer preferences into the wholesale market, smoothing out peaks and optimizing load factors (and curbing the exercise of supplier market power along the way). Furthermore, allowing demand reduction to bid into capacity markets can reduce the construction of new generation and transmission capacity, and is therefore a good long-run strategy for conservation of resources and for making investment more efficient. Demand response is the Swiss Army Knife of the electricity policy world – it is one compact tool that does a lot of things in a very parsimonious way.

Many of the relevant factors that add to or subtract from system reliability are well understood. Most of these factors are attributed to, or could be measured and attributed to, the responsible party. The responsible party could then be either charged or paid an appropriate amount. The key is to bring reliability into the commercial realm, where choices can be made in the presence of relevant tradeoffs.

7 Reliability, resource adequacy, and capacity markets

Introduction

This chapter focuses on a particular regulation-driven market design question that is unique to electricity – capacity markets. The question of resource adequacy is an intertemporal supply/demand coordination problem. The basic question is how to facilitate optimal future consumption and resource allocation. In addressing this challenge, our toolkit essentially consists of four tools: more generation, more transmission, less demand, and technological change that could affect any or all of the other three tools. No one knows the optimal combination of those four tools, and that combination is likely to be very local depending on the existing resource portfolio, customer characteristics, and so on. A capacity market is frequently discussed as a way to use price signals to induce investment in generation, and is in use in three of the RTOs/ISOs in the U.S. (Besser *et al.* 2002; Hobbs *et al.* 2001).

Fueled by the glacially incremental restructuring process in the states and concerns about service reliability in this persistent policy limbo, states and regional system operators (RTOs/ISOs) have explored a variety of means of providing forward-looking reliability incentives in the absence of the historical regulatory mandate to vertically-integrated utilities. One incremental approach is capacity markets.

In a capacity market, system operators solicit offers from generators to provide a guarantee of future capacity to provide power, based on the system operator's need to meet a specified, engineering-determined reserve margin over and above forecast demand. In capacity markets that have been implemented or proposed in the U.S., the forward timeframe can range from one day to four years.

Capacity markets have grown out of other regulatory decisions affecting wholesale power markets. The introduction of competition into the U.S. electricity industry has taken place in a very piecemeal and political fashion. Part of the political bargain in return for liberalizing wholesale power markets has been a multi-year (typically six to ten years) retail price cap for residential customers. This price cap provided both cost certainty for customers and revenue certainty for their load-serving entities (LSEs, typically the incumbent utility). With the widely-held expectation that wholesale markets would lead to lower wholesale prices, this type of restructuring was intended to ensure utility profitability in the long, slow transition to fully-integrated wholesale and retail competition.

The rosy expectations of these flawed models have not been met. The California crisis of 2000–2001 remains the worst example of a flawed wholesale-focused restructuring model (Sweeney 2002). Even in other states and regions that have not had such dramatic problems, the liberalization of wholesale markets has led to wholesale price volatility. This volatility is largely a consequence of the institutional design choices implemented in the various restructuring models used in the U.S. All of these market designs focus on short-term products (day-ahead and day-of markets) and spot markets; in all organized commodity markets throughout history, short-term and spot markets have been characterized by the most volatile prices. Couple this spot market focus with a requirement that LSEs and independent power producers participate in the organized markets instead of arranging bilateral contracts (to ensure liquidity), and with an absence of strong demand-side bidding due to retail price caps, and this market design is highly likely to reinforce and propagate wholesale spot market price volatility. This sensitivity of outcomes to market design shows why electricity restructuring in the U.S. is a dramatic case study for the NIE arguments for why institutions matter.

With some variation in design, this general model characterizes U.S. restructuring in the past decade: retail price caps to "protect consumers" and to ensure incumbent profitability in expectation, the associated lack of active demand-side bidding in wholesale markets, and wholesale market rules focused on liquidity. Price volatility ensued as market participants explored these new markets and discovered where profit opportunities existed, exacerbated by exogenous increases in underlying fuel costs since 2002.

The policy response to this wholesale price volatility has not been to re-examine and revise market designs to enable participants to manage or reduce price volatility more effectively. Uniformly across all organized wholesale markets in the U.S., market operators and regulators have chosen a politically expedient approach and have imposed prices caps.[1] These caps have varied by market and by design, ranging from a blanket $250/MW imposed in the California ISO in 1999 (Sweeney 2002, p. 130), to an automated mitigation procedure (AMP) price cap dependent on the historical average price in that hour in the New York Independent System Operator's territory (Kiesling and Wilson 2007).

Price caps are extremely problematic, particularly in burgeoning markets. Applying the decentralized coordination framework to critique price caps, they clearly silence the transmission of diffuse private knowledge among the many heterogeneous agents participating in the market. Price caps stifle the discovery process. In newly-formed markets like those in electric power, most agent behavior is motivated by discovery, because of the novelty (and to apply North's term, the non-ergodic nature) of the institutions and the environment. Price caps stifle the communication of economic knowledge and the ability of agents to coordinate:

[G]overnmentally-imposed obstacles to price flexibility not only ... prevent prices from telling the truth – they smother the emergence of those disequilibrium-price-generated incentives upon which the system depends for its very ability to discover and announce the truth.

(Kirzner 1992, p. 149)

Instead of taking price volatility as a signal to reconsider and revise the fundamental market institutions, the politically-charged restructuring environment has led to an inferior but politically expedient "solution."

This knowledge aggregation and discovery critique is only one of the pressing criticisms of price caps. Another criticism, and one that forms the basis of this chapter, is the role that wholesale market price caps play in distorting intertemporal information and investment incentives. In a misguided approach to curb market power, by preventing spot market prices from moving freely, price caps distort the intertemporal scarcity signals that entrepreneurs take as information about where profitable investment opportunities exist. When price caps reduce the producer surplus that indicates potential profitable investment opportunities, at the margin less investment occurs. Lower investment leads to higher prices in the future. Furthermore, specific to network infrastructure industries, lower investment can lead to lower future expected reliability and quality of service.

In an industry without such a deeply-embedded regulatory control culture, adjustment to entrepreneurial mistakes in perceiving profitable investment opportunities is more organic – consumers punish reliability and quality failures by taking their business elsewhere, and the threat of that happening induces firms *ex ante* to invest in the resources that provide reliability and quality of service.[2] However, even though wholesale markets are competitive or contestable and the issue of a single physical infrastructure is irrelevant to the effect of investment on the reliability of supply of the electricity commodity, RTOs/ISOs as system and market operators are charged with the regulatory responsibility of ensuring long-term resource adequacy, as defined in Chapter 6. This responsibility perpetuates the traditional regulatory mandate on the vertically-integrated utility to perform "integrated resource planning"; in regions with organized wholesale markets, the RTO/ISO has taken on this function.

Thus from the perspective of the RTO, the long-term investment incentive effect of price caps is problematic, because it means that spot market price caps may undercut long-term resource adequacy and make their resource adequacy planning much more difficult, both economically and politically. This tension is the origin of the capacity market concept. A capacity market is one way to deal with the regulatory distortion imposed by price caps, but in many ways it is inferior to integrated forward energy markets.[3]

The analysis of the issues surrounding capacity market design in this chapter starts from a context of the importance of increasing the integration of wholesale and retail markets in electric power. The objective is to create the preconditions for a robust, reliable network during and after the transition toward integrated, competitive wholesale and retail markets. In that transition, we face:

- Concerns about long-term reliability and the investment to provide reliability;
- A perceived need for a centralized resource adequacy planning process;
- Immature integrated physical and financial wholesale markets;
- Immature demand-side participation in both wholesale and retail parts of the value chain; and
- Reluctance to allow wholesale energy spot price fluctuations to signal investment opportunities to entrepreneurs.

Capacity markets are meant to address these considerations; however, experiences in the Northeastern markets where capacity markets have been implemented have been mixed. While New York has seen some new generation and some retirements, New England generally has not seen any increased investment, and PJM has seen some delayed retirements in transmission-constrained areas. The reliability benefits that this new investment may produce are coming at increasingly higher costs. Moreover, the need for regulatory involvement persists, despite supporters' claims that the Northeastern capacity markets either are or will be market-based.

There are numerous foreseeable and potential drawbacks to adopting a flawed capacity market approach that relies on an artificial, administratively-determined demand curve like that used in New York, New England, and PJM. While the primary function of a capacity market is to create price signals so as to compensate for the absence of active demand-side participation in the wholesale market, a capacity market ironically will inhibit price signals for demand response. A capacity market focuses solely on supply resources and relies on an administratively set demand curve, so the price signal that is actually transmitted will be distorted, potentially leading to inefficient investment outcomes. These problems are particularly acute when a capacity market is coupled with the regulatory distortion caused by price caps, as it would be in California.

Investors are especially wary of committing capital resources in areas that have combined price caps and capacity markets. Such an institutional design is likely to stunt investment in a diverse portfolio of supply-side and demand-side resources that could contribute toward the state's resource adequacy. It is also likely to stifle the development of workably competitive wholesale and retail markets, as well as to discourage investment in new technologies. These negative effects could easily end up costing consumers billions over the long term. And while some analysts tout the benefits of a capacity market in terms of disciplining market power, even a relatively small amount of demand elasticity would have a greater effect.

Capacity markets do have benefits in terms of increasing price transparency and market liquidity, as well as providing a platform for load-serving entities (LSEs) to buy and sell capacity. Rather than adopt a capacity market that is based on an artificial demand curve, however, the best resource adequacy policy is to eliminate the current regulatory barriers that impede demand-side participation in the wholesale *and* retail markets (i.e., participation by end-use customers and LSEs). A second priority should be to develop integrated spot and forward energy market platforms that transmit accurate price signals to investors and entrepreneurs. While achieving these two priorities will take time, a transitional approach that employs known, tested financial instruments, such as call options, could bridge that gap. By accommodating generation, transmission, and new demand-side resources and technologies in a flexible and adaptive way, this recommended approach is more likely to generate long-run benefits for customers than an artificial capacity market that would be both costly to implement and difficult to dismantle once it became obsolete.

The information requirements to make that decision in a centralized manner are large, as the knowledge required to discover the optimal resource portfolio is diffuse, distributed among the market participants, customers, and entrepreneurs who are the agents in the electric power network. The best way to access, aggregate, and get action on that distributed knowledge is to use market processes to determine the resource portfolio. But there is a twist – the intertemporal nature of the problem, and the time that some resources take to build, mean that the market in question has to be a market with delivery commitment in the future. That means integrated spot and forward energy markets.

This chapter proposes a vision of integrated spot and forward energy markets, and a transition path to move in that direction. The desired end state is an information-rich signal for investment that incorporates the value given by retail customers and their actively bidding LSEs, to the spot, future, reserves, and ancillary markets without the need for artificial constructs. This framework can reduce price volatility and attract more of and a variety of infrastructure investment that will promote resource adequacy. If a capacity market relying on an administrative demand curve is necessary to get us there, it has to be thoughtfully designed, carefully tested, and retired when obsolete. During the transition period, it is critical that there be parallel development of active demand. Besides removing regulatory barriers, this will require clear definition of the property rights and other rights and obligations of LSEs. And regulators must also guard against the entrenchment of the capacity market as an end in and of itself. To that end, regulators must stipulate milestones for the sunsetting of the capacity market as integrated, liquid markets develop.

A capacity market relying on an administrative demand curve is merely a band-aid for the absence of active demand and the ability to contract for differentiated reliability; it does nothing to advance a sustainable market design. Indeed, in the presence of pre-existing price caps, capacity markets are an attempt to remedy the consequences of a distortionary policy with another distortionary policy. While deliverable capacity commitments obviously can provide reliability insurance to customers, integrated spot and forward energy markets do a better job of providing insurance in a flexible, cost-effective way. Thus, instead of becoming a permanent regulatory fixture, a capacity market should only serve as a bridge to integrated, transparent spot and forward energy markets that enable participants to make investment choices, assume risks, and plan appropriately – on both the supply side and the demand side.

Why capacity markets?

Resource adequacy market design initiatives are meant to achieve a complex set of objectives. The primary objective is to ensure cost-effective reliability to retail customers via the presence of sufficient future resources, while promoting wholesale market transparency, avoiding market manipulation and incentives for collusion, and creating an environment in which demand can participate actively.

The question of resource adequacy is an intertemporal supply/demand coordination problem. At any given point in time, the interaction of cost (supply) and value (demand) determine price. But markets are also institutions that enable that interaction to occur in a forward-looking way, across time, to take expectations of where that interaction will occur in the future as reflected in price signals to induce investment where it is needed, and is therefore profitable.

The basic question is how to facilitate optimal future consumption and resource allocation. Four types of resources combine to meet this challenge: more generation, more transmission, less demand, and technological change that could affect any or all of the other three tools. No one knows (or can know) the optimal combination of those four tools, and that combination is likely to be very local depending on the existing resource portfolio, customer characteristics, and other factors. A capacity market construct with locational product definition is frequently discussed as a way to use price signals to induce investment in generation. Such a capacity market is one way to deal with the regulatory distortion imposed by price caps, but in many ways it is inferior to integrated spot and forward energy markets. To the extent that it deters or stifles the evolution of integrated markets, then, a capacity market should only be pursued with extreme caution, and with specific guidelines for its transition into integrated markets.

Although all network industries are important parts of our daily lives, none of the deregulated network industries – trucking, railroads, airlines, telecommunications – have faced the long-term investment price signal issues that we have created for ourselves in electric power. In other network industries, investment in future capacity has occurred through active double-sided markets, with investor capital flowing in where its providers perceive a likely return on investment. Investment-backed reliability has not been a policy challenge in these other industries, while in electric power, investors are wary of committing capital resources in areas that have combined price caps and capacity market constructs (Woodley 2003).

The goal of resource adequacy policy should be to enable a forward-looking supply/demand balance that is efficient. Supply-focused solutions, such as capacity markets with artificial, administered demand curves, are not efficient and thus end up being more costly over time for customers. Recent research indicates that supply-focused resource adequacy approaches cost U.S. customers $19 billion more than a market-based approach, and cost California customers alone almost $4 billion (Sutherland and Treadway 2005).

By focusing on generation resources to the exclusion of other alternatives, this approach may fail to attract an efficient portfolio of resources, as well as stifling the development of workably competitive wholesale and retail markets.

As an alternative, this chapter proposes a vision of integrated spot and forward energy markets, and a transition path to move in that direction. This transition involves the use of call options on capacity that can develop without significant regulatory interference. The desired end state is an information rich signal for investment that incorporates the value given by retail customers and their actively bidding LSEs, to the spot, future, reserves, and ancillary markets without the need for artificial constructs.

Capacity market designs in the U.S.

Capacity markets are a recent policy innovation intended to ensure investment in network reliability by addressing two elements of electricity markets that have yet to evolve: rate structures and installed technologies to empower active demand, and rate structures and technologies that enable retailers to sell differentiated reliability to different customers. PJM, the New York Independent System Operator (NYISO), and ISO New England (ISO-NE) have adopted forms of capacity markets in the past several years, and PJM and ISO-NE have recently revised their capacity market designs. Other wholesale market operators, including ERCOT and the Midwest ISO, have chosen to follow the Australian model and develop bilateral forward contracting through energy-only markets, in conjunction with rules for the active participation of demand in wholesale markets.

The New York ISO wholesale market has had a monthly capacity market since its inception in 1999; this market used a locationally-based demand curve, but it was vertical and set at the reserve margin requirement. That requirement determines the installed capacity (ICAP) requirement. In 2002 NYISO changed the capacity market design to incorporate a downward-sloping administrative demand curve, with the parameters of the demand curve updated on a three-year cycle. This modification has led to some new generation serving New York City, largely on long-term contract with load-serving entities (LSEs). It has also led to some retirements, suggesting that the market is not necessarily inducing existing generation to continue operation in order to receive a capacity payment.

PJM has offered a capacity market for several years, and like the NYISO its structure derives from the markets it has been operating since 1927. PJM uses an auction to determine the price of an annual capacity obligation. Its installed capacity (ICAP) payments to generators were not differentiated by location, and the demand curve used is vertical at the ICAP requirement.

In 2005 PJM proposed a new Reliability Pricing Model (RPM) to replace its existing ICAP requirement; the RPM is intended to address the deficiencies of the ICAP approach. The RPM began operating in June 2007 and had its first three auctions in late 2007.

The RPM uses a downward-sloping administrative demand curve and a four-year forward timeframe for generation planning and delivery. It also implements locational differentiation among generation resources. The RPM design met with stakeholder criticism, ranging from Commission critiques of the testing of the administrative demand curve, to demand-side concerns that demand resources cannot participate equivalently with generation.[4] Some stakeholders are also skeptical that the RPM can evolve to an energy-only market. Finally, retail providers cannot hedge congestion risk with sufficient precision, which creates a costly risk and harms the development of retail competition. Sener and Kimball (2007) provide a thorough description of the RPM and the results of its first capacity auctions.

ISO-NE's capacity market development parallels NYISO's. ISO-NE opened its bid-based wholesale markets in 1999, including an hourly operable capacity (OpCap) market and a monthly installed capacity (ICAP) market. The design of the OpCap market led to local generator market power and was an easily manipulated design, so the capacity market was discontinued in 2000 and the forward price signal carried out through a reserve market and the ICAP.

In 2007, after a lengthy regulatory and legal battle, ISO-NE implemented a locationally-based capacity market (LICAP) to replace their existing installed capacity market. The LICAP design incorporates both locational pricing and an administrative demand curve; as in the PJM case, the LICAP proposal met with stakeholder criticism.[5] The objectives of the LICAP are to ensure three-year resource adequacy, to meet that objective through a portfolio of supply and demand resources, and to provide a long-term commitment to those resource owners to encourage investment (LaPlante 2007). More so than in other capacity markets, demand is treated as a resource and can participate equivalently with generation (although PJM continues to adjust its RPM to increase demand-side participation).

These experiences indicate that capacity market design is incremental and costly. The incremental nature of the design is reflected in the persistence of the regulatory involvement in decision-making, including the persistence of the engineering standard and reserve margin forecast upon which the ICAP is based. Although the ICAP model has become discredited and capacity market supporters claim that their designs are market-based, they remain driven by regulatory mandate that has little, if any, relationship to customer value for system reliability.

Critique of the capacity market concept

Costs and benefits of capacity markets

Proponents of capacity markets argue that they replace investment incentives that are missing from existing power markets. Capacity markets send an otherwise absent intertemporal price signal to communicate the value of future generation resources. Communicating this value provides incentives for investment in these resources that might otherwise not be brought to market. Transmitting the value of future resources also reduces the retirement of units in locally constrained areas until either new transmission, generation, or demand reduction resources can be constructed and commercialized. This price signal is a crucial inducement for investment in future resources of all kinds, not just generation.

Another frequent argument for capacity markets is that they reduce the ability of generators to exercise market power by ensuring the presence of adequate generation capacity.[6] However, market power can still exist with excess capacity if there are other distortions in the supply chain, such as inadequate transmission price signals. Furthermore, such arguments do not address the cost at which capacity markets limit market power, nor do they address the issue of buyer market power (monopsony power). Capacity markets simply do not deliver as much value in disciplining market power as even a little demand elasticity. The most parsimonious and cost-effective means of controlling market power is via active demand for a small share of total demand. Rassenti *et al.* (2003) demonstrated that having as little as 16 percent of peak load on a simple interruptible contract was sufficient to eliminate all exercise of market power in an experimental wholesale power market. In addition to the reliability that such contracts provide, the natural market power mitigation arising from demand–supply interaction can be achieved at a lower cost than constructing an entire artificial market framework.

The reluctance to allow wholesale energy spot and forward price fluctuations to signal investment opportunities to entrepreneurs creates an artificial need for a capacity market construct. Fear of the exercise of market power, leading to the use of price caps, further stunts investment in a diverse portfolio of supply-side and demand-side resources that could provide resource adequacy. In the presence of a pre-existing price cap, capacity markets are an attempt to remedy the consequences of a distortionary policy with another distortionary policy.

Supply shortages are not the only consequence of price caps and capacity markets. By distorting price signals, price caps and capacity markets can disrupt investment portfolio choices. Although the focus of policy has been on providing incentives to increase the level of investment, the composition of investment also matters. Even if capacity markets were to succeed in increasing generation investment, they still fail to reflect accurate incentives and opportunity costs for investment in other resources – demand reduction, transmission, and technological innovation – that may be more economically efficient.

Do capacity markets actually succeed in increasing generation investment? The evidence in the Northeast regions is mixed; New York has seen some new generation construction and some retirements, while New England has generally not seen increased generation investment (Joskow 2005b). In PJM much of the effect has been in delaying retirements in transmission-constrained areas. Furthermore, market participants and stakeholders increasingly find that what reliability the generation investment provides comes at a high cost. These concerns have led to contentious capacity market redesign processes in ISO-NE and PJM. In contrast, Texas has seen investment in generation capacity in the absence of either a capacity market or an official resource adequacy policy.

Capacity markets also do not address the layered distortions in relative prices across resources and across markets that currently exist. The inadequate price signals for the construction of transmission provide the most notable example of this layered distortion, and compound the problems that arise from a generation-specific focus in a capacity market. The existing congestion revenue structure provides no incentive to transmission owners to relieve congestion by building transmission. The existing cost-recovery-based, regulatory pricing of transmission provides perverse incentives that spill over into energy markets and provide further distortions of investment signals.

As an institutional alternative to the development of integrated spot and forward financial markets, capacity markets have many negative features. Two of their limitations – their focus solely on supply resources and their reliance on an administered demand curve – mean that the price signal that is actually transmitted via capacity markets will be distorted, and will thus lead to dynamically inefficient investment outcomes. Put another way, capacity markets restrict the resource adequacy focus to one of the four tools available, emphasizing generation to the exclusion of transmission, demand reduction, and technological innovation. Market rules that focus on inducing generation investment and ignore other resources will lead to more generation investment (and less investment in other resources) than is efficient. In cases where generation would be used at the expense of demand reduction, transmission, and innovation, and those three options would have been less expensive, then the generation-focused approach would lead to an inefficient outcome. Consequently, the long-run cost of generation-focused resource adequacy would be higher than the long-run cost of a portfolio of resources induced and constructed through a balanced market with active supply-side and demand-side participation.

Active demand-side participation, particularly by large customers, can be implemented more quickly and cheaply than a capacity market. It also does a better job of targeting resources to peak hours, which are precisely the hours in which achieving sufficient returns on investment are the most challenging. In 2005, only 32 hours occurred in which the peak load came within 2000 megawatts of the peak load resources forecasted by the CAISO. The most economically efficient resource to serve this load is demand reduction. Two thousand megawatts of peaking capacity cannot be installed for just 30 to 50 hours per year and receive an acceptable return under current market rules; however, using demand response to reduce peak demand by two thousand megawatts is already feasible. Not only does demand response provide an alternative to investment in new costly peaking capacity, it can also offer an effective program that will improve the system capacity load factor and serve to benefit system operations.

Administrative demand curve: a poor substitute for active demand

RTOs with capacity markets now use a downward-sloping "administrative demand curve" in the capacity market as a substitute for active demand-side participation. This administrative demand curve uses demand and resource forecasts, in conjunction with the required reserve margin to meet reliability standards, to estimate the value of new generation resources over time. The administrative demand curve takes the basic economic concept of downward-sloping demand, but applies it in an artificial way that does nothing to represent or to induce the expression of true preferences for the installation of new supply capacity in the future. At best it is an approximation based on little data; at worst, it is a bureaucratic substitute for the empowering opportunity for customers and entrepreneurs to make their own decisions through free, active markets. Reeder (2006) and King *et al.* (2007) make similar arguments.

At its core, the reason for the demand curve disconnect in a capacity market is that the artificial capacity product has no intrinsic value to customers, so developing a demand side would be similarly artificial. In other words, RTOs have no estimate of the economic value that customers place on different degrees of reliability, so they cannot infer a value of future capacity with any precision. Instead, they implement a regulatory reserve margin target, typically 12.5–17 percent of peak demand. To the extent that the required reserve margin is disconnected from any information about how customers value reliability, the "good" being exchanged in the capacity market is one that has an unknown intrinsic value to customers. What is exchanged in a capacity market is derived entirely from an engineering definition of reliability, and unless that engineering definition and customer values map into each other exactly, the capacity market will not reflect customer values for reliability. Given that, how can we be confident that a capacity market sends a meaningful price signal at all?

Another crucial consideration relating to the administrative demand curve is its ability to stifle the development of actual, active demand participation in the capacity market, and later, in integrated spot and forward energy markets. If a capacity market relies on an administrative demand curve, what incentive or opportunity will exist for active demand participants to bid in that market as technologies and markets evolve? Much of the stakeholder concern about capacity market redesign in PJM and ISO-NE hinges on this exact entry barrier.

Proponents of administered demand curves accurately claim that demand-side resources, and the market rules to empower them to participate in a capacity market, are not yet sufficiently developed to lead to a healthy, robust, liquid capacity market. If an administered demand curve is required to substitute in the short run for demand-side incompleteness in a capacity market, then setting the parameters of the demand curve will be a crucial exercise. RTOs bear the responsibility of constructing, setting parameters, testing, and implementing the administrative demand curve – a costly and bureaucratic process.

Alternatives to administered capacity markets

This chapter proposes an alternative institutional design for resource adequacy policy. Integrated spot and forward energy markets with active supply and demand participants can deliver resource adequacy using decentralized market processes. Note that this design is the same as the double-sided market design articulated in Chapter 6.

Using such active markets also provides direct benefits to retail customers by empowering them with a way to communicate their preferences and values through retail markets to wholesale markets. Achieving resource adequacy through integrated markets is efficient because it relies on the transmission of accurate price signals to induce investment, instead of relying on bureaucratic estimates of customer demand for capacity derived from an engineering definition of reserve margins. Efficiency through integrated markets means delivering resource adequacy to customers at the lowest feasible long-run cost. Developing such markets must occur in parallel with the ongoing development of metering and communication to enable customers to provide active demand in markets. If a capacity market construct with an administrative demand curve must exist as a bridge to active, integrated markets, then a preferred interim approach to achieve the desired end state would be the use of call options on capacity that can develop without significant regulatory interference. The desired end state is an information-rich signal for investment that incorporates the value given by retail customers and their actively-bidding LSEs, to the spot, future, reserves, and ancillary markets without the need for artificial constructs.

Market-based resource adequacy

The most forward-looking and robust alternative to a capacity market is to allow spot and forward prices to communicate investment signals in integrated, double-sided markets. Simply put, a double-sided market is an institution that enables buyers and sellers to find each other and to consummate transactions for mutual benefit. Think, for example, of ebay, a market platform that simultaneously accommodates multiple supplier listings and buyer bids. Details of double-sided market designs can vary – in most retail transactions, for example, double-sided markets take the form of retailers posting prices for goods and potential buyers looking at those prices as "take it or leave it" offers. In financial markets, multiple buyers and sellers make simultaneous bids and offers, using a set of pre-determined rules to govern the consummation of transactions. Also, the consumer is determining his or her value of the option of winning or losing the bid and of their otherwise alternative to a win. For example, if a customer has flexibility in a residential daytime schedule, he or she might move load from the peak readily and value the lower bill. If a business values the avoided cost more than using the power on peak, it will bid to be interrupted at a value set by it. We see this in many other previous network industries such as consumers' choices of cell phone plans by peak/off peak minutes. Also consumers now choose whether they will pay less by booking an airline flight in advance, knowing that for a change fee, he or she has the option to change it. The government no longer decides whether consumers will pay more per ticket to have plenty of extra seats.

An active demand and supply market institution is in direct contrast with the supply-oriented, single-sided market that is typical in electric power, and is the dominant form of capacity market design. In wholesale power markets we have become familiar with generators submitting offer curves, or a schedule of offers for different portions of their generation capacity, but without active bidding on the demand side it is still only a single-sided market. Single-sided electricity markets are prone to market power because they do not permit customers to voice their preferences. The motivation for such is the fundamental incentive in utility regulation providing a return on investment to shareholders for supply-side investments. Without a similar incentive on upgrading the wires or enabling demand response, the supply side, and less efficient model, will be perpetuated.

The double-sided market envisioned in the alternate model set forth here is one in which economic agents on the supply side submit offers, economic agents on the demand side submit bids, and a computer algorithm (designed and administered by the system operator) coordinates the bids and offers to determine the market-clearing price and the amount sold. The most important detail in this model that is substantially missing from existing electricity markets is active demand. Active demand means customers in retail markets making bids, in which they essentially state a set of prices above which they do not wish to purchase any more power. Their load-serving entities take those active bids into the wholesale markets (both spot and forward), and bid on behalf of the bids their customers have submitted. Furthermore, sophisticated retail customers can also participate, although no LSE or customer would be forced to participate, which proved the death-knell for the California Power Exchange design (Sweeney 2002). Imagine such a customer, with on-site generation and advanced metering, able to bid its willingness to pay on the demand side, and also able to offer demand reduction as a resource on the supply side.[7] Such customers, and many ESPs, are nimble enough to provide cost-effective, decentralized, distributed reliability throughout the network through increased liquidity and participating actively on both sides of integrated markets.

Note the crucial difference here between active demand participation and bidding in the wholesale market on the basis of load shaping and average profiles. Active bidding communicates more precise information about the preferences of consumers into both retail and wholesale markets, integrating them and consequently leading to better decisions and more efficient resource allocation. That process makes customers better off and provides the necessary pressure to reduce long-run costs in the most economical way.

Consider a wholesale electric power market environment in which several integrated markets coexist. Real power (the actual energy flow) markets, both spot and forward, would enable buyers and sellers to transact over sales of electric power in the short run, in long-term contracts, and in financial instruments to hedge price risk. Reserve markets for reserve availability at various time intervals would also provide the necessary reliability of supply to ensure system balancing. Such reserve markets would range from ten-minute to day ahead, and could accommodate long-term contracts in which generators supply reserves in conjunction with real power sales for which they have entered into long-term contracts. Similarly, markets for ancillary services would enable buyers and sellers to transact over the provision of voltage support through reactive power or other services that complement the sale of real power. In other words, the market design would not restrict the creativity of market participants if they come up with a mutually beneficial transaction innovation in either real, reserve, or ancillary power markets. The forward nature of these markets would communicate the value of investments to all participants. In such an information-rich market environment, investment signals incorporate the relative value of spot energy, future energy, reserves, and ancillary services, without the need for an artificial capacity construct.

The demand side in this portfolio of markets would be the LSEs. Active LSE bidding in forward markets sends a very rich, informative price signal regarding the value of investment in resources to meet future demand. In a true double-sided market in which all resources can participate equivalently, that price signal might bring a diverse portfolio of investments to market, including generation (traditional and renewable), transmission, demand reduction, and innovation in all three areas.

Even in the absence of price caps, integrated spot and forward markets reduce price volatility. Price volatility is a consequence of excess demand or inadequate supply, and these conditions can occur even in the presence of excess capacity due to constraints in other parts of the supply chain (such as transmission). However, that volatility is a short-run phenomenon, beyond the capability of capacity markets to absorb. Integrated spot and forward markets can absorb volatility and spread price risk and outage risk over time, thereby increasing volatility.

One of the most widespread benefits of double-sided markets is the increase in the number of market participants by empowering active demand. By actively representing customer interests, increased LSE participation in markets disciplines prices, provides added liquidity, and makes customers better off by increasing efficiency.

A transparent legal environment

Double-sided markets rely on a foundation of clearly-defined property rights. Buyers need a clear legal environment in which their rights and obligations are laid out; that clarity is lacking in existing market models for electricity. Although some attempts have been made to do so, the legal environment in which LSEs and sophisticated customers could buy in integrated markets remains uncertain. This claim is particularly true with respect to utilities entering long-term contracts.

In addition to the market institution, the legal institutions in which this double-sided market model operates matter a great deal. The LSEs on the demand side, either by contract with retail customers or by their obligation to serve, should have the legal obligation to meet end-user demand. According to Coase (1960) and subsequent law and economics scholars, a legal framework that defines the rights and obligations of both buyers and sellers transparently creates the most possible economic value, because such clarity of property rights increases the possibility of mutually beneficial exchange.[8] It also reduces uncertainty that can prevent a party from entering a market. Thus clarifying the legal rights and obligations of LSEs would reduce transaction costs and improve their ability to enter as buyers in both spot and forward double-sided markets.

This definition of property rights seems to contradict the legal reality that utilities do not guarantee service to customers. For this reason, the idea of legal liability for reliability resting with LSEs should accompany contracts that enable customers to purchase the quality of service that they desire. If they are with a utility with the obligation to serve, the regulator can impose the level of reliability that these captive customers must buy. For consumers of competitive LSEs, it should be by contract. A competitive LSE would meet the same requirements of a completely firm customer, but could differentiate in contract for interruptible and need not buy or show capacity for such. In other words, ultimately, LSEs should be free to sell reliability as a differentiated product to customers with different preferences, through an instrument like reliability insurance. Technology will increasingly enable us to privatize many aspects of reliability, opening up the opportunity to create value by selling reliability-differentiated electric power retail service, as will be discussed in Chapter 8.

While creating an environment in which participants can transact freely, these legal institutions impose commensurate obligations on market participants. Both parties to a transaction must face clear consequences for contractual non-performance. On the demand side, LSEs must also treat the bids they make to buy in the wholesale market as financial and legal obligations. The suppliers face similar legal obligations to meet the terms of their transactions, implying legal liability if they fail to deliver as agreed to in a transaction. The ISO should have a legal obligation to provide a transparent and technology-neutral market platform and operating environment for the facilitation of these transactions. Double-sided markets in such an environment remove the incentive problems that face system operators when they participate in markets as both system operators and principals.

The market-based model in practice

Examples from other states and countries indicate that this model is being implemented, resulting in benefits for customers.[9] Australia's national wholesale markets opened in December 1998; these markets do not include a capacity construct, relying instead on integrated spot and forward energy markets and an integrated wholesale and retail environment to provide investment signals and induce participants to focus on risk management. The spot market has a AU$10000 bid cap, coupled with disclosure requirements to increase information and market transparency. Australia developed this wholesale market in conjunction with a retail market with no reliability obligation, but with simultaneous development of advanced metering to empower demand participation in markets. Most of Australia's population can access full retail competition. As a consequence of this integrated spot and forward market design in an integrated wholesale and retail environment, Australia has not experienced the wholesale price volatility observed in regional U.S. markets. Furthermore, forward prices are also stable. Since the markets opened in 1998, net generating capacity has increased by 13 percent, provided largely by private investment in Queensland, Victoria, and South Australia. Transmission interconnection has increased by 33 percent, and although peak demand has increased by 18 percent due to economic growth, wholesale market prices have generally fallen. Australia has successfully created a decentralized, market-based approach to reliability via risk management.

In the U.S., Texas and the Midwest ISO are in the midst of determining their resource adequacy policies, and they are considering approaches largely informed by the Australian experience of decentralized, integrated markets. Recently, the Texas PUC has decided to pursue an energy market approach to resource adequacy.[10] In 2006 Texas implemented a new resource adequacy policy incorporating both a high wholesale price cap and integrated energy markets with bilateral forward contracting. Texas has enjoyed more success in implementing electricity restructuring than any other U.S. state, including robust retail competition and the presence of price-responsive demand (Kiesling and Kleit 2008).[11] Given that environment, the resource adequacy policy raised the wholesale market price cap to $1000/MWh to allow scarcity pricing. It also did not create a capacity market, relying instead on bilateral forward contracting in energy markets (Schubert *et al.* 2006). The Public Utility Commission of Texas coupled this institutional design with the establishment of an independent wholesale market monitor to enforce rules against the exercise of market power in the presence of such a high price cap (Kleit 2008).

Although still a work in progress, the current Midwest ISO market design does not include a capacity market.[12] In both cases, equivalent treatment of supply and demand resources characterize the market construct, and the focus is on the creation of a transparent environment for forward contracting.

Required transition out of administered capacity markets

Even if an RTO chooses to implement an interim capacity market as a transition to integrated spot and forward markets, it should design and test the construct carefully. To achieve the goals of reliability and market transparency for customers at the lowest achievable long-run cost, the resource adequacy policy should therefore focus on the capacity market as a transition to integrated spot and forward energy markets. This transition must involve parallel development of active demand, based on metering and rate structure activities already under way in California, and must guard against the entrenchment of the capacity market as an end in and of itself, with the corresponding sense of entitlement to receive payments that is likely to develop on the supply side of the capacity market.

The feasible alternative thus is to stipulate milestone-based sunsetting provisions for the capacity market, as integrated, liquid markets develop and active demand increases in the ISO-sponsored market and in bilateral forward contracting. For example, Texas sunsetted the price to beat cap for small customers, and is now developing the long-term rules for default service to replace such a cap. The only condition under which a capacity market structure should be approved is the parallel and simultaneous development of market platforms that incorporate active demand and embed rules that allow demand-side resources to participate equivalently with supply-side resources.

Capacity markets may be a valuable short-run mechanism while demand-side participation develops, property rights clarify, and forward energy markets evolve that will take on their proper role of providing intertemporal resource allocation signals. If that is the case, however, the design of that capacity market is crucial. The capacity market design must treat generation, transmission, demand reduction, and new technologies equivalently. Also, enshrining a capacity market for all time does not contribute to a resilient, agile, flexible network or set of markets. Imagine if 1850s law had dictated the existence in perpetuity of a capacity market for the production of whale oil. The extinction of the capacity market construct as integrated financial markets evolve is one key to industry robustness and adaptability, and to ensuring the long-term investment that will deliver reliability to customers cost-effectively. One way to implement the reduction of the capacity market is to establish transparent rules for its decreased use as the volume of forward commitments in financial markets approaches the desired reserve margin.

Known, proven financial instruments provide a transition approach that may bridge the gap between capacity obligations and integrated markets. Oren (2005) presents a set of financial tools and a resource adequacy market design that would enable California to implement this vision and transition to integrated spot and forward energy markets. Oren's approach uses call option obligations as an alternative to capacity payments to generators. A call option gives the holder the right to buy energy at a specific price (the strike price), but the holder is not obligated to make the purchase. Similarly, a call option commits the seller to sell at the strike price if the buyer chooses to exercise the option. Call options typically specify the quantity, location, and time of delivery, and in electric power call options are usually defined in terms of a continuous delivery stream over a particular amount of time. Call options are common, known financial instruments for sharing risks between buyers and sellers. Using such familiar financial instruments may create more certainty and a consequently higher expected return on investment to attract new capital; as John Woodley notes,

> Many argue that this [option] value is insufficient to ensure the financing and construction of supply. However, it is exactly and solely this value that has caused Morgan Stanley to finance, construct and operate not one but three peaking power plants. All three are in regions where no mandated capacity payment was expected and no price caps were expected
>
> (Woodley 2003, p. 4)

In the case of resource adequacy, the buyers of call options would be LSEs purchasing on behalf of their end-use customers. The sellers could be generators, and they could also be LSEs who can commit to a particular volume of demand reduction. Thus call options provide a natural path to market for demand-side and interruption contracts to serve as reliability resources. Call options can be constructed so that the options perfectly hedge the exposure to capacity and energy that an LSE has to its customers, thereby providing flexibility and accommodating the migrating nature of competitive retail sales.

A call option approach to resource adequacy provides a natural platform that does not require an administrative demand curve, because the call option provides customers with a good that has intrinsic value: insurance. LSEs, who are the customers in resource adequacy, would receive insurance against both price risk and outage risk through call options; the strike price provides a credible alternative to paying spot prices (and thus also helps discipline supplier exercise of market power), and by providing forward price signals through the price of the call option, investment can occur to provide reliable delivery. The price of the call option would decrease as available capacity increased, thus naturally capturing the downward-sloping demand instead of imposing it administratively.

In Oren's proposal, the transitional regulatory instrument is the strike price, and the ISO can serve as a purchasing intermediary while LSEs develop their capability to participate and enter into bilateral forward contracts; however, liquidity on both sides of the option market is crucial for this alternative to work. As with capacity markets, this function should sunset as integrated financial markets develop. Such a financial and risk management approach to resource adequacy would smooth the transition from generator capacity obligations to true double-sided markets.

Conclusion

The most important and valuable resource adequacy policy in electricity is to eliminate the regulatory barriers that impede demand-side (customers and LSEs) participation in markets, both wholesale and retail. The second priority, in conjunction with the first, should be to develop integrated spot and forward energy market platforms so that accurate, not artificial, price signals can transmit crucial investment opportunities to entrepreneurs. If achieving these two priorities will take time, a transitional approach that employs known, tested financial instruments, such as call options, would bridge that gap. By accommodating generation, transmission, and demand resources, and new technologies flexibly, this approach is more likely to generate long-run benefits for customers than an artificial capacity market that would be costly to implement and difficult to remove once obsolete.

A capacity market runs the risk of undermining the development of robust, integrated, double-sided markets. Deliverable capacity commitments provide insurance to customers, but integrated spot and forward energy markets do a better job of providing insurance in an adaptive, cost-effective way. A capacity market is an artificial band-aid to address the absence of active demand and contracts for differentiated reliability; however, it does nothing to advance market design toward bringing about active demand and differentiated reliability

This discussion of contracts, demand, and product differentiation is very different from the policy discussion of resource adequacy for the past five or so years, in which the discussion and action have all been on the supply side, and have involved construction of elaborate capacity markets as a substitute for forward contracts in financial markets. In electricity, policy has not applied the lessons and tools of other industries, the most relevant of which being that integrated spot and forward markets provide the most robust and fluid way to send those investment signals that lead to network reliability. The focus on building generation also retains the narrow physical asset definition of the "electric power network"; it does not acknowledge that the network is actually composed of assets and humans, and the network is a function of the interaction of physical assets and human actions.

The typical argument offered for the implementation of capacity markets invokes the lack of retail demand response, which makes active, double-sided forward markets impossible, and the lack of developed, liquid, integrated spot and forward energy markets. Notwithstanding the chicken-and-egg nature of this conundrum, implementing a capacity market in isolation, based on an artificial demand curve (regardless of its slope), does not do anything to reduce the barriers to active retail demand. Furthermore, technological advances and increasing numbers of retail demand projects discussed in Chapter 4 show that empowering demand response is not as expensive or as distant a task as capacity market advocates claim.

Another cautionary note for capacity markets comes from their focus on providing the "missing incentives" for investment in generation capacity for the future. But there are four resources in the portfolio of resources that we can use to ensure future system reliability: generation, transmission, demand reduction, and technological innovation that can affect any or all three of the other resources. Creating incentives for generation leads to inefficient distortions in cases where one of the other resources might be better suited to a particular case, or might be less expensive, or might be more flexible and adaptable on the network.

The target institutional design for resource adequacy is a market process in which generation, transmission, demand, and new technology can all participate in producing electric power (or its equivalent in demand reduction), in which a consummated forward transaction commits the agents in the transaction to meet the agreed obligation by the date specified in the contract. Note that this is a decentralized contractual approach to the resource adequacy question, not a centralized regulatory approach.

The crucial demand-side agents are the ones who will value the future delivery of the capacity resources. This is where property rights definitions become important – which agents have the legal liability in the event of a reliability failure due to insufficient resources? Here the insights of new institutional economics (NIE) become valuable; the market rules should minimize transaction costs and assign legal liability clearly to the least-cost avoiders of the harm. In this transaction, that agent is the load-serving entity (LSE). In a forward market for future capacity, whether a capacity market or an energy market, LSEs should be the demand side of the market, and the clarity of the property right definition would provide them with appropriate intertemporal incentives to procure forward commitments to meet their anticipated forward obligations.

The important wholesale market design elements should be clear from this discussion:

- A double-sided market in which the transaction is the capacity to deliver an additional MW in X years (where X is determined in the financial contract);
- LSEs on the demand side with clear property rights and legal definitions of obligations;
- Generation, transmission, demand reduction, and new technology resources all free to participate on the supply side; and
- Transparent market rules governing the submission of bids and offers and determining the market clearing price.

This transaction, like many other similar transactions in other infrastructure industries, can occur through existing financial markets without constructing capacity markets, if property rights are well defined, transaction costs are low, and regulatory barriers to the equivalent participation of generation, transmission, demand reduction, and new technologies are low.

However, these three assumptions do not currently hold. So ISOs/RTOs use capacity markets instead of clarifying property rights definition, reducing transaction costs in existing financial markets, and reducing regulatory barriers to the equivalent participation of all resources in markets. Many of these decisions do not fall within the jurisdiction of ISOs/RTOs.

If this analysis is correct, then capacity markets may be a valuable short-run mechanism while demand-side participation develops, property rights clarify, and forward energy markets evolve that will take on their proper role of providing intertemporal resource allocation signals. If that is the case, however, the design of that capacity market is crucial. First, the capacity market design must treat generation, transmission, demand reduction, and new technologies equivalently. For example, PJM's four-year timeframe may not enable transmission resources to offer into the market. Second, the capacity market must be allowed to evolve, dare I say atrophy, as integrated spot and forward financial markets evolve. Enshrining a capacity market for all time does not contribute to a resilient, agile, flexible network or set of markets. Imagine if 1850s law had dictated the existence in perpetuity of a capacity market for the production of whale oil. We do a very bad job in this industry of letting dinosaurs go extinct, but the extinction of the capacity market construct as integrated financial markets evolve is one key to industry robustness and adaptability. One way to operationalize the reduction of the capacity market is to establish transparent rules for its decreased use as the volume of forward commitments in financial markets approaches the desired reserve margin.

Instead of a capacity market in perpetuity, the capacity market should serve as a bridge to integrated, transparent spot and forward energy markets that enable participants to make investment choices, assume risks, and lay off risks on risk management entrepreneurs, both on the supply side and the demand side. Such markets are more likely than an administered capacity market to bring about outcomes that benefit retail customers through efficient resource allocation, efficient investment, and dynamic technological innovation. If a capacity market is a bridge connecting our current situation to that future vision, then its rules must address how that transition will occur. Otherwise, a capacity market is likely to stifle the development of integrated spot and forward markets, of active demand, and of technological innovation.

Forward markets are the key to a resilient and agile industry and provide the clearest price signals to investors. Forward energy markets are superior to generator-specific capacity markets precisely because they provide the lowest-cost means of transmitting intertemporal opportunity cost information to parties with the widest variety of possible ways to respond. If a capacity market is necessary to get us there, it has to be thoughtfully designed, carefully tested, and allowed to retire.

8 Is network reliability a public good?[1]

Introduction

The preceding chapters have illuminated several aspects of electricity policy in which the combination of technological change and economic dynamism have made existing policy ineffectual, irrelevant, or counterproductive. Such changes make it important to challenge the fundamental assumptions on which these regulatory institutions rest. This chapter explores one such assumption: in network industries like electric power, the assumption the interconnectedness of agents means that all agents *necessarily* experience the same quality of service (such as, for example, reliability) on the network. In particular, the AC electric power network is physically constructed such that all agents on the network experience the same voltage and frequency conditions. This powerful assumption undergirds much of the centralized physical control paradigm.

Policy discussions of electric system reliability often assert that reliability is a public good. The claim is usually followed by the assertion that, therefore, all agents should share the costs of providing reliability. Increasingly, this claim is used to support the idea of making reliability rules mandatory, i.e., enforceable by regulators. Rarely do the authors of these claims pause to analyze or explain the public good character of reliability on the grid. In this chapter I define reliability as the probability of receiving service, which is 1-(probability of service interruption). Ensuring a particular level of reliability and a commensurate probability of receiving service requires investing in network capacity.

Oren defines short-term reliability, or security, as a public good:

> From an economic point of view security and adequacy are quite distinct in the sense that the former is a public good while the latter can potentially be treated as a private good. Security is a system wide phenomenon with inherent externality and free ridership problems. For instance, it is not possible to exclude customers who refuse to pay for spinning reserves from enjoying the benefits of a secure system. Hence, like in the case of other public goods such as fire protection or military defense, security must be centrally managed and funded through some mandatory charges or self-provision rules.... Adequacy provision on the other hand ... amounts to no more than

insurance against shortages, which in a competitive environment with no barriers to entry translate into temporary price hikes. Such insurance can, at least in principle be treated as a private good by allowing customers to choose the level of protection they desire.

$(2003, p. 5)^2$

Many institutional design decisions in electric power are based on the argument that electric power service has public goods aspects. Although most analysts and regulators do not think about the problem this way, at its core the problem here is the combination of incomplete and uncertain property rights with the interdependence of agent behavior in a network.

This chapter focuses on the implications of the failure of this assumption to hold for network reliability. In network industries, reliability of the network is frequently considered to be a public good, and this conclusion is largely based on the assumption of necessary shared consumption of the same good within the network. Based on standard public good theory, this argument holds that because networks are nonexcludable (and nonrival up to a point, for congestible networks), individual network agents do not face sufficient incentives to undertake actions or investments that contribute to optimal network reliability. Consequently, a regulatory approach is required that induces investment up to a particular, shared, common reliability standard.

This argument pervades electricity policy, particularly concerning short-term service security and long-term resource adequacy At the distribution level, the physical layout of the electric power network is arranged such that large groups of customers (typically all customers on a substation) consume a shared level of reliability. Occasionally this argument is inappropriately extended to the claim that "we all get the same level of reliability, so the cost of providing it should be shared equally across everyone." Similarly, on a transmission network, all interconnected load-serving entities (LSEs) face the same voltage and frequency conditions (Joskow and Tirole 2007).

By focusing solely on the supply of a shared degree of reliability, such an approach ignores the theoretical and practical implications of the potential excludability and rivalry of the electric power network. The wires network is a congestible, rival resource, and is not a public good. In a network with capacity constraints the claim of nonrivalry is false, and technological change increasingly makes the claim of nonexcludability false. Furthermore, this focus on common reliability also ignores the fact that different customers have different preferences, and this heterogeneity can itself promote reliability through resiliency and willingness to be interrupted if system reliability requires it.

Most public goods claims in electricity policy pertain to the wires portion of the value chain, as seen in the example of reliability described above. In this chapter I argue that these public goods claims are largely incorrect, and that instead of having public goods aspects, the wires are actually a congestible common-pool resource.[3] While this distinction may appear subtle, it leads to different policy implications and different institutional design choices. With a common-pool resource, the institutional design challenge is to create and enforce a system of use rights, which increases the excludability of the resource and makes it more of a private good. Moreover, the fact that our behavior in the wires network is interdependent is insufficient to support the contention that the wires network is a public good. This contention is based on the idea that a public good is an extreme case of externality, where one agent's actions affect the outcomes of others. The existence of this effect, though, does not necessarily imply inefficient provision of the good.

Electric network reliability is a congestible common-pool resource, which means that it is a rival in consumption but that excluding agents from consumption is costly. Exclusion costs are not fixed, which is one of the reasons why the pure public good theory fails to be generally applicable. In particular, technological change can, and has, reduced exclusion costs in many network industries, including television, communications, and highways. A congestible good is one that is not perfectly nonrival, but that becomes increasingly rivalrous as consumption approaches some upper bound. Any good with a limited capacity is congestible, including highways, swimming pools, and electricity distribution networks.

Policies based on the contention that the wires have public good traits fail to analyze the core problem, which is the inability to define and enforce property rights fully in an AC wires network. They also fail to consider two important issues that are the focus of this chapter. First, institutions can help us manage the problem of incomplete and uncertain property rights through the establishment of use rights. Second, technological change can decrease the costs of defining and enforcing property rights, thereby decreasing the extent to which the wires network has public good characteristics.

This chapter describes public goods, club goods, and common-pool resources to ensure that the distinction among them is clear. It then uses the concept of relevant and irrelevant externality from Buchanan and Stubblebine (1962) to show how wires networks can have private good aspects. It then presents the argument that instead of being public goods, wires networks should be more accurately modeled as common-pool resources; as such, the institutional design challenge facing policymakers should be to devise a system of use rights. Finally, I discuss how technology and the ability to sell customers service with differentiated levels of reliability turns reliability into a private good. The combination of technological change and institutional design can bring about decentralized coordination, even with a common-pool resource like network reliability.

Public goods, club goods, and common-pool resources

An extensive literature in economics is devoted to exploring the nature of public goods, to assessing the problems and opportunities that such goods present, and to devising mechanisms and institutions to overcome the problems and exploit the opportunities present in public goods. Applying this literature to issues of reliability on the grid necessitates more careful analysis of the public good character of grid reliability, including examining the relevance of the assumptions underlying the public good model and the effects of technological change on the relevance of that model.

According to the now-standard approach to public goods in economics, a pure public good is characterized by nonexcludability and nonrivalry.[4] A good is nonexcludable if others cannot be excluded from the effects of the good, or can only be excluded at great expense. A good is nonrival in consumption if the use or enjoyment of the good by one person does not diminish the ability of others to also use the good. In consequence, once a pure public good is provided by anyone, it is available to everyone. National defense is the canonical example of a public good.

Note that excludability is another way of referring to the ability to define and enforce property rights. Defining a property right as belonging to one agent implies excluding all other agents from consumption, unless the owner chooses to share the resource.

Clearly the production of pure public goods unavoidably has external effects, or effects on "third parties." Following Pigou, an externality arises when one agent's action affects another agent's value, positively or negatively (Pigou 1921, pp. 166–168).[5] The concepts of externalities and public goods are closely related, but strictly speaking a public good is a subset of the more general category of externality in economics. A pure public good is a particular type of externality in which excluding non-payers is not feasible, and all third-party agents are affected.

The existence of public goods could create problems with market processes because of the possibility of free riding. A free rider is an agent that does not contribute to a public good, but intends to enjoy the benefits of other agents' efforts to provide the public good. An example in an electric power network would be a load-serving entity (LSE) that does not make any investments in network reliability, but instead relies on the contributions of other LSEs to keep the grid stable and power flowing to its customers. Since Samuelson's (1954) pioneering articulation of neoclassical public good theory, the conclusion drawn from the model has been that the free rider problem leads to the underprovision of the good in equilibrium.

While the pure public good definition is a useful theoretical construct, such goods rarely exist. The two defining characteristics – nonexcludable and nonrival consumption – do occur, though, so it is important to expand the conceptual space to include club goods and common-pool resources (CPR), both of which have some measure of one or the other trait. Figure 8.1 shows the taxonomy of goods depending on the extent to which they possess these two traits.

Public and private goods are diametrically opposed; private goods are both excludable and rival, such as food. Club goods, or toll goods, are excludable but nonrival; once an agent pays the membership fee he can consume the good without diminishing the consumption of others. Judiciously determining the size of the club can prevent the consumption from becoming rival through congestion. A common-pool resource, on the other hand, is nonexcludable but rival. An

	Less rival	More rival
Less excludable	Public goods	Common-pool resources
More excludable	Club goods	Private goods

Figure 8.1 Taxonomy of public, private, and hybrid goods (source: adapted from Ostrom 2005, Figure 1.3).

agent cannot be excluded from consuming a CPR, but that consumption reduces the amount of the resource available to others. Thus CPRs are prone to overexploitation, such as Hardin's infamous "tragedy of the commons" (1968). Fish, water, and oil deposits are examples of CPRs. Both club goods and CPRs are hybrid goods that have both public and private characteristics.

The CPR category is particularly relevant in electric power networks, because for a CPR the material questions are the resource's use rate relative to capacity (which is a static efficiency question), and the incentives facing agents to invest in capacity expansion when it is valuable (a dynamic efficiency question). It is helpful to think of the CPR as a warehouse of goods, where individual units are produced, placed on the shelves, and taken off the shelves for shipment and sale. The key is to isolate a production rate that is equal to, or greater than the shipment rate, by which the resource units leave the warehouse. The resource's overall units represent its "stock," where the shipment or extraction rate represents the resource's "flow" (Ostrom 1990, p. 30). She summarizes this stock/flow definition by observing that "[r]esource systems are best thought of as stock variables that are capable, under favorable conditions, of producing a maximum quantity of a flow variable without harming the stock or the resource system itself" (Ostrom 1990, p. 30). Think, for example, of the use of irrigation water per user on an irrigation network. The questions facing those agents are whether in total they will use (or overuse) the water in a given season, and the incentives they have to expand irrigation capacity over time. These questions mirror the network reliability and capacity issues that arise in electric power.

These hybrid categories of goods are relevant to electricity policy, and call into question the extent to which the public good model is the right model for understanding network reliability and for designing regulatory institutions. Both the general theoretical framework and the application to electricity that relies on public good theory overstate the public good characteristics of network reliability. That overstatement overlooks the crucial ways that reliability is a private good, and policies overlooking the private good characteristics of reliability are also likely to lead to inefficient outcomes. Reliability is both a public good and a private good, a composite good with dimensions involving both system security and commodity delivery. This application of public good theory is misguided, and the resulting policy implications are likely to be inappropriate and costly (and therefore produce inefficient outcomes).

The private good aspects of the wires network

Critiques of neoclassical public good theory

The primary fallacy in the traditional public good/externality argument is that it ignores the direct comparison that an individual supplier makes between the marginal private benefit he or she gains and the marginal private cost of the additional unit of the public good. Regardless of whether others contribute or free ride, if that supplier's marginal benefit is at least as great as the marginal cost, then the supplier will provide that additional unit, unless the supplier chooses to behave strategically to try to induce payment by others to reduce his or her own private costs.

The neoclassical public good model suggests that without policy intervention, no amount of the good will be provided. This conclusion ignores the marginal private benefit–cost calculation that each agent makes. Unlike the traditional treatment of public good market failure, we are unlikely to see the infinite reversion of public good provision to zero if enough providers are willing to incur the costs to receive the benefits, or if a few providers have intense enough preferences that they will provide the good regardless of the actions of others. In such a case, the remaining important policy question is whether or not the marginal benefits that are not reflected in the supplier's choice would change the supplier's decision. Only in the cases where they would change that decision should the effect be considered potentially policy relevant.

The standard public good argument fails to take into account this distinction between relevant and irrelevant externalities. Take an example of an environmental amenity – the view of a forest on an island by passing ships.[6] The view is a public good (both nonexcludable and nonrival in consumption), so the standard conclusion is that the island's owner would underprovide forest relative to other uses of the land, such as pasture for beef cattle (an economic commodity). Thus by the neoclassical public good argument, to achieve the optimal level of forest to reflect the benefits to passing ships, the island's owner should be subject to land use regulation that increases the amount of forest beyond what she would choose independently, and the passing ships should be taxed to pay for the increase in forest acreage.

However, consider the fact that the island's owner has preferences over both the financial and the non-financial benefits of the land use. She may place high (marginal and total) value on the view (and smell and sound and fauna habitat) of the forest. How likely is it that the preferences (marginal benefits) of those on the passing ship will be higher than the owner's? Only if the marginal benefit of an additional acre of forest is higher for the ship passengers than for the owner, and the transaction costs are high enough to prevent them from negotiating with the owner, will the neoclassical public good argument hold. That special case is the *only* case in which free riding is economically relevant.

This argument is derived from Buchanan and Stubblebine's (1962) analysis of relevant and irrelevant externalities. Buchanan and Stubblebine start from a standard neoclassical model, where agents maximize utility subject to their budget constraints. But, as in the case of public goods, their agents have interdependent utilities in the sense that one good is consumed jointly, and the total amount available for consumption is a function of the choices of all of the agents. They then use their model to derive efficient provision levels and optimality conditions.

Buchanan and Stubblebine provide major insights in analyzing the reasoning underlying the result of equilibrium underprovision. The flaw in this logic is a straightforward consequence of economic thinking; it overlooks the fact that if the agent's marginal benefit from making the investment exceeds the marginal cost, she will make the investment, regardless of whether or not she can capture *all* of the marginal benefits. As long as she enjoys enough of them herself, she'll invest in reliability assets, and there will be no underprovision in equilibrium. Some other agents enjoy benefits without paying for them, but even if they did pay, if their benefits are small relative to hers their payments will not change her investment.

The implications of this insight for electricity policy and institution design are profound. First, it takes advantage of the fact that different agents on the network are going to have different preferences over reliability. These different preferences mean that for a given, shared level of reliability, some agents will have high marginal benefits and some will have low marginal benefits. That heterogeneity of preferences means that reliability can be both a public good and a private good. Individual production and consumption of reliability are interdependent, but when we recognize the diversity of preferences over reliability, the next logical step is to acknowledge that for high marginal value agents, reliability is a private good for which they are willing to pay beyond the lower levels that low marginal value agents would prefer. A salient example from retail electricity markets is the use of uninterruptible power supplies (UPSs) by residential customers. Using UPSs in critical locations in the home (on a main computer and the house's computer firewall, for example) indicate that the customer has more intense preferences over reliability than the common, shared level that is provided by the electric retailer; installing UPSs is an expression of a higher willingness to pay for more reliability at the margin.

That observation leads to the second major implication of the Buchanan and Stubblebine argument. If some agents are willing to pay for more reliability given that it does have private good aspects, then if left to their own investment choices, high marginal value agents would invest to a level beyond what would satisfy low marginal value agents. In other words, high-value agents choosing to pay for higher reliability would satiate low-value agents. Thus in the sense in which reliability is a public good, cases can arise in which the marginal value of additional reliability to a low-value agent is essentially zero. In that case the low-value agent is satiated, there is no externality at the margin, and any interdependency/externalities at the margin occurred at lower levels of reliability. High-value agents would not stop at that level, though, if their private marginal benefit from reliability were still higher than their private marginal cost. Technically, this equilibrium condition equating marginal benefit and marginal cost means that the interdependence between low-value agents and high-value agents experienced on the way to getting to equilibrium is a case of inframarginal externalities. Such externalities do not affect the amount of reliability provided in equilibrium, because at the margin the high-value agents determine that level, and the low-value agents are satiated. In other words, the benefits that accrue to the low-value agents are irrelevant externalities.

The policy implication of irrelevant externalities is that low-value agent free riding is irrelevant to the equilibrium outcome. It does not affect the efficient outcome, if the environment is structured in such a way that the incentives facing high-value agents are aligned such that they are willing and able to invest in reliability; markets with well-defined property rights are an example of such an environment (but, as we will see later, it is possible to design institutions to create such an environment even in the absence of well-defined property rights). If, on the other hand, a policy exists that forces the low-value agents to invest, in the worst case the outcome is over-investment in reliability, and in the best case there is an income transfer from the low-value agents to the high-value agents. These cases violate the efficiency and fairness conditions that purportedly drive regulatory policy.

The third implication of this argument is that in an efficient equilibrium, there will still be un-internalized externalities; however, the un-internalized effects, which are inevitable consequences of interdependence on networks, are small enough at the margin that even if they were internalized, they would not change the actual outcome, the actual investment in reliability. In networks, not all externalities can, or should, be internalized.

The fourth implication is that the only externalities that should matter, i.e., be policy relevant, are those that would affect the actual outcome in equilibrium and its efficiency. If there are relevant externalities, or effects on agents' values at the margin (if a failure to invest in reliability has a significant effect on another agent's utility), then there are unrealized gains from trade between the agent doing the investing and the one reaping the external benefit. They are leaving money on the table if they do not negotiate and figure out how to internalize the effects. They could self-internalize by one paying the other to invest, and if the payment is high enough, investment increases. If it is not high enough, then the investment shouldn't occur anyway, because the external benefit is not high enough to induce the agent to pay for it. This idea should sound familiar, because this is where the Buchanan and Stubblebine and the Coase "Problem of Social Cost" (1960) arguments dovetail. Externalities are not policy relevant if transaction costs are sufficiently low that we can negotiate to self-internalize them. In such cases contractual approaches to policy will lead to superior outcomes relative to regulatory approaches, such as the imposition of mandatory reliability standards on all agents. The institutional design implication of this insight is to focus on rules that reduce transaction costs and foster the development of markets, formal and informal, through which network agents can self-internalize the relevant, inevitable, effects on each other of their interdependence.

Applying this critique to the electric power network

Suppose a group of agents are connected on a network, and their participation in the network generates benefits for each of them. In the case of electric power, being connected to the grid enables agents to buy power from agents who produce and sell power, meaning either that consumers do not have to produce it themselves, or that they do not have to buy it from the nearest producer.[7]

Being connected through a network generates benefits for the connected agents, but at a cost. In addition to the cost of building the network, there is an additional cost of ensuring that the network will operate reliably for the agents using it. Ensuring a particular level of reliability requires investing in network capacity, particularly in peak hours, because one of the biggest causes of reliability reduction on all networks (electric, cell phone, Internet, highways, airports, etc.) is congestion. Does the network have sufficient capacity to provide reliable service in high-congestion periods?

Several different means exist for providing this capacity. One is to build more transmission wires, so the overall capacity constraint becomes less binding. Another is to build generation closer to consumer agents, using the network less. These approaches are costly in several ways. First, obviously, is high capital costs. Second, building more generation capacity closer to load has NIMBY (Not In My Backyard) costs, and in a large sense defeats the purpose of being interconnected on a network.

Other means of providing capacity do exist, though. We can use voltage-management technologies as springs or shock absorbers at various points in the network. We can ensure that we have good incentives and good capacity for reactive power to balance local network flows. Most importantly, we can use active demand response as a form of capacity building, empowering customers to choose from among a portfolio of contracts that could include real-time pricing, TOU pricing, or fully-loaded flat-rate pricing (as discussed in Chapters 4 and 6). Such pricing flexibility has proven and demonstrable benefits for networks, particularly in optimizing the capacity utilization of the existing network capacity without risking too much loss of reliability. In other words, demand response promotes reliability by using price to increase the network's load factor. Voltage management technologies and reactive power capacity also enhance network load factor without a cost of loss of reliability. They represent investments in reliability.

On an interconnected network, though, when one network agent invests in one of these reliability assets, all of the rest of the connected agents benefit, and the one who pays cannot always exclude the others from benefiting. This important factor is the basis for the argument that reliability is a public good. Applying standard neoclassical public good theory implies that the fact that reliability is nonexcludable and nonrival means that no one will want to invest in reliability, because he/she will not capture all of the additional benefits from the additional investment. This lack of investment is the manifestation of the free rider problem in network reliability. Thus we can expect underprovision of reliability unless we have some central coordination to require network agents to pay for the investments in reliability that benefit all of them. For example, on a network of interconnected load-serving entities (LSEs), if LSE_A makes an investment that benefits LSE_B, LSE_B reduces its investment. Anticipation of such free riding induces LSE_A not to invest. Thus the policy prescription of the neoclassical public good model is to require LSE_A and LSE_B to contribute to reliability-related investments determined through a central authority.

Now consider this thought experiment in the context of the irrelevant externality discussion presented above. The crucial distinction between policy-relevant and policy-irrelevant externalities rests on the difference between total benefit and marginal benefit. In order for an externality to be relevant, or to influence the optimal amount of the public good, the marginal benefit of the party not being considered in the decision has to be positive. In other words, just because LSE_A benefits from LSE_B's investments in reliability, that positive externality is not sufficient reason for LSE_A to pay toward LSE_B's investment. LSE_A's marginal benefit, not total benefit, has to be positive at the reliability level that LSE_B provides in order for LSE_A's preferences to make a difference. The crucial question is: at the level of reliability that LSE_B has provided (where, presumably, LSE_B's marginal benefit is nonnegative), is LSE_A's marginal benefit positive? If not, then LSE_B's reliability provision is enough for LSE_A, and if LSE_A is required to pay LSE_B it is simply a transfer of surplus from LSE_A to LSE_B.

Thus the policy-relevant case is one in which LSE_A's marginal benefit is still positive at the level of reliability that LSE_B's investments have provided. Now suppose that LSE_A's marginal benefit is small, smaller than the incremental cost of providing additional reliability through a centrally planned regulatory framework. Then the least-cost way for LSE_A to get the reliability it wants is to enable LSE_A to take small actions on its own that will satisfy its preferences for additional reliability, such as offering interruptible contracts and/or installing decentralized voltage management technology. But the transaction costs of increasing reliability through a centralized institution, such as long-term capacity auctions, may be high enough to leave LSE_A dissatisfied and unable to get that small, incremental amount of reliability benefit.

Now suppose that LSE_A's marginal benefit after LSE_B's actions is positive and large. Then LSE_A would benefit from investing in reliability, and would do so up to the point that equalizes LSE_A's marginal benefit and marginal cost from the incremental investment. In other words, incremental investments in reliability need not be subject to underprovision simply because others are simultaneously investing.

The preceding analysis relies on two assumptions that differ from the assumptions that typically underlie simple public goods analysis – that agents have homogeneous preferences, and that agents necessarily consume the same amount and quality of the public good. Instead, we have assumed that agents have a variety of preferences for the public good and we have assumed that reliability levels can differ across the grid. It is worth examining these two points more explicitly.

An LSE's demands for grid reliability, like its demand for power, are derived demands that arise from the end-use demands of the LSE's customers. Some of these customers will be very tolerant of variations in power quality and power supply interruptions, and some customers will be less accepting of power problems. At the retail residential level the difference may be as simple as one customer has a gas heater rather than electric, and a wind-up alarm clock, while another is all-electric for both heater and alarm clocks. A mid-winter power interruption might only mildly inconvenience the first customer, while the second customer's life could be seriously disrupted. At the commercial and industrial levels, the financial stakes will be much higher and the range of risk exposure much greater. Variation among end-use consumer exposure to risks from network-based disruptions will lead to variation among LSE preferences for the public good.

Recent market design efforts within regional power market operators have tended to move in a non-public good direction on assignment of costs, toward particularizing the provision of some reliability resources. For example, efforts under way in the Northeastern U.S. markets incorporate locational elements into both reserves and capacity markets.[8] These efforts arise out of practical attempts to address reliability issues on the grid, but these efforts, too, typically do not explicitly address the public- and private-good characteristics of network reliability.

In standard price theory we would say that the inframarginal agents have captured consumer surplus. Why, then, when modeling the inframarginal agents in the market for network reliability, do we model these same agents as free riders? We should only consider their free riding to be a problem if the incremental preferences of those agents over the public good are decision-relevant. Only then, and only in the presence of sufficient transaction costs to prevent negotiation, will a lack of reflection of their preferences in the ultimate choice lead to underprovision.

If it is possible, or even highly likely, that there are enough risk-averse agents in an electricity network to ensure optimal reliability without central planning, then enshrining a central planning mandate in federal policy can be inefficient, or even counterproductive. A more robust and flexible approach may be to hold all network agents jointly and severally legally liable for any lapses in reliability. Technology has made it easier and cheaper to discern whose actions, or inactions, have contributed in what way to a reliability failure. Such decentralized liability and responsibility would deter network agents from free riding. Legal liability would make network agents more risk averse, thus making network reliability less prone to free riding. Legal liability rules governing risk-averse agents are a decentralized institutional alternative to an inflexible central planning framework that is prone to creating costly excess reliability.

Agents with high marginal values will invest, agents with low marginal values will not and will free ride, but so what? At the margin, these are the efficient responses. Taking into account transaction costs and information costs, a bureaucratic response mandating a single level of reliability and using centralized institutions to bring it about is likely to result in an inefficient level of reliability and more costly provision than using decentralized incentives and contractual approaches to enable high marginal value agents to invest in network reliability.

The wires network and reliability: congestible common-pool resources

Rather than being public goods, both the wires network itself and service reliability are common-pool resources (CPRs). Although common-pool resources and public goods share certain characteristics, they remain distinct, and that distinction matters when modeling the policy treatment of reliability. Recall the central concepts defining public goods and CPRs, excludability and rivalry.[9] If it is easy to keep individuals from benefiting from a good or service without paying a fee, it is said to be *excludable* (Ostrom *et al.* 1994, p. 6). A good is *rival* if the use of the resource by one person diminishes another's ability to enjoy it (Ostrom 1990, p. 32; Ostrom *et al.* 1994, p. 6). CPRs differ from public goods because the consumption by one individual precludes another user from consuming that same unit; in other words, CPRs are rival but nonexcludable. Costly exclusion and a high level of rivalry combine to determine a good as a common pool resource (Ostrom *et al.* 1994, pp. 6–7). Recall also that costly exclusion also implies costly definition and enforcement of property rights; thus goods for which defining and enforcing property rights is difficult are often CPRs.[10] Public goods, in contrast, are both nonexcludable and nonrival.

In the case of the electric wires network, defining and enforcing property rights is both technically and economically challenging. The wires network, and its reliability, are CPRs because excluding interconnected agents from using it is costly, and consumption can reduce the amount available for others because of capacity constraints and congestion. Kirchoff's Law means that fully-defined property rights are impossible over the actual electricity commodity (the resource units, in Ostrom's terminology), and the economies of scale in transportation of the electricity over a shared physical network means that the system is subject to the problems of shared use that characterize a CPR. These features of the AC wires network as a system imply directly that property rights cannot be fully defined, and that transacting agents cannot specify a complete contract path. Because incomplete property rights definition and incomplete contracting characterize this environment, we can, and should, model the wires network as a CPR.

Costly exclusion and difficulty defining and enforcing property rights can lead to overuse of a CPR, diminishing consumption for all agents (Hardin 1968; Dietz *et al.* 2003). Take the canonical example of grazing animals on a common pasture in a medieval village. At the margin each resident has an incentive to add another animal to the pasture as long as the marginal benefit is positive, even if the additional animals reduce the grass available to the other pastured animals. Once they reach the pasture's carrying capacity constraint, additional animals reduce the grass available to all.

The policy challenge facing the users of the CPR is devising a set of rules, designing an institution, to enable them to avoid the overuse that is the "tragedy of open access" in a CPR (Haddock and Kiesling 2003). Institutional design to govern the commons is the objective (Ostrom 1990). Overuse problems arise in CPRs because exclusion and property rights definition are costly. Institutional design is the key to effective CPR governance: can the users of the CPR design an institution to make the CPR excludable? Such an exclusion institution typically takes the form of a system of use rights and a means of enforcing those rights. In the common pasture example, a community norm limiting the number of animals allowed per family, coupled with branding or some other way of identifying animal ownership, creates a system of use rights over the CPR.

The analogy applies to a wires network if the interconnected agents could send and receive power without paying for using the wires. In such a case congestion, and system failure during peak hours, would be the likely result in the short run, and underinvestment in network capacity would be likely in the long run. Recall that in AC power systems the property rights over the electricity itself is incomplete.[11] Thus the form that a system of use rights takes in electricity is more like that typical of an irrigation system – agents have rights to inject or to remove power at a specific time.[12] Reliability and physical system balancing require that the injection right and the withdrawal right pertain to a precise time interval. In fact, this paired right to inject/right to withdraw power is the fundamental concept underlying the system of firm transmission rights (FTRs) used in RTOs in the U.S. (Stoft 2002). Thus we see that by modeling the wires network as a CPR we can understand FTRs as a system of use rights that the RTO, as a centralized control organization, uses to govern the commons.

More specifically, how does this CPR model relate to reliability policy? Reliability is a service characteristic that is a consequence of the use of the (CPR) wires network, but is reliability a CPR in its own right? In order for reliability to be a CPR, it has to have costly exclusion while being rival in consumption. The rivalry is the key question here – if we add a (consumer) agent to the network, does that additional consumer diminish reliability? Up to a point, adding more consumers has barely perceptible effects on the probability of service interruption or fluctuation, but as consumption and production near the capacity constraint, consumption becomes rival. The reliability of all consumers who have not self-insured (by installing UPSs, as discussed above) suffers.

At this general level reliability does have the nonexcludability and rivalry features of a CPR. If that is the case, then the policy challenge is to see whether exclusion by defining use rights is possible, or if exclusion costs are too high. Is it possible to exclude some network users from reliability levels for which they have not paid? Historically the answer has been no, with two caveats. The first caveat is the evidence discussed above that consumers do not consume the same level of reliability, either within RTO regions or across regions.

The second caveat picks up on the use of technology to self-insure by customers who are willing to pay for higher reliability. Technology is increasingly enabling different consumers to be able to experience differential probabilities of interruption or service fluctuation. In the terms of the CPR model, technologies that enable different users to consume different levels of the good increase the excludability of the good. By reducing exclusion costs and property rights definition costs, technological change can turn reliability into more of a private good and less of a CPR. Moreover, these same technologies, coupled with institutions that enable the retail sale of reliability as a differentiated product, contribute to our ability to achieve short-term system security and long-term resource adequacy through more decentralized coordination and less central control. If we are to achieve decentralized coordination in the use and expansion of the wires network, the institutions we employ to define and enforce use rights in the network matter a great deal.[13]

Institutional design implications[14]

Now introduce two other features to this narrative model. First, take the important starting point from earlier in this chapter: assume that agents have heterogeneous preferences over reliability. For simplicity, as before, think of there being high-value agents and low-value agents.[15] Second, note that digital current flow metering, monitoring, and interruption technologies have become increasingly available and affordable, which make implementing the delivery of different levels of reliability to different agents feasible. Black argues that congestion-related reliability problems can, and should, be addressed using technology and decentralized market processes rather than treating the congestible resources as a public good:

> Protection schemes are implemented almost exclusively at the grid level. For fault isolation, this may be efficient in most cases. For relieving congestion in contingencies, however, it is possible to reduce the impact on loads of curtailments by moving the protection controls inside the residence, building, or factory and targeting specific portions of load (e.g. energy based) rather than bluntly curtailing essential and non-essential services for the same purpose.
>
> (2005, p. 114)

A question related to the public good nature of network reliability is whether the fact that something has public good characteristics necessarily implies that it should be provided to all at a uniform level. Again, not necessarily. Imposing a uniform reliability standard to deal with the alleged public good features of networks does disservice to the diverse, heterogeneous preferences that agents have over reliability. A uniform standard is likely to underprovide to high-value agents and overprovide to low-value agents, and costly inefficiency ensues. Instead, consider the extent to which reliability can be marketed, bought, and sold as a differentiated product.

To see the point, consider how reliability is provided as a differentiated product in another industry – Internet service. When you flip the light switch, does the electricity to power the light flow to you on demand? When you want to access a webpage, does your network have the capacity to satisfy your demand in the time that you want it to? Intuitively the Internet makes grasping this argument easier – different agents on a network have different preferences over the degree of reliability of the network on which they operate. A high-demand agent is more likely to pay for larger broadband capacity, signaling to the Internet service provider that they should similarly invest in network capacity to meet the level of reliability for which the agent has contracted. A low-demand user will choose a slow connection, and will pay a correspondingly lower price. In this example, both the high-demand and the low-demand agent want on-demand access. In Internet networks the measure of reliability is more about upload and download speed than it is about on-demand availability of the network.

The case of electricity is slightly different, because of the nature of electrons and the physics of AC power flows. In the case of electricity, thinking about reliability essentially boils down to thinking about the probability of interruption, with no issue of connection speed. In this way electric network reliability is similar to, and different from, Internet network reliability.

What value do electricity consumers place on reliability, and does that value vary across consumers? It is not clear that anyone knows whether a typical electricity consumer in the United States or Canada would rather have more reliability at higher power prices or less reliability and lower power prices; nor is it clear that anyone knows the distribution of reliability values across consumers. As Black notes,

> Regulators and/or system operators typically determine a uniform reliability standard for their jurisdictions/control areas. These reliability standards are based on estimates of what the "correct" level of reliability for all consumers should be. There is currently little or no direct consumer feedback or choice as to these estimated reliability standards. Surveys may be used to estimate costs of outages, but consumers may not know or be able to articulate their costs of outages accurately.
>
> (Black 2005, p. 122)

More to the point, some consumers would probably be willing to pay more to have more reliable service, and others would choose lower prices even if service quality went down a little. The existing top-down system offers few avenues for suppliers, operators or policymakers to gather information on how different customers value reliability. Nor does the regulatory system offer many opportunities to energy consumers wishing to buy different levels of reliability; instead industry and its regulators tend to see reliability as a "one size fits all" characteristic, and to implement top-down uniform reliability regulations and spread the costs accordingly.[16]

If reliability is defined as the local electric company being willing and able to supply uninterrupted electric power, at a price and on demand, it is possible for neighboring customers to have differing reliability. An industrial customer may be willing to be cut back on power consumption when the system is stressed, contractually agreeing that the electricity provider can reduce service under certain circumstances. The customer is in effect accepting lower local reliability to allow the electric company to provide added reliability to other customers.

This interruptibility option still embodies a supply-side view of reliability. If reliability is defined as the uninterrupted provision of services to the consumer from electric appliances, then we can see even more clearly the limitations of the "one size fits all" view of reliability. Consumers who have specific needs for reliable power can, for example, purchase battery-backup power supplies to help keep computers up and running even if the local power company is having problems with delivery: these consumers are paying a little more to have more reliable service from a select appliance or two, and as a result would feel less of a need for uninterrupted electric power services from the local power company. Consumers also may have similar tolerances for service interruptions, for instance, being able to tolerate periods of having their air conditioners turned off during the summer. Devices are available that would enable a consumer or third-party energy management company to control air conditioner loads remotely, or to automate changes in consumption in response to a price signal. Businesses do the same thing on a larger scale, with companies that have special needs for highly-reliable electric power spending millions of dollars to secure their supplies, and similarly can install complex energy management systems to control power consumption. This focused demand-side approach provides targeted power reliability.

These consumer-side choices have the potential to reveal more information about consumer values for reliable electric power system service, but current approaches to providing targeted reliability services usually prevent the local utility from being directly involved. As a result, few avenues exist for consumer reliability choices to percolate up through the market, informing the system-wide choices about reliability that distribution and transmission system operators need to make appropriate maintenance and investment decisions. Chao and Wilson (1987) and Fumagalli *et al.* (2004) have suggested a "priority insurance" system that would produce this kind of information.[17]

In such an environment, treating reliability as a differentiated product becomes feasible, and may even be preferable to the extent that it enables increased value creation through better meeting the diverse preferences of network agents. Note that even in the current regulatory environment, high-value agents can buy more reliability – even single-family households can install UPSs (uninterruptible power supplies) to power their computers in the case of a blackout. But there's an asymmetry, in that it's difficult for low-value agents to pay less and buy less reliability than is provided under a uniform standard. That is where the idea of priority insurance comes in.

When something is scarce, priority insurance is a way for suppliers to ration the scarce resources among customers who have essentially bought a place in line. Think of priority insurance as a menu of contracts where customers choose a price and a probability of service. Put another way, if you are willing to be interrupted, you may pay a lower price, and if there is deficient supply, you will have a lower priority for being served than others who were willing to pay a higher price. Chao and Wilson model priority insurance as a menu of contracts in which each customer's selection of one contract from the menu determines the customer's service order or priority. In the case of a contingency or threat to system reliability, the seller rations supplies by serving customers in order of their selected priorities until the supply is exhausted or all customers are served. Chao and Wilson then point out that priority insurance means that the product being sold can be a differentiated product, differentiated on the dimension of your willingness to be interrupted. Put another way, priority insurance in electric networks makes reliability a differentiated product, not a uniform product that has to be provided to all agents on the network at the same level. Priority insurance empowers agents on a network to choose either higher or lower levels of reliability, depending on their willingness to pay.

Note also that priority insurance provides a means of inducing customers to reveal information about their preferences over reliability. This kind of information is extremely absent today, and its absence means that policymakers have little or no idea of how customers really value reliability. Thus policymakers are making decisions about reliability policy on electric networks without having any good idea about what "the right" level of reliability is, or how costly it is to impose a single level of reliability in the face of diverse agent preferences over the level of reliability.

The essence of priority insurance is to pay consumers when the lights go out. From a contractual perspective, in a market with competitive retailers and a single wires company, the retailers contract with consumers to pay them, and they also include terms in their contracts with the wires company for determining which party is responsible for the outage. If the wires company is responsible, it pays the retailer, which pays its customers.

Paying customers is a simple idea, but Chao and Wilson add a twist: the electric company offers different qualities of service. For a higher price, a customer can obtain a lower probability of being cut off when the system is short of power (and a higher payment from the electric company when the lights go out); pay a lower price, get a higher probability of being cut off (and a lower payment). Customers would be able to make a tradeoff between price and reliability based on their individual preferences and private knowledge. When the embedded premiums are set appropriately, each customer class can be assured of being no worse off than before, and they may be made better off.[18] Noussair and Porter (1992) tested a version of this idea experimentally against a simple system of proportional rationing of shortages, and found that their version of priority insurance was more efficient than proportional rationing.[19]

Black (2005, p. 126) and Fumagalli *et al.* (2004, pp. 1290–1291) describe how circuit breaker and recloser technology can be used to implement priority insurance contracts. Distributed reclosers throughout the distribution network can be particularly useful in implementing priority insurance because they reset automatically after temporary faults (Fumagalli *et al.* 2004, p. 1290). This example illustrates the use of technology to increase exclusion costs on the distribution network, and how technology can help create a system of use rights in the CPR. The technology exists to enable us to value and sell reliability as a differentiated product; however, until we have regulators and market institutions that enable us to value reliability separately from delivery, we will fail to make investments in technologies that can improve reliability in this decentralized, targeted way.

While one benefit of priority insurance is that it allows the retailer to allocate a shortage efficiently by having customers prioritize their own use, a larger benefit comes from the information created by the consumer actions. Priority insurance allows consumers to evaluate energy and service reliability separately, allowing the company to distinguish what customers are willing to pay for power from what they are willing to pay for reliability; in other words, selling reliability as a differentiated product would create knowledge that we do not currently have about the value customers place on reliability. Companies could target investments where they provide the most long-term value to consumers instead of simply ensuring sufficient generation capacity to meet the regulation-mandated reserve margin. This information about how customers value reliability is crucial to getting the efficient amount and kind of system infrastructure investment.

Conclusion

If a good (or service) has public good characteristics, does that fact necessarily imply that its provision should be centrally coordinated through regulation? Not necessarily. Nor does that fact imply that the good is a public good. Electric wires networks and network reliability are actually common-pool resources (CPRs) and not public goods. That difference changes the policy implications and institutional design choices that should be implemented in reliability policy.

The public good model fails to account for features of network reliability that are important for deriving policy implications from the model. Specifically, the combined public/private good aspect of reliability means that a more general model is needed. I propose a model based on Ostrom's (1990) continuum of property rights definition over common-pool resources, with the associated focus on institutional design to create a system of use rights over the CPR.

Network reliability is not as much of a public good as is assumed in the policy institutions governing the electric power industry. The assertion that at least some aspects of network quality are shared by all network users, and that each user's actions on the grid have "external" effects, is common. However, public goods, as the term is understood in economics, require more than just the presence of an externality, and the presence of an externality is insufficient in itself to justify regulatory action.

This analysis suggests that even network reliability (the portion of reliability capturing the voltage, frequency, and stability conditions of the network) is both a congestible CPR and a private good. The importance of locational interaction and the increasing ability to use technology to manage voltage in a decentralized manner reinforces this conclusion. Furthermore, the public good characteristics of network reliability may not necessitate cost-sharing or some other centralized approach, because the heterogeneity of agent preferences and the private good aspects of reliability may make the public good characteristics an irrelevant externality. In fact, attempts to mandate cost sharing can themselves lead to inefficient outcomes in complex dynamic systems, particularly where the boundary between the public good aspects and the private good aspects differs across agents and shifts dynamically over time.

The electric power network is a complex interaction of human agents and physical interconnections, with many real-time characteristics and constraints. It is precisely this interaction of the human and the physical that makes the integration of markets into networks so crucial. Markets are a key human institution for making this complex system into a complex adaptive system. The rules governing the use of such a network can exploit these decentralized, distributed resources and incentives to enhance the stability and reliability of the grid. However, mandatory uniform reliability standards and legacy reserve margin requirements do nothing to take advantage of the very real fact that human agents on the network have diverse preferences over their use of the network.

In that paradigm, the control room operator is the primary decision-maker, because system stability is paramount, and in that paradigm the only way to maintain system stability is through centralized control to deliver a common quality of service to all. However, as shown in Chapter 4 and discussed further here, digital technologies exist (and are increasingly becoming less expensive) that enable decentralized coordination and decision-making. Such technology opens up the possibility that agents can choose for themselves what quality of service they experience, independent of the quality available on the network. For example, an agent could install a power-conditioning system if s/he finds it valuable to ensure less voltage or frequency fluctuation than is available as the standard power quality level. On the other hand, an agent can also install price-responsive automation technology that reduces or shuts off some or all power use at an agent's premises in response to a price signal.

In traditional centralized control, such reductions constitute reduced reliability. In a technology-enabled distributed control environment, though, the agent is empowered to choose a lower level of reliability when consumption is just not sufficiently valuable to the agent.

In this truly decentralized coordination paradigm, the agent is the primary decision-maker. One of the institutional design challenges in network industries will be to craft regulatory institutions that increase the likelihood that the aggregation of individual agent decisions in this distributed control environment leads to system stability – to emergent order.

A more contractual approach to the electric power network, rather than the legacy regulatory approach of uniform standards and reserve margins, can take advantage of agent heterogeneity, and can also increase the transparency of property rights assignment. One particular application of a contractual approach, namely priority insurance, holds great promise for harnessing the decentralized preferences and incentives of network agents to enhance network stability and reliability.

Given these conclusions, a more dynamic and constructive policy approach to network reliability is to use the heterogeneous and locational characteristics of reliability to bolster system and grid security and stability. A system of priority insurance (or reliability insurance) would do just that, recognizing reliability as a differentiated product from the point of view of end-use customers and the load-serving entities selling services to them.

The second assumption – that reliability can differ across the grid – is in some respects just saying that reliability is not a pure public good. While at first glance it may appear that all network users are in the same boat, metaphorically speaking – after all, the network is either working or it is not – turns out to be an oversimplified approach. Consider the August 14, 2003 blackout in the Midwestern and Northeastern United States and parts of Canada. Despite being the largest such network failure in history, the network failure was in some respects contained. While service was out for many millions of customers, several million more customers continued to receive service.

Much of the impetus for this argument arises from the realization that network reliability actually differs across the grid. Such a realization opens up the analysis such that we can look at policies that contribute to more or less network reliability at particular places, we can examine how actions taken by producers and consumers connected to the grid add to or subtract from reliability (both for themselves and for their neighbors on the network), and we can compare efforts to improve grid reliability to a fuller range of alternatives that consumers face in making trade-offs between power consumption, need for reliable service, and overall expense.

Of course, the "realization" that network reliability differs across the grid is not news to the engineers and managers working with the grid on a day-to-day business, nor likely to anyone else. The point has been underemphasized in policy discussions. This connection is important in order to develop the implications of this difference in demand for reliability, and to better apply the economics of CPRs and public goods to understanding reliability policy.

Reliability is a crucial element in enabling those power markets to continue developing, but that does not mean that reliability is a "one size fits all" characteristic of the network. Treating reliability as a public good leads to conflicts, treating it as a private good could avoid those conflicts. The metering, monitoring and switching technology exists to treat reliability as a differentiated, private good. Now the institutional and legal structure must adapt and evolve to take advantage of these opportunities.

Consumers are the sleeping giant of electric reliability. Retail rate regulation has put the demand side to sleep, but it is time for consumers to wake up. Retail pricing, including the separate pricing of energy and reliability, is a crucial component of a healthy, dynamic electricity industry, and a reliable grid.

Offering consumers service choices in a range of prices would make diverse consumers better off, and bolster system reliability.

Technology contributes to making reliability less of a public good, because it reduces the cost of defining and enforcing property rights and use rights in the network. Technology also makes it easier and more potentially attractive to market and sell reliability of service to end-use customers as a differentiated product. This product differentiation would create value for consumers, increase dynamic efficiency, and reduce strains on the existing physical infrastructure.

Appendix 8.1

Ostrom's institutional design principles

In this chapter I argue that reliability is a common-pool resource (CPR), and consequently that governance institutions for defining and enforcing use rights are important when designing reliability policy. In Chapter 3 of *Governing the Commons*, Ostrom distills some institutional design principles from case study analysis of several long-enduring CPR institutions (1990, Table 3.1, p. 90). She does not claim that these design principles are either necessary or sufficient, but that experience of robust CPR institutions suggests that these design principles increase the probability of success.

Ostrom cautions, "Given that CPR appropriators in some of the cases ... do switch back and forth between arenas, we must drop the framing assumption that analysis at single level will be sufficient" (Ostrom 1990, p. 50). In other words, agents make choices in the face of specific day-to-day rules as well as more abstract rules that affect their decisions more broadly. To understand agent behavior and incentives requires thinking about institutional design as these different levels.

Ostrom introduces the concept of "nested institutions," by first defining "institutions" as, "The sets of working rules that are used to determine who is eligible to make decisions in some arena, what actions are allowed or constrained, what aggregation rules will be used, what procedures must be followed, what information must or must not be provided, and what payoffs will be assigned to individuals dependent on the actions" (Ostrom 1990, p. 51). Just as there are different levels of analysis for CPRs, there are also different levels of rulemaking and enforcement. Governance of a CPR comes from formal legislation, as well as informal norms established by the community. At times these informal norms, known as "working rules," may depart from the "formal rules" established by legislators (Ostrom 1990, p. 51). Nonetheless, working rules are not entirely independent of formal rules, as "All rules are nested in another set of rules that define how the first set of rules can be changed" (Ostrom 1990, p. 51). The author cautions that while changing one set of rules, the rules in which others are nested remain unaltered. Additionally, reformulating the rules at a deeper level presents greater challenges to managers (Ostrom 1990, p. 52).

The three levels of rules can be thought of as different spheres of influence, which are encased in one another. *Constitutional rules* represent the outermost sphere, as they dictate the structure of governance and the overall political organization of the system. *Collective-choice rules* are nested within *constitutional rules*; they concern policymaking and management decisions. Lastly, *operational rules* involve the daily decisions within the CPR, as they involve monitoring, enforcement, and other actions on the ground level. *Operational rules* are the innermost sphere and thus, are nested in *collective-choice* and *constitutional rules*.

Ostrom confronts the fatalist attitudes often displayed by property-rights theorists. These scholars believe that only two outcomes are possible for communal actors who determine their own use rights. (1) Communal actors will either fail to establish a high enough degree of exclusion, or (2) they will succeed in outlining rules, but only at prohibitively high costs (Ostrom 1990, pp. 60–61). The author counteracts these notions through the study of cases where local stakeholders set rules and monitor their adherence. From these case studies Ostrom outlines eight design principles illustrated by long-enduring CPR institutions.

(1) *Clearly defined boundaries*: *Individuals or households who have rights to withdraw resource units from the CPR must be clearly defined, as must the boundaries of the CPR itself.*
The most concrete example of this point is the case of licensing, where managers grant formal legal access to the CPR. Ostrom warns, "Without defining the boundaries of the CPR and closing it to 'outsiders,' local appropriators face the risk that any benefits they produce by their efforts will be reaped by others who have not contributed to those efforts" (Ostrom 1990, p. 91). Licensing and other forms of limiting access to the commons establish rights to the commons; however, the strategies do not provide rules for extraction. The author explains why limiting access is not enough to protect the resource, "Making this attribute one of seven, rather than a unique attribute, put its importance in a more realistic perspective" (Ostrom 1990, p. 92). Thus, the definition of boundaries requires other efforts on the part of organizers. Note that this principle relies on a very crucial distinction in both CPRs and networks: the distinction between property rights and use rights. Either by choice or physical necessity a group of agents can treat a resource as a CPR while still defining very specific, clear, transparent use rights. This principle is very important in a network context.

(2) *Congruence between appropriation and provision rules and local conditions*: *Appropriation rules restricting time, place, technology, and/or quantity of resource units are related to local conditions and to provision rules requiring labor, material, and/or money.*
Local conditions matter greatly. In places where water is stored in a dam, the irrigators purchase resource units based on an hourly rate, where they know from experience how the level of water in the dam dictates the flow rate (Ostrom 1990, p. 92). In contrast, systems without stored water often rely on a rotation, where irrigators take the amount they need one at a time. These two

systems are in close proximity, but the two cases illustrate that the individuality of the resource requires rules tailored to the locality. We have millennia of human history, with the most poignant and painful being the Soviet experience, showing how the top-down imposition of external institutions that do not respect or incorporate local knowledge and local conditions will make people worse off and are ultimately doomed to costly failure. This design principle gets at the institutional design question at the core of this analysis: robust institutions are organic in nature. They derive from the decentralized interactions of those with strong interests and good local knowledge. Local knowledge and local conditions differ, even on an electric power network. Furthermore, some of that local knowledge is going to be tacit and difficult or impossible to communicate, reinforcing the important knowledge problem points raised in Chapter 3.

(3) *Collective-choice arrangements: Most individuals affected by the operational rules can participate in modifying the operational rules.*
This principle is best understood as direct democracy, where stakeholders propose, debate, and agree upon rules that govern themselves. The process of community rule-making grants a level of efficacy not often experienced in cases where rules are dictated to stakeholders by an outside authority. The benefits continue further as "CPR institutions ... are better able to tailor their rules to local circumstances, because individuals who directly interact with one another and with the physical world can modify the rules over time so as to better fit them to the specific characteristics of their setting" (Ostrom 1990, p. 93). Although the presence of collective-choice arrangements does promote stewardship, it does not guarantee compliance. Agents affected by the institutions should have opportunities to modify the institutions. Otherwise the institutions stagnate as networks evolve, and the institutions become obsolete at great cost (both financial cost and opportunity cost) to the network agents.

(4) *Monitoring: Monitors, who actively audit CPR conditions and appropriator behavior, are accountable to the appropriators or are the appropriators.*
Monitoring and enforcement are not taken care of by an omnipresent and omnipotent being; thus, CPRs require resources dedicated to oversight. Monitoring is important but costly, and should be done in a way that the monitors are accountable to the network agents. In many of the CPR cases Ostrom analyzes appropriators themselves do the monitoring, although it's important to have a third party responsible for enforcement and punishment. In a network context like electricity, where everyone's actions are to some degree interdependent, self-monitoring arrangements should be relatively cheap, but getting the incentives right for the monitor is a challenge. Additionally, monitoring efforts should be carried out with transparency and justice, as corruption can unsettle a successful CPR institution. Ostrom encapsulates Levi's central argument, "Strategic actors are willing to comply with a set of rules ... when (1) they perceive that the collective objective is achieved, and (2) they perceive that others also

comply" (Ostrom 1990, p. 95). From this point, it is understood that resource harvesters are inclined to monitor others' behavior, as it informs their own decisions. In addition to offsetting informational asymmetries, informal monitoring may also bring higher status to an appropriator who reports others who do not comply (Ostrom 1990, p. 96). However, this elevation in status can only arise when there are means of dealing with noncompliance.

(5) *Graduated sanctions: Appropriators who violate operational rules are likely to be assessed graduated sanctions (depending on the seriousness and context of the offense) by other appropriators, by officials accountable to these appropriators, or by both.*
Graduated sanctions allow for appropriators to address and punish rule-breakers in proportion to the infraction. Punishment escalates with the severity of the violation.

(6) *Conflict-resolution mechanisms: Appropriators and their officials have rapid access to low-cost local arenas to resolve conflicts among appropriators or between appropriators and officials.*
This principle is an obvious off-shoot of principles 4 and 5, as rules and punishments require a means of enforcement and due process. CPRs require a process that is not encumbered by overly complex rules of order. Without such mechanisms, stakeholders will begin to categorize rules as either weak or unjust. These mechanisms can be formal or informal, from courts to local self-administered arbitration. In different contexts different conflict-resolution mechanisms will have the credibility to make their decisions stick, so this design principle also builds on the local conditions/knowledge one discussed above.

(7) *Minimal recognition of rights to organize: The rights of appropriators to devise their own institutions are not challenged by external governmental authorities.*
Higher levels of government cannot undermine the autonomy of local managers in cases where robust institutions govern common property. As previously discussed, there are often three different sets of rules, each representing a separate sphere of influence. In order for local institutions to succeed, the outer shells need to support and not encumber the system. The rights of local agents to develop and arrange their own institutions are not challenged by central government authorities. This principle is difficult in a network context like electric power that occurs in multiple political jurisdictions, and with this history of 85 years of symbiotic codependency of the regulator and regulated. It is important, though, because this is a pressure valve that allows for the evolution of institutions and the adoption of designs that are better suited to local conditions and/or changing and unknown conditions. Government-based institutions do not typically face competition from different institutional arrangements, but that competition is crucial (and is one of the important foundations of the "laboratory of the states" defense of federalism).

(8)* *Nested enterprises: Appropriation, provision, monitoring, enforcement, conflict resolution, and governance activities are organized in multiple layers of nested enterprises.*
*for CPRs that are parts of larger political systems or jurisdictions

Once again, the spheres of influence come into play. This principle is best illustrated by the federal system, where laws and policy are created and coordinated at different levels of government. The idea once again is not to hamper the abilities of the inner sphere, but to lend any need oversight or authority when necessary. I interpret "nested enterprises" as analogous to the concept of federalism, with local knowledge and local institutions prevailing where appropriate but nested within an institutional structure to accommodate larger and broader interests.

These design principles can inform how we design institutions in electric power that have more organic features, and are more likely to be flexible enough to evolve beneficially in the face of unknown and changing conditions.

9 Facilitating technology-enabled decentralized coordination

The preceding chapters highlight several areas in the electric power industry in which economic and technological dynamism have made the existing natural monopoly regulatory institutions and business models obsolete. A more dynamic model based on decentralized coordination can, and should, take their place. We can use the ideas in this work to think differently about regulation in the electric utility industry, to imagine and design regulatory institutions that are more focused on establishing preconditions for decentralized coordination and allowing innovation to occur. Institutions that do so focus primarily on transparent contract enforcement rules (including consumer protection rules), on information provision, and on reducing the transaction costs that prevent mutually beneficial exchange from occurring.[1]

This work has two overarching connected themes. The first theme is that pervasive economic and technological dynamism mean that regulatory institutions must be adaptive, or they become inefficient and obsolete. The second theme follows naturally from that observation: the analyses presented here challenge the assumptions underlying the existing regulatory institutions that are based on static, neoclassical natural monopoly theory. One objective of this work is to challenge the assumptions on which the existing regulatory institutions are built. Those assumptions include taking technology as exogenously given, full information available to all agents, zero transaction costs, and full definition and costless enforcement of property rights.

Regulatory institutions based on neoclassical natural monopoly theory and premised on unrealistic static assumptions are ill-suited to enable the electricity industry to serve customers and maximize value creation in this constantly changing world. While natural monopoly theory had some value in crafting a policy framework that resulted in widespread electrification and low retail prices, its static focus limits its ability to help us understand the dynamic interaction of regulation, retail competition, and technological change. If the static neoclassical model on which they are based does not capture salient features of this dynamic environment, then we should rethink the regulatory model. I suggest rethinking regulation along the lines of facilitating mutual coordination.

Recall that the coordination framework used in this analysis has the following defining ideas:

1   *Heterogeneous agents with diffuse private knowledge*;
2   The benefits of *decentralized coordination*;
3   The possibility of *emergent order*, both economic and physical, in electric power systems;
4   *Technological change* makes decentralized coordination and emergent order possible;
5   *Institutions* play a crucial role in enabling heterogeneous agents with diffuse, private knowledge to achieve decentralized coordination and emergent order; and
6   Institutions must have the *capacity to adapt* to unknown and changing conditions.

Framing the economic problem as the coordination of heterogeneous agents with diffuse private knowledge is the crucial starting point for adaptive regulatory institutional design. Static neoclassical models, with outcomes evaluated based on resource allocation (allocative, or static, efficiency) take the fundamental economic problem to be the allocation of scarce resources; a more dynamic focus on processes instead of outcomes takes the fundamental economic problem to be the coordination of the decisions of distributed, heterogeneous agents with private knowledge.

Technology affects whether decentralized coordination and emergent order are possible; the dramatic transformation of digital technology in the past few decades has decreased transaction costs and increased the extent of feasible decentralized coordination in this industry. Institutions, which structure and shape the contexts in which such processes occur, provide a means for creating this coordination. Regulatory institutions affect whether or not this coordination can occur. Thus effective regulation should not focus on allocation, but rather on decentralized coordination and how to bring it about. A focus on decentralized coordination means a focus on market processes, which are adaptive institutions that evolve along with technological change. But regulatory institutions should also be adaptive themselves, and policymakers should view regulatory policy as a work in progress so that the institutions can adapt to unknown and changing conditions.

Technological changes in generation, transmission, distribution, and metering over the past two decades (coming from outside the industry) have accelerated the obsolescence of the traditional regulatory model. Changes in other public policies, such as the increasing political support for wind power and other energy sources seen as environmentally friendly, are also spurring policy adjustments.[2] Much of the vision guiding recent electric industry restructuring efforts emerged from the deregulatory impulse of the late 1970s, was refined in the 1980s, and became implemented in bits and pieces up through 2000.[3] While restructuring has stalled in the wake of the California electricity crisis and Enron scandal, unrelenting technological change in other parts of the economy make stagnation in this industry even more costly.

One of the most effective institutional changes to enable decentralized coordination is to open retail electricity markets to competitive entry, and to separate the distribution wires transportation transaction from the retail transaction. This separation has been at the root of successful restructuring, most notably in England and Wales and in Texas (Kiesling and Kleit 2008). Removing retail entry barriers and enabling retail competition would facilitate the promulgation of dynamic pricing options and product differentiation that could include green power and priority insurance, among other things.

The decentralized and distributed network of retailers and customers can also contribute to grid resiliency and flexibility, through more active participation in the market. Active, engaged customers could choose anything from a fixed price that incorporates an insurance premium to full real-time pricing, in which the customer bears the financial risk of price volatility, and they could see electricity bills fall by shifting or reducing use.[4] Several ongoing demand response and retail pricing pilots have demonstrated that even residential customers do change their behavior in response to prices. Even if the magnitude of the shift is small, the effect may be large because of the nonlinear relationship between peak load reductions and network reliability. A small load reduction at just the right time can keep the system from hitting capacity, can increase capacity utilization, and in the long run can reduce required investment in peak resources that sit idle much of the year. Letting go of some of the centralized economic and physical control would increase the resiliency of the system.

Using this coordination framework to think about technological dynamism and regulation leads to implications for institutional change and policy recommendations. In general, to .".. enhance effective problem-solving ... Instead of central direction, what is needed are policies that enhance the accuracy and reliability of information, that provide low-cost conflict resolution, and that develop the authority to govern resources at multiple levels" (Ostrom 2005, p. 240). The coordination framework suggests the following alternative criteria by which to evaluate regulatory institutions and market designs:

- Adaptability to unknown and changing conditions;
- Enabling coordination of distributed, individual plans and actions;
- Enabling agents to self-organize; and
- Reducing the transaction costs that prevent private parties from engaging in mutually beneficial exchange.

Regulatory institutions that meet these criteria will do a better job of enabling new value creation to come from unanticipated areas and sources. Regulation that focuses on creating an environment for thriving, integrated wholesale and retail markets serves consumers by decreasing entry barriers and transaction costs that obstruct the process of innovation in services and technologies.

This industry and its regulatory organizations are highly risk averse and resistant to change, despite all of the potential value creation that they are foregoing by resisting change. Lasting changes in institutions and behavior requires overcoming status quo bias. How do we overcome this historical, cultural, and economic inertia?

The first step is to recognize the shortcomings of the existing regulatory institutions and business models. Those shortcomings include overinvestment to build to meet peak capacity, which leaves underutilized assets for most of the year; higher levels of pollution than we might otherwise experience because of the lack of product differentiation to allow green products and the lack of dynamic pricing that correlates with true marginal costs of electricity consumption; and a resource portfolio mix that is too supply oriented, too dominated by central generation, and too divorced from consumer preferences because of the truncation of retail price signals. The next step in overcoming this inertia is in recognizing that we do not know the future and cannot pick specific outcomes. Traditional regulation picks an outcome, which stifles innovation and drives it outside of the industry.

Given these realizations, it is important to re-focus the regulatory mission away from protecting consumers by mandating low, stable prices for a regulated commodity service, and toward a mission of protecting consumers by facilitating the growth and operation of integrated wholesale and retail markets that can adapt to change. This dynamic mission relies on reducing entry barriers and transaction costs.

By establishing preconditions for markets to function and creating an institutional environment in which they thrive, regulation will adapt to change because markets are complex adaptive systems that achieve ordered outcomes through decentralized coordination. By allowing markets to function, regulation will also benefit consumers by delivering differentiated products and services at different price points; note also that competition-facilitating regulation also enables entrepreneurial producers to profit from meeting the needs of consumers (who have diverse preferences and diffuse private knowledge). Market processes are positive-sum interactions in ways that traditional regulation cannot anticipate or duplicate.

A final recommendation arising from this coordination framework is humility. As analysts and policymakers, "we need to ... be better facilitators of building adaptive institutional design – in contrast to presuming we are the experts who can devise *the* optimal design to solve a complex problem" (Ostrom 2005, p. 254). Adaptive institutional design that allows the agents in the electric power network to achieve decentralized coordination while allowing new services to develop and diffuse is consistent with a dynamic, forward-looking, modernized industry that creates benefits for consumers and entrepreneurs alike.

Notes

1 Introduction

1 Recall, for example, the benefits from deregulation in telecommunications, airlines, rail, trucking, package delivery, and financial services in the 1980s and 1990s.
2 Order can take many forms in a complex system like electricity – keeping the lights on (short-term reliability), achieving economic efficiency, optimizing transmission congestion, longer-term resource adequacy, etc.
3 Although this is the most common way to generate electricity, it is not the only one. Renewable technologies like wind and solar, for example, operate differently.
4 Deadweight loss is the loss in economic surplus associated with an inefficient market outcome.
5 Joskow (1989) disagreed on this point two decades ago, but technological change can reduce economies of scope. Later chapters explore this issue in further detail.
6 For example, contrast the changes that the Internet has wrought in retailing relative to the electricity industry. Digital technology and the Internet have brought profound and relatively quick changes to economic activity, and the electricity industry has been slower to adapt than most industries.
7 We even have choice in our consumption of water; we can use the water from our wells or our local water utility, but we can also buy bottled water at the store, or from a delivery service. Even the highway system and air traffic control, examples of network infrastructure industries in which no choice exists, do have substitutes in more broadly-defined markets (the market for travel and transportation).
8 One exception is Westfield (1970), which takes a standard Solow residual model of technological change and interacts it with regulatory constraints and with the concept of Hicks-neutral innovation. Another exception is Rose and Joskow (1990), which focuses on the adoption of new generation technology in the electricity industry; however, they do not model or analyze the relationship between regulation and innovation specifically.
9 Personal correspondence with author, 24 July 2007.
10 Note that this issue in networks is different from one of demand complementarity and the potential for "lock-in," which has been extensively studied in the context of software and operating systems. See, for example, Shy (2001).
11 Boettke (1998) provides a useful collection of survey articles.
12 The following definition draws heavily on Holland 1995, pp. 6–10.

2 A brief history and theory of electric utility regulation in the United States

1 For a more thorough discussion of the technical aspects of natural monopoly, see Kahn 1988, vol. II, pp. 119–125. For an illustration of how Samuel Insull's

turbogenerators created economies of scale in the early twentieth century, see Platt 1991, pp. 212–213.

2 For comparison, in 1987 retail revenues were $150 billion ($222.78 billion in 2005 dollars) (Joskow 1989, p. 128). This comparison implies an average annual growth rate in revenues of 0.55 percent, just over one-half of 1 percent. This low revenue growth rate reflects both low growth in costs and the persistence of retail price caps for most end-use customers. The composition of demand in 1987 was residential 40 percent, commercial 30 percent, industrial 27 percent, and other 3 percent (Joskow 1989, p. 128, fn. 3). The composition shift from commercial and industrial toward residential is consistent with the argument in Chapter 4 that insulating residential customers from dynamic pricing makes residential customers less likely to monitor their electricity use or engage in conservation.

3 For more extensive analyses of the origins of the electric power industry in the U.S., see Hirsh (1999), Hughes (1983), and Platt (1991).

4 See also Martimort (1999) for a recent model of dynamic repeated interactions of political principals, regulators, and interest groups to generate regulatory capture.

5 For a thorough and fascinating analysis of the political process to get PURPA passed, see Hirsh (1999), Chapter 4.

6 The ISOs are the California ISO, the Electricity Reliability Council of Texas (ERCOT), the Florida Reliability Coordinating Council, and the New York ISO. The RTOs are the Midwest ISO (MISO), ISO-New England, PJM Interconnection (which is primarily in the mid-Atlantic), and the Southwest Power Pool (SPP).

7 Notice the difference between the average cost of production, which is the same for all the units produced, and the marginal cost, which is almost literally the cost of the last unit produced.

8 The social surplus is defined in the economic literature as the weighted sum of all consumers' valuation for the goods provided and the firm's profits. Usually, the firm's profits are weighted down in comparison with the consumers' surplus. There are two common alternative motivations for this assumption. First, the assumption embodies an intrinsic preference of the regulator for the consumers' surplus. This preference can be motivated on distributional grounds (see Baron and Myerson 1981). Second, this assumption applies when direct transfers to the firms are costly, or even unfeasible. Costly transfers are motivated by the costly nature of tax raising, which generates distortion in the economy in order to raise the funds to finance the firm (see Laffont and Tirole 1986). Also, there are political economy considerations for motivating the unfeasibility of direct transfers from the government to the firm. The Ramsey–Boiteux basic problem (discussed below) is defined in a situation in which such transfers are not feasible.

9 As pointed out in the last footnote, this assumes that the regulator cannot make direct transfers to the firm.

10 The economic literature defines "mark-up" as the difference between a product's price and its marginal cost, divided by the product's price.

11 Specifically, $\eta = -\dfrac{\partial q_k(p)}{\partial p_k} \cdot \dfrac{p_k}{q_k(p)}$. Where $q_k(p)$ is the demand function of good k, and p

is the vector of prices of all the goods. The demand elasticity measures the response of the quantity demanded to an increase in a particular price. The own-price demand elasticity measures this response to an increase in the price of the same good. However, given that the demand of one good could eventually depend on the demand of other related goods (if the demands are interdependent; i.e., they could be complementary or substitute goods), the definition is more general.

12 This refers to the existence of substitute goods *outside* the bundle of products offered by the firm. See next paragraph.

13 And, naturally, when there is a price decrease, the effect is the exact opposite in each

of the cases. For a more concrete definition of the response of quantities to prices see footnote 11 above.

14 For a more in-depth review of this literature see Armstrong and Sappington (2007).

15 Armstrong and Sappington (2007) contains an analysis of the robustness of the mechanism to the strategic manipulation by the firm. Sappington (1980) was one of the first contributions to raise those concerns, which have been addressed in many other later works.

16 See, for example, Laffont and Tirole (1996).

17 The long-run marginal cost is the derivative (with respect to quantity) of the long-run cost function.

18 For example, Panzar (1976) assumes a different type of production function, leading to a different pricing structure.

19 And the cross-price demand elasticities when the multiple products are related (i.e., if they are substitute or complement).

20 The treatment of the regulator is ad hoc in the sense that the decision-making of the regulatory body is not modeled explicitly. Therefore, the regulated rate of return is basically exogenously imposed to be greater than the opportunity cost of capital and lower than the monopolistic rate of return.

21 Or it assumes that the regulator is almost completely uninformed, knowing only *ex post* the effective rate of return realized by the firm (through a process of auditing, for example).

22 A bit more precisely, the regulator may use, for example, a detailed analysis of the own-firm cost reports, the information of firms with similar cost structures (the so-called "yardstick competition"), or the assessment of third party experts.

23 If the prices would be adjusted to costs instantaneously (let's think of this as a theoretical exercise), the firm would have no incentive to reduce costs, given that all the savings would be passed to the consumers through price reductions.

24 There is another type of model in which the firm has an informational advantage about the state of the market (i.e. demand). See, for example: Lewis and Sappington (1988a and 1988b). However, the focus of this review is on the types mentioned in the text.

25 The definition of effort does not intrinsically refer to a concrete measure (it could be, for example, managerial effort). However, we can think that any deviation from the minimum cost achievable, the efficiency frontier, as the (inverse) measure of the managerial effort. Of course, in this case the measure will be stated in monetary units.

26 In Armstrong and Sappington (2007) there is an extensive literature review about a broader class of models. Besides what is pointed out in footnote 20, the asymmetries can involve the regulator's incomplete information about marginal costs, fixed costs or both of them simultaneously.

27 The important paper of Laffont and Tirole (1986) was one of the first in establishing this particular definition of information asymmetry.

28 Recall that "type" refers to the ability of the firm to reduce costs. The name is given because it refers to an intrinsic feature of the firm, which could be determined by technology, quality of inputs, etc. A *high type* will refer to a firm with a very limited ability to reduce costs, while a *low type* will refer to the opposite case. Given the same level of effort, a high-type firm will have a greater cost level than a low-type firm.

29 The name of profit sharing comes from the fact that if $b < 1$, the firm is only partially rewarded for any cost reduction, so it is said that profits are shared with consumers.

30 Of course the specific values should be selected according to the consumer's surplus and firm's cost function which apply in each case. Additionally, note that in more general theoretical models the contracts would not necessarily be linear in C.

31 Also it is worth pointing that under the assumptions of the model, the optimal menu is a menu of *linear* contracts to be offered to the firm, exactly like the one described in the preceding paragraphs.

3 A decentralized coordination framework for analyzing regulatory institutions

1 As noted in Chapter 2, the private knowledge aspect of a firm's costs is the primary critique of existing cost-based regulatory institutions and is the foundation of the Bayesian regulation literature.

2 Decentralized coordination is an area of intersection between Austrian economics and complexity science. See Hayek (1967), Lavoie (1989), Koppl (2000), and Arthur *et al.* (1997).

3 Note that this type of coordination is the primary reason why the double auction design, in which buyers and sellers make simultaneous bids and offers that are visible to all agents, is the most efficient market design; its information richness provides ample opportunity for feedback mechanisms to enable enhanced coordination.

4 Elinor Ostrom captures this idea eloquently:

> Humans do not have fixed characteristics. What makes understanding human behavior so difficult is exactly our capacity to try out multiple norms, heuristics, or strategies,... Like all creatures honed by millennia of evolutionary processes, humans do seek beneficial outcomes for themselves. Information search is costly, and the information-processing capabilities of human beings are limited. Individuals, therefore, often must make choices based on incomplete knowledge of all possible alternatives and their likely outcomes.
>
> (2005, p. 118)

See also Simon (1996), Williamson (1985), and Smith (2007)

5 Note that the Bayesian regulation literature discussed in Chapter 2 captures a small part of the problem – the inability of the regulator to observe firm costs. However, this literature assumes that the costs are a draw from a known probability distribution, and that the firm observes them perfectly. The Bayesian regulation literature in no way incorporates the regulatory challenge of coordination in the face of dispersed knowledge and unknown ignorance facing both the regulator and the firm.

6 One can also think about equilibration processes as algorithms, which incorporate the idea that humans make decisions using induction and following rules that help us to structure our choices in the face of uncertainty and distributed knowledge.

7 Emergent order is another area of substantial overlap between complexity science and Austrian economics.

8 Since the mid-eighteenth century, this concept in economics has also been known as *spontaneous order*. For more background on spontaneous order research in economics, see Boettke (1998).

9 The electricity wires network has this communication capability already, which is the basis on which broadband over power line (BPL) technology operates, and enables electricity wires owners to compete with broadband providers.

10 Eggertsson (1990, p. 15) offers an illustrative list of types of transaction costs.

11 This claim makes sense even in the context of a simple property rights model – only property rights that have very low (or, in the limit, zero) definition and enforcement costs would be fully-defined private property rights.

12 The *Oxford English Dictionary* defines a stochastic process as ergodic if it has "the property that the probability of any state can be estimated from a single sufficiently extensive realization, independently of initial conditions; statistically stationary." Thus a non-ergodic process is one for which the probability of any state cannot be estimated independently of its initial conditions; it is also not stationary.

13 In complexity science, this idea of getting stuck at a focal point and having difficulty moving from one to another arises in models involving fitness landscapes, such as Kauffman (1993) or Axelrod and Bennett (1997).

14 Mechanism design is an exception to this criticism, as is the industrial organization literature on product differentiation.

4 Rethinking retail regulation: enabling active demand and retail choice

1 This discussion extends the analyses found in Kiesling (2007).
2 Another way to think about this question is using the Pareto efficiency criterion – are resources allocated such that they cannot be reallocated without someone being made worse off? While useful as a theoretical construct, the Pareto criterion is difficult (if not impossible) to apply empirically.
3 Two complicating factors arise here, though: (1) monthly service charges typically do not recover 100 percent of fixed costs, the balance being recovered in the variable portion of the rate; and (2) monthly service charges within customer classes typically do not reflect the differences in investment between serving a 60 amp vs. a 400 amp residential service. Therefore, the price signals are skewed beyond just RTP energy charges.
4 Chapter 6 discusses the reliability aspects of active demand in more detail. The additional capital expense is often hidden; only when the total cost of meeting an "uncontrolled" peak is concentrated in the peak does it appear as expensive as it truly is, and only then can people make intelligent decisions about peak consumption.
5 From the utility's and the regulator's applied perspective, the traditional averaged rate is the cost of production (not of the commodity) plus fixed costs of establishing and maintaining the infrastructure. That traditional rate can be resolved into components that include the commodity price and the risk premium.
6 By "excess capacity" I mean generation, transmission, and distribution assets that are fully utilized in peak periods and underutilized the rest of the time, as distinct from reserves. Maintaining reserves to ensure a particular level of service reliability does not constitute excess capacity in the sense that I am invoking the concept here, although the extent to which distributed digital technology reduces the optimal reserve margin is an open research and policy question.
7 The exception to this claim is the TOU contract where the rate structure is known in advance. However, even on such a simple dynamic pricing contract, devices that allow customers to see their consumption and expenditure in real time instead of waiting for their bill can change behavior.
8 See also Reiss and White (2003).
9 I am indebted to my co-author at PNNL, David Chassin, for the preliminary quantitative analysis reported here.

5 Organizational form and the wires

1 This chapter draws on extensive conversations with Vernon Smith, as well as on joint work with Federico Boffa (Boffa and Kiesling 2008).
2 A theoretical discussion of this characteristic of legislatively-created organizations is in Hayek (1976), Chapter 1.
3 A new technology, broadband over power lines (BPL), is beginning to change the transaction specificity of the network assets, but its development and implementation at this point is limited.
4 These ideas will also arise in Chapter 8, in the exploration of the extent to which network reliability is a public good.

6 Network reliability and short-term security: decentralized coordination using demand as a resource

1 This chapter is an extension of the analysis in Smith and Kiesling (2005).
2 Recommendation 13: DOE should expand its research programs on reliability-related tools and technologies (U.S.–Canada Power System Outage Task Force 2004, p. 149).

3 A resource is dispatchable if a physical control-room operator can rely on its presence if called on.
4 Note that the LSEs could send other price signals to customers, thereby taking some wholesale price risk themselves and providing a risk management service to their customers.
5 See Hirst (2002b), Smith and Kiesling (2003), and Black (2004, 2005).
6 See Reiss and White (2003), Bushnell and Mansur (2005), and Rassenti *et al.* (2003).

7 Reliability, resource adequacy, and capacity markets

1 In all states except Texas the relevant regulator is FERC, which has the responsibility of ensuring "just and reasonable" prices in wholesale markets. In Texas ERCOT is the organized wholesale market platform, and it is contained entirely within the state with only a few direct current interties beyond state boundaries, so FERC forebears from exercising jurisdiction and the Public Utility Commission of Texas regulates wholesale power markets in ERCOT.
2 Investment in the wireless telecommunications industry provides an example of this process. Reliability failures (dropped calls) do induce customers to change providers, and firms invest both *ex ante* and *ex post* to reduce the likelihood of such loss of market share occurring.
3 For a general discussion of resource adequacy that touches on this issue, see Bushnell (2005).
4 See, for example, the extensive analysis of the RPM performed by the Maryland Public Service Commission and their subsequent position statements:
www.pjm.com/committees/working-groups/pjmramwg/downloads/20050210-maryland-rpm-comments.pdf;
www.psc.state.md.us/psc/aboutus/Press/RPMPosition.htm;
www.psc.state.md.us/psc/Reports/8980FinalCommissionPositionPaper.pdf;
www.psc.state.md.us/psc/aboutus/Press/MDPSCRPMApr182005ResponseLetter.pdf;
www.psc.state.md.us/psc/aboutus/Press/RPMApril182005.pdf.
5 For a clear discussion of the deficiencies of installed capacity markets as seen in New England, see Cramton (2000). For an institutional design proposal for ISO-New England that informed the ultimate design, see Cramton and Stoft (2005).
6 Bushnell (2005) notes that capacity requirements can have market power implications, because capacity markets create market power for the sellers of capacity
7 This feature is already in use in some regions, and is implemented with particular success in Texas, as ERCOT's Load as a Resource (LAAR) principle.
8 A work that surveys the application of this concept in many ways is Ménard and Shirley (2007).
9 Information on Australia's market design and experience, as well as links to further information, is available from Peter Adams, "The Australian Market," Presentation at PUCT Resource Adequacy Workshop, 20 April 2005. Available at www.puc.state.tx.us/rules/rulemake/24255/042005/2-Adams.pdf.
10 All materials in the three-year resource adequacy process at the Public Utility Commission of Texas are available at www.puc.state.tx.us/rules/rulemake/24255/24255.cfm.
11 The Public Utility Commission of Texas is also currently working with the electricity industry and customer stakeholders to facilitate the installation of advanced metering infrastructure (AMI) and other smart grid technology that will enhance price responsiveness even further.
12 The Midwest ISO's Business Practices Manual for Resource Adequacy is available at www.midwestmarket.org/publish/Document/20f443_ffd16ced4b_7e630a3207d2?rev =7.

8 Is network reliability a public good?

1 This chapter draws upon the collaborative work in Giberson and Kiesling (2004a, 2004b), Kiesling and Giberson (2005), and Salies *et al.* (2007).

2 See also Joskow (2005a), Joskow and Tirole (2007), and Cowart *et al.* (2001).

3 Black (2005, Chapter 3) makes a similar claim for ancillary services (such as spinning reserves) in electric power networks, which are a crucial aspect of network reliability.

4 This section draws upon Cornes and Sandler (1996) and Musgrave (1969). Cowen (1992) reprints the key Samuelson (1954) article and other classic works in public goods and externality theory.

5 Pigou argued that remedying the allocative inefficiency arising from this interdependence requires the use of "bounties and taxes" to realign the incentives of the offending agent to address "uncompensated services and uncharged disservices."

6 Haddock (2003) extends this analysis and discusses this example, and others, in greater detail.

7 This general articulation of the problem abstracts from the distinction between LSEs as agents interconnected on a transmission network and end-use consumers as agents interconnected on a distribution network.

8 Proposals for locational reserves, locational capacity requirements, and arguments for participant funding of grid upgrades are examples of such initiatives. If these resources were pure public goods, then the location of the reliability resources would not matter. Of course, they are not pure public goods, but these efforts provide evidence that reliability resources are not even pure network goods. Depending on the location of a reliability resource, some networked loads will benefit and others may not. Note also efforts to develop "participant funding" mechanisms to pay for transmission system improvements, which reveal a belief in the non-public nature of some system improvements.

9 Rivalry is synonymous with subtractability, another term used to indicate the possible extent of simultaneous consumption, as used in Ostrom *et al.* (1994) and Ostrom (2005).

10 Lowered excludability is characteristic of open access in the cases of CPRs and public goods (Ostrom 1990, p. 32).

11 In other words, there is no equivalent of branding, or of attaching digital packet headers and footers, as is done with digital communication networks.

12 Note, though, that in most irrigation systems the water is exogenously determined and all agents are extractors or appropriators, withdrawing water from the system. But irrigation systems share with electric power systems the inability to define property rights over specific units of the resource (water or electricity).

13 For another argument about the importance of institutional design, in this case the importance of market design in electric power (see Wilson (2002)).

14 Appendix 8.1 summarizes useful institutional design principles from Ostrom (1990).

15 This idea can generalize to a continuum of preferences, very much like is done in discrete and continuous models of product differentiation in Hotelling-style models (Thisse and Norman 1994).

16 Hunter *et al.* (2003) suggest that consumers that have relatively reliable power would rather see improvements in call center waiting times, and other service improvements, rather than still more reliable power. Hamachi LaCommare and Eto (2004), and Eto *et al.* (2001) provide assessments of the value of reliability.

17 See also Chao and Peck (1998).

18 Chao and Wilson describe how to set the rates to ensure this result. The significant question is empirical: How much better off can consumers become, and how certain can we be that consumers will be sufficiently better off?

19 Nossair and Porter added another twist in that in their version the number of levels of service and price levels were endogenous to the customer evaluations.

9 Facilitating technology-enabled decentralized coordination

1 An example of such institutions in practice is the set of principles-based regulatory institutions that the Commodity Futures Trading Commission (CFTC) uses to regulate futures transactions and exchanges.
2 See FERC Notice of Proposed Rulemaking, Docket No. RM05–4-000, *Interconnection for Wind Energy and Other Alternative Technologies* (January 2005); FERC Staff Briefing Paper, *Assessing the State of Wind Energy In Wholesale Electricity Markets*, Docket No. AD04–13–000 (November 2004).
3 In different ways the policy oriented work of Joskow and Schmalensee (1983), and the technical work of Schweppe *et al.* (1988), contributed to the vision that has guided restructuring the industry.
4 Hirst (2002a).

References

Aigner, D. and Hirshberg, J. (1985) "Commercial/Industrial Customer Response to Time of Use Prices: Some Experimental Results," *Rand Journal of Economics*, 16: 341–355.

Alger, D. (1998) "Open Ownership, Not Common Carriage," working paper, New Zealand Institute for the Study of Competition and Regulation.

Alger, D. and Toman, M. (1990) "Market-Based Regulation of Natural Gas Pipelines," *Journal of Regulatory Economics*, 2(3): 263–280.

Armstrong, M. and Sappington, D. (2007) "Recent Developments in the Theory of Regulation," in Armstrong and Porter (eds) *Handbook of Industrial Organization, Vol. 3*, North Holland: Amsterdam.

Arthur, W.B., Durlauf, S., and Lane, D. (1997) "Introduction," in Arthur, W.B., Durlauf, S., and Lane, D. (eds) *The Economy as an Evolving Complex System II*, Reading, MA: Addison-Wesley: 1–14.

Averch, H. and Johnson, L.L. (1962) "Behavior of the Firm under Regulatory Constraint," *American Economic Review*, 52: 1059–1069.

Axelrod, R. and Bennett, S. (1997) "Choosing Sides: A Landscape Theory of Aggregation," in Axelrod, R., *The Complexity of Cooperation*, Princeton: Princeton University Press.

Bailey, E.E. and White, L. (1974) "Reversals in Peak and Off-Peak Prices," *The Bell Journal of Economics*, 5: 75–92.

Bajari, P. and Tadelis, S. (2001) "Incentives Versus Transaction Costs: A Theory of Procurement Contracts," *Rand Journal of Economics*, 32: 387–407.

Baker, G., Gibbons, R., and Murphy, K. (2002) "Relational Contracts and the Theory of the Firm," *Quarterly Journal of Economics*, 117: 39–84.

Baron, D. and Myerson, R. (1981) "Regulating a Monopolist with Unknown Costs," *Econometrica*, 50(4): 911–930.

Bastiat, F. (1995 (1848)) "What is Seen and What is Not Seen," in Bastiat, F., *Selected Essays on Political Economy*, Irvington-on-Hudson, NY: The Foundation for Economic Education. Online. Available at www.econlib.org/library/Bastiat/BasEss1.html (accessed January 11, 2008).

Baumol, W., Panzar J., and Willig, R. (1982) *Contestable Markets and the Theory of Industry Structure*, New York: Harcourt Brace Jovanovich, Inc.

Beinhocker, Eric (2006) *The Origin of Wealth*, Oxford University Press.

Besser, J., Farr, J., and Tierney, S. (2002) "The Political Economy of Long-Term Generation Adequacy: Why an ICAP Mechanism is Needed as Part of Standard Market Design," *Electricity Journal*, 15(7): 53–62.

Black, J. (2004) "Demand Response as a Substitute for Electric Power System Infrastructure Investments," paper presented at Electricity Transmission in Deregulated Markets: Challenges, Opportunities, and Necessary R&D Agenda, Carnegie-Mellon University.

Black, J. (2005) "Integrating Demand into the U.S. Electric Power System: Technical, Economic, and Regulatory Frameworks for Responsive Load," Ph.D. dissertation, Massachusetts Institute of Technology.

Boettke, P. (ed.) (1998) *The Elgar Companion to Austrian Economics*, London: Edward Elgar.

Boffa, F. and Kiesling, L. (2008) "Network Regulation Through Ownership Structure: An Application to the Electric Power Industry," mimeo. Available at http://ssrn.com/abstract=1123772.

Boiteux, M. (1956) "Sur la Gestion des Monopoles Publics Astreints à l'Equilibre Budgétaire," *Econometrica*, 24: 22–40; trans. (1971) "On the Management of Public Monopolies Subject to Budgetary Constraints," *Journal of Economic Theory*, 3: 219–240.

Boiteux, M. (1960) "Peak-Load Pricing," *Journal of Business*, 2: 157–179.

Borenstein, S. (2005) "The Long-Run Efficiency of Real-Time Electricity Pricing," *Energy Journal*, 26(3): 93–116.

Borenstein, S., Jaske, M., and Rosenfeld, A. (2002) "Dynamic Pricing, Advanced Metering, and Demand Response in Electricity Markets," Center for the Study of Energy Markets Working Paper 105. Online. Available at http://repositories.cdlib.org/ucei/csem/CSEMWP-105 (accessed September 6, 2007).

Bosselman, F., Rossi, J., and Weaver, J.L. (2000) *Energy, Economics, and the Environment: Cases and Material*, New York: Foundation Press.

Braeutigam, R. (1989) "Optimal Policies for Natural Monopolies," in Schmalensee and Willig (eds) *Handbook of Industrial Organization, Vol. 2*, North Holland: Amsterdam.

Bretsen, S. and Hill, P.J. (2007) "Irrigation Institutions in the American West," *UCLA Journal of Environmental Law and Policy*, forthcoming.

Buchanan, J. and Stubblebine, C. (1962) "Externality," *Economica*, 29: 371–384.

Burton, J. (1997) "The Competitive Order or Ordered Competition?: The 'UK Model' of Utility Regulation in Theory and Practice," *Public Administration*, 75: 157–188.

Bushnell, J. (2005) Electricity Resource Adequacy: Matching Policies and Goals," *Electricity Journal*, 18(8): 11–21

Bushnell, J. and Mansur, E. (2005) "Consumption Under Noisy Price Signals: A Study of Electricity Retail Rate Deregulation in San Diego," *Journal of Industrial Economics*, 53(4): 493–513.

Carlton, D. and Salop, S. (1996) "You Keep On Knocking But You Can't Come In: Evaluating Restrictions On Access To Input Joint Ventures," *Harvard Journal of Law and Technology*, 9: 319–351.

Carlton, D.W. and Klamer, J.M. (1983) "The Need for Coordination Among Firms, with Special Reference to Network Industries," *University of Chicago Law Review*, 50: 446–465.

Caves, D. and Christensen, L. (1980) "Residential Substitution of Offpeak for Peak Electricity Usage under Time-of-Use Pricing," *Energy Journal*, 1: 85–142.

Caves, D., Christensen, L., and Herriges, J. (1981) "The Neoclassical Model of Consumer Demand with Identically Priced Commodities: An Application to Time-of-Use Electricity Pricing," *Rand Journal of Economics*, 18: 564–580.

Caves, D., Herriges, J., and Keuster, K. (1989) "Load Shifting Under Voluntary Residential Time-of-Use Rates," *Energy Journal*, 10: 83–99.

Chao, H. and Peck, S. (1998) "Reliability Management in Competitive Electricity Markets," *Journal of Regulatory Economics*, 13: 189–200.

Chao, H. and Wilson, R. (1987) "Priority Service: Pricing, Investment, and Market Organization," *American Economic Review*, 77: 899–916.

Charles River Associates (CRA) (2005) *Impact Evaluation of the California Statewide Pricing Pilot.*

Coase, R.H. (1937) "The Nature of the Firm," *Economica*, 4: 386–405.

Coase, R.H. (1960) "The Problem of Social Cost," *Journal of Law and Economics*, 3: 1–44.

Colander, D. (ed.) (2000) *The Complexity Vision and the Teaching of Economics*, Northampton, MA: Edward Elgar.

Cornes, R. and Sandler, T. (1996) *The Theory of Externalities, Public Goods, and Club Goods*, 2nd Edition, Cambridge University Press.

Cowart, R., Harrington, C., Moskovitz, D., Sedano, R., Shirley, W., and Weston, F. (2001) "Efficient Reliability: The Critical Role of Demand-Side Resources in Power Systems and Markets," Regulatory Assistance Project, The National Association of Regulatory Utility Commissioners.

Cowen, T. (ed.) (1992) *Public Goods & Market Failures: A Critical Examination*, New Brunswick: Transaction Publishers.

Cramton, P. (2000) Affadavit, Federal Energy Regulatory Commission EL00–62–000, May 2000. Online. Available at www.cramton.umd.edu/papers2000–2004/cramton-affidavit-on-icap.pdf (accessed online September 6, 2007).

Cramton, P. and Stoft, S. (2005) "A Capacity Market That Makes Sense," *Electricity Journal* 18(7): 43–54.

Dahle, D. (2003) "A Brief History of Meter Companies and Meter Evolution" Online. Available at www.watthourmeters.com/history.html (accessed September 6, 2007).

Datamonitor (2006(*Industry Profile: Electricity in the United States*. Online. Available at www.reportbuyer.com/energy_utilities/electricity/electricity_united_states.html (accessed September 7, 2007).

Dietz, T., Ostrom, E., and Stern, P. (2003) "The struggle to govern the Commons," *Science*, 302: 1907–1912.

Doane, M. and Spulber, D. (1994) "Open Access and Evolution of the U.S. Spot Market for Natural Gas," *Journal of Law and Economics*, 37(2): 477–517.

Eggertsson, T. (1990) *Economic Behavior and Institutions*, Cambridge: Cambridge University Press.

Eggertsson, T. (2003) "Open Access versus Common Property," in T. Anderson and F. McChesney (eds) *Property Rights: Cooperation, Conflict, and Law*, Princeton: Princeton University Press.

Energy Information Administration, U.S. Department of Energy (2000) *The Changing Structure of the Electric Power Industry: An Update*. Online. Available at www.eia.doe.gov/cneaf/electricity/chg_stru_update/update2000.html (accessed September 6, 2007).

Energy Information Administration, U.S. Department of Energy. *Electric Power Industry Overview*. Online. Available at www.eia.doe.gov/cneaf/electricity/page/prim2/toc2. html (accessed September 6, 2007).

Erdi, P. (2007) *Complexity Explained*, Berlin: Springer-Verlag.

Eto, Joe, Koomey, T., Lehman, B., Martin, N., Mills, E., Webber, C., and Worrell, E. (2001) *Scoping Study on Trends in the Economic Value of Electricity Reliability to the U.S. Economy*, LBNL-47911, Lawrence Berkeley National Laboratory, Berkeley, CA.

Fumagalli, E., Black, J., Vogelsang, I., and Ilic, M. (2004) "Quality of Service Provision in Electric Power Distribution Systems through Reliability Insurance," *IEEE Transactions on Power Systems*, 19(3): 1286–1293.

Gale, I. (1994) "Price Competition in Noncooperative Joint Ventures," *International Journal of Industrial Organization*, 12(1): 53–69.

Gale, R., Poirier, J.L., Kiesling, L., and Bodde, D. (2007) *The Path to Perfect Power: New Technologies Advance Consumer Control*, Galvin Electricity Initiative Report. Online. Available at www.galvinpower.org/resources/galvin.php?id=88 (accessed September 6, 2007).

George, S. and Faruqui, A. (2002) "The Economic Value of Market-Based Pricing for Small Consumers," paper presented to the California Energy Commission, March 2002.

Giberson, M. and Kiesling, L. (2004a) "Analyzing the Blackout Report's Recommendations: Alternatives for a Flexible, Dynamic Grid," *Electricity Journal*, 16: 51–60.

Giberson, M. and Kiesling, L. (2004b) *Mercatus Center Public Interest Comment on Midwest ISO Proposal Concerning Reactive Power Procurement*.

Ginsburg, D. (2006) "Synthetic Competition," *Media Law and Policy* 16: 1–24.

Goldman, C., Hopper, N., Bharvirkir, R., Neenam, B., Boisvert, R., Cappers, P., Pratt, D., and Butkins, K. (2005) *Customer Strategies for Responding to Day-Ahead Market Hourly Electricity Pricing*. Online. Available at http://drrc.lbl.gov/pubs/57128.pdf (accessed September 6, 2007).

Goldman, C., Hopper, N., Sezgen, O., Moezzi, M., Bharvirkir, R., Neenam, B., Boisvert, R., Cappers, P., and Pratt, D. (2004a) *Customer Response to Day-ahead Wholesale Market Electricity Prices: Case Study of RTP Program Experience in New York*. Online. Available at http://drrc.lbl.gov/pubs/NMPC_LBNL_54761.pdf (accessed September 6, 2007).

Goldman, C., Hopper, N., Sezgen, O., Moezzi, M., Bharvirkir, R., Neenam, B., Pratt, D., Cappers, P., and Boisvert, R. (2004b) *Does Real-Time Pricing Deliver Demand Response? A Case Study of Niagara Mohawk's Large Customer RTP Tariff*. Online. Available at http://drrc.lbl.gov/pubs/54974.pdf (accessed September 6, 2007).

Government Accountability Office (2004) *Electricity Markets: Consumers Could Benefit From Demand Programs, But Challenges Remain*. Online. Available at www.gao.gov/new.items/d04844.pdf (accessed September 6, 2007).

Grossman, S. and Hart, O. (1986) "The Costs and Benefits of Ownership: A Theory of Vertical and Lateral Integration," *Journal of Political Economy*, 94(4): 691–719.

Gunderson, L. and Holling, C. (2001) *Panarchy: Understanding Transformations in Human and Natural Systems*. Washington: Island Press.

Haddock, D. (2003) "Irrelevant Internalities, Irrelevant Externalities, and Irrelevant Anxieties," Law & Economics Research Paper 03–16, Northwestern University Law School. Online. Available at http://papers.ssrn.com/sol3/papers.cfm?abstract_id=437221 (accessed September 6, 2007).

Haddock, D. and Kiesling, L. (2003) "The Black Death and Property Rights," *Journal of Legal Studies*, 32: S545-S587.

Hamachi, LaCommare, K. and Eto, J.H. (2004) *Understanding the Cost of Power Interruptions to U.S. Electricity Consumers*, LBNL-55718, Lawrence Berkeley National Laboratory (Berkeley, CA).

Hammerstrom, D., Ambrosio, R., Brous, J., Carlon, T., Ghassin, D., DeSteese, J., Guttromson, R., Horst, G., Järregren, O., Kajfasz, R., Katipamula, S., Kiesling, L., Le, N., Michie, P., Oliver, T., Pratt, R., Thompson, S., and Yao, M. (2007) *Pacific Northwest GridWise™ Testbed Demonstration Projects, Volume I: The Olympic Peninsula Project*. Online. Available at http://gridwise.pnl.gov/docs/op_project_final_report_pnnl17167.pdf (accessed January 9, 2008).

Hardin, G. (1968) "The Tragedy of the Commons," *Science*, 162: 1243–1248.

Hart, O. and Moore, J. (1998) "Cooperative vs. Outside Ownership," NBER Working Paper 6421.

Hausman, W. and Neufeld, J. (1984) "Time Of Day Pricing in the U.S. Electric Industry at the Turn of the Century," *Rand Journal of Economics*, 15: 116–126.

Hausman, W. and Neufeld, J. (1991) "Property Rights Versus Public Spirit: Ownership and Efficiency of U.S. Electric Utilities Prior to Rate-of-Return Regulation," *Review of Economics and Statistics*, 73: 414–423.

Hausman, W. and Neufeld, J. (2002) "The Market for Capital and the Origins of State Regulation of Electric Utilities in the United States," *Journal of Economic History*, 62: 1050–1073.

Hayek, F. (1945) "The Use of Knowledge in Society," *American Economic Review*, 35(4): 519–530.

Hayek, F. (1948) "The Meaning of Competition," in F. Hayek, *Individualism and Economic Order*, Chicago: University of Chicago Press.

Hayek, F. (1967) "The Theory of Complex Phenomena," in F. Hayek, *Studies in Philosophy, Politics and Economics*, Chicago: University of Chicago Press.

Hayek, F. (1976) *Law, Legislation, and Liberty*, Chicago: University of Chicago Press.

Hayek, F. (1978) "Competition as a Discovery Procedure," in F. Hayek, *New Studies in Philosophy, Politics, Economics, and the History of Ideas*, Chicago: University of Chicago Press.

Hayek, F. (2005 (1944)) *The Road to Serfdom*, London: Routledge.

Herriges, J., Baladi, M., Caves, D., and Neenan, B. (1993) "The Response of Industrial Customers to Electric Rates Based Upon Dynamic Marginal Costs," *Review of Economics and Statistics*, 75: 446–454.

Heyes, A. and Liston-Heyes, C. (1998) "Price-cap Regulation and Technical Change," *Journal of Public Economics*, 68: 137–151.

Hirsh, R. (1999) *Power Loss: The Origins of Deregulation and Restructuring in the American Electric Utility System*, Cambridge, MA: MIT Press.

Hirst, E. (2002a) "The Financial and Physical Insurance Benefits of Price-Responsive Demand," *Electricity Journal*, 15(4): 66–73.

Hirst, E. (2002b) "Reliability Benefits of Price-Responsive Demand," *IEEE Power Engineering Review*, 22(11): 16–21.

Hirst, E. and Kirby, B. (2001) *Transmission Planning for a Restructuring U.S. Electricity Industry*. Report prepared for the Edison Electric Institute.

Hobbs, B., Iñón, J., and Stoft, S. (2001) "Installed Capacity Requirements and Price Caps: Oil on the Water, or Fuel on the Fire?," *Electricity Journal*, 14(6): 23–34.

Holland, John (1995) *Hidden Order: How Adaptation Builds Complexity*, New York: Addison Wesley.

Hughes, Thomas (1983) *Networks of Power: Electrification in Western Society, 1880–1930*, Baltimore: Johns Hopkins University Press.

Hunter, R., Melnik, R., and Senni, L. (2003) "What Power Consumers Want," *The McKinsey Quarterly* (3).

Hutcheson, F. (1747) *Philosophiae Moralis Institutio Compendiaria, with A Short Introduction to Moral Philosophy*, L. Turco, ed. Indianapolis: Liberty Fund. Online. Available at http://oll.libertyfund.org/title/2059 (accessed January 11, 2008).

Jarrell, G. (1978) "The Demand for State Regulation of the Electric Utility Industry," *Journal of Law and Economics*, 21: 269–295.

Joskow, P. (1988) "Asset Specificity and the Structure of Vertical Relationships: Empirical Evidence," *Journal of Law, Economics and Organization*, 4: 95–117.

Joskow, P. (1989) "Regulatory Failure, Regulatory Reform, and Structural Change in the Electrical Power Industry," *Brookings Papers on Economic Activity, Microeconomics*, 125–208.

Joskow, P. (1991) "The Role of Transaction Cost Economics in Antitrust and Public Utility Regulatory Policies," *Journal of Law, Economics and Organization*, 7: 53–83.

Joskow, P. (1997) "Restructuring, Competition and Regulatory Reform in the US Electricity Sector," *Journal of Economic Perspectives*, 11: 3.

Joskow, P. (2005a) "Transmission Policy in the United States," *Utilities Policy*, 13: 95–115.

Joskow, P. (2005b) "Why Capacity Obligations and Capacity Markets?" Online. Available at http://econ-www.mit.edu/files/1177 (accessed January 8, 2008).

Joskow, P. (2007) "Regulation of Natural Monopolies," in A.M. Polinsky and S. Shavell (eds) *Handbook of Law and Economics*, Amsterdam: North Holland.

Joskow, P. and Schmalensee, R. (1983) *Markets for Power: An Analysis of Electric Utility Deregulation*, Cambridge: MIT Press.

Joskow, P. and Tirole, J. (2007) "Reliability and Competitive Electricity Markets," *Rand Journal of Economics*, 38(1): 60–84.

Kahn, A. (1988) *The Economics of Price Regulation: Principles and Institutions (Vol. I)*, Cambridge, MA: MIT Press.

Kauffman, S. (1993) *The Origins of Order: Self-Organization and Self-Selection in Evolution*, New York: Oxford University Press.

Kiesling, L. (2005) "Using Economic Experiments to Test Electricity Policy," *Electricity Journal*, 18: 43–51.

Kiesling, L. (2007) "The Role of Retail Pricing in Electricity Restructuring," in A. Kleit (ed.) *Electric Choices: Deregulation and the Future of Electric Power*, London: Rowman & Littlefield.

Kiesling, L. and Giberson, M. (2005) "Electric Network Reliability as a Public Good," paper presented at *Electricity Transmission in Deregulated Markets*, Carnegie-Mellon University.

Kiesling, L. and Kleit, A. (eds) (2008) *Electricity Restructuring: The Texas Story*, Washington, DC: American Enterprise Institute Press.

Kiesling, L. and Wilson, B. (2007) "An Experimental Analysis of the Effects of Automated Mitigation Procedures on Investment and Prices in Wholesale Electricity Markets," *Journal of Regulatory Economics*, 31(3): 313–334.

King, M., King, K., and Rosenzweig, M. (2007) "Customer Sovereignty: Why Customer Choice Trumps Administrative Capacity Mechanisms," *Electricity Journal* 20(1): 38–52.

Kirby, B. and Kueck, J. (2003) *Spinning Reserve from Pump Load: A Technical Findings Report to the California Department of Water Resources*, ORNL-TM/2003/99, Oak Ridge National Laboratory (Oak Ridge, TN).

Kirzner, I. (1992) *The Meaning of Market Process: Essays in the Development of Modern Austrian Economics*, London: Routledge.

Kirzner, I. (1997) "Entrepreneurial Discovery and the Competitive Market Process: An Austrian Approach," *Journal of Economic Literature*, 35(1): 60–85.

Klein, B., Crawford, R., and Alchian, A. (1978) "Vertical Integration, Appropriable Rents, and the Competitive Contracting Process," *Journal of Law and Economics*, 21: 297–326.

Kleit, A. (2008) "Market Monitoring, Texas Style," in Kiesling, L. and Kleit, A. (eds) (2008) *Electricity Restructuring: The Texas Story*, Washington, DC: American Enterprise Institute Press.

Koppl, R. (2000) "Policy Implications of Complexity: An Austrian Perspective," in Colander, D. (ed.) *The Complexity Vision and the Teaching of Economics*, Northampton, MA: Edward Elgar.

Laffont, J.J. and Tirole, J. (1986) "Using Cost Observations to Regulate Firms," *Journal of Political Economy*, 94(3): 614–641.

Laffont, J.J. and Tirole, J. (1993) *A Theory of Incentives in Procurement and Regulation*, Cambridge: MIT Press.

Laffont, J.J. and Tirole, J. (1996) "Creating Competition through Interconnection: Theory and Practice," *Journal of Regulatory Economics*, 10: 227–256.

Laffont, J.J. and Tirole, J. (2000) *Competition in Telecommunications*, Cambridge: MIT Press.

LaPlante, David (2007) "New England's Forward Capacity Market," presentation to the Harvard Electricity Policy Group Forty-Eighth Plenary Session. Available at www.ksg.harvard.edu/hepg/Panel%203/David_LaPlante.pdf (accessed January 8, 2008).

Lavoie, D. (1989) "Economic Chaos or Spontaneous Order? Implications for Political Economy of the New View of Science," *Cato Journal*, 8: 613–635.

Lewis, T. and Sappington, D. (1988a) "Regulating a Monopolist with Unknown Demand," *American Economic Review*, 78(5): 986–998.

Lewis, T. and Sappington, D. (1988b) "Regulating a Monopolist with Unknown Demand and Cost Functions," *Rand Journal of Economics*, 18(3): 438–457.

Loeb, M. and Magat, W. (1979) "A Decentralized Method for Utility Regulation," *Journal of Law and Economics*, 22(2): 399–404

Lyon, T.P. and Hackett, S.C. (1993) "Bottlenecks and Governance Structures: Open Access and Long Term Contracting in Natural Gas," *Journal of Law, Economics and Organization*, 9(2):380–398.

McClean, Bethany and Elkind, P. (2003) *The Smartest Guys in the Room: The Amazing Rise and Scandalous Fall of Enron*, New York: Penguin.

Mansur, E. and Holland, S. (2008) "Is Real-Time Pricing Green? The Environmental Impacts of Electricity Demand Variance," *Review of Economics and Statistics*, forthcoming.

Martimort, D. (1999) "The Life Cycle of Regulatory Agencies: Dynamic Capture and Transaction Costs," *Review of Economic Studies*, 66: 929–947.

Ménard, C. and Shirley, M. (2007) *Handbook of New Institutional Economics*, New York: Springer-Verlag.

Mokyr, J. (1990) *The Lever of Riches: Technological Creativity and Economic Progress*, New York: Oxford University Press.

Mokyr, J. (2002) *The Gifts of Athena: Historical Origins of the Knowledge Economy*, Princeton: Princeton University Press.

Mulherin, J.H. (1986) "Complexity in Long Term Contracts: An Analysis of Natural Gas Contractual Provisions," *Journal of Law, Economics and Organization*, 2(1): 105–117.

Musgrave, R. (1969) "Cost–Benefit Analysis and the Theory of Public Finance," *Journal of Economic Literature*, 7: 797–806.

Nicita, A. (ed.) (2001) *The Evolution of Economic Diversity* (Routledge Siena Studies in Political Economy, 2), London: Routledge.

North, D. (1984) "Government and the Cost of Exchange in History," *Journal of Economic History*, 44: 255–264.

North, D. (1990) *Institutions, Institutional Change and Economic Performance*, Cambridge: Cambridge University Press.

North, D. (2005) *Understanding the Process of Economic Change*, Princeton: Princeton University Press.

Noussair, C. and Porter, D. (1992) "Allocating Priority with Auctions: An Experimental Analysis," *Journal of Economic Behavior and Organization*, 19(2): 169–195.

Olson, M. (1965) *The Logic of Collective Action*, Cambridge: Harvard University Press.

Oren, S. (2001) "Market Based Risk Mitigation: Risk Management vs. Risk Avoidance," Proceedings of a White House OSTP/NSF Workshop on Critical Infrastructure Interdependencies, Washington DC, June 14–15, 2001.

Oren, S. (2003) "Ensuring Generation Adequacy in Competitive Electricity Markets," University of California Energy Institute, Working Paper EPE-007, June 3, 2003.

Oren, S. (2005) "Generation Adequacy via Call Options Obligations: Safe Passage to the Promised Land," *Electricity Journal*, 18(9): 28–42.

O'Sheasy, M. (2002) "Real Time Pricing at Georgia Power Company," in Borenstein, S., Jaske, M., and Rosenfeld, A. (eds) *Dynamic Pricing, Advanced Metering, and Demand Response in Electricity Markets*, Center for the Study of Energy Markets Working Paper 105, October 2002. Online. Available at http://repositories.cdlib.org/ucei/csem/CSEMWP-105. (accessed September 6, 2007).

Ostrom, E. (1990) *Governing the Commons: The Evolution of Institutions for Collective Action*, Cambridge: Cambridge University Press.

Ostrom, E. (2005) *Understanding Institutional Diversity*, Princeton: Princeton University Press.

Ostrom, E., Gardner, R., and Walker, J. (1994) *Rules, Games, and Common Pool Resources*, Ann Arbor: University of Michigan Press.

Outhred, H. (2003) "The Australian Approach to Electricity Industry Restructuring and Outcomes to Date," paper presented at Interdisciplinary Center for Economic Science, George Mason University.

Pacific Northwest National Laboratory (2003) *GridWise: The Benefits of a Transformed Energy System*, PNNL-14396, September 2003. Online. Available at www.pnl.gov/energy/eed/etd/pdfs/pnnl-14396.pdf (accessed September 6, 2007).

Panzar, J. (1976) "A Neoclassical Approach to Peak Load Pricing," *The Bell Journal of Economics*, 7: 521–530.

Pigou, A.C. (1921) *The Economics of Welfare*, London: Macmillan.

Platt, H. (1991) *The Electric City: Energy and the Growth of the Chicago Area, 1880–1930*, Chicago: University of Chicago Press.

Polanyi, M. (1969) *Knowing and Being*, Chicago: University of Chicago Press.

Polanyi, M. (1983) *Tacit Dimension*, London: Peter Smith.

Ramsey, F. (1927) "A Contribution to the Theory of Taxation," *Economic Journal*, 37: 47–61.

Rassenti, S.J., Reynolds, S.S., and Smith, V.L. (1994) "Cotenancy and Competition in an Experimental Market for Natural Gas Pipeline Networks," *Economic Theory*, 4: 41–64.

Rassenti, S.J., Smith, V.L., and Wilson, B.J. (2003) "Controlling Market Power and Price Spikes in Electricity Markets: Demand-Side Bidding," *Proceedings of the National Academy of Science*, 100: 2998–3003.

Reeder, M. (2006) "Want to Put an End to Capacity Markets? Think Real-Time Pricing," *Electricity Journal*, 19(6): 38–48.

Reiss, P.C. and White, M.W. (2003) *Demand and Pricing in Electricity Markets: Evidence from San Diego During California's Energy Crisis*, NBER Working Paper No. 9986, Online. Available at www.nber.org/papers/w9986 (accessed September 6, 2007).

Romer, P. (1990) "Endogenous Technological Change," *Journal of Political Economy*, 98: S71–S102.

Rose, N. and Joskow, P. (1990) "The Diffusion of New Technologies: Evidence From The Electric Utility Industry," *Rand Journal of Economics*, 21(2): 354–373.

Salies, E., Kiesling, L., and Giberson, M. (2007) "L'électricité est-elle un bien public?," *Revue de l'Observatoire Francais des Conjonctures Economiques*, 101: 135–152.

Sampson, R. (2004) "Organizational Choice in R&D Alliances: Knowledge-Based and Transaction Cost Perspectives," *Managerial and Decision Economics*, 25: 421–436.

Samuelson, P.A. (1954) "The Pure Theory of Public Expenditure," *Review of Economics and Statistics*, 36: 387–398.

Sappington, D. (1980) "Strategic Firm Behavior under a Dynamic Regulatory Adjustment Process," *The Bell Journal of Economics*, 11(1): 360–372.

Schelling, T. (1978) *Micromotives and Macrobehavior*, New York: W.W. Norton.

Schmalensee, R. (1989) "Good Regulatory Regimes," *Rand Journal of Economics*, 20(3): 417–436.

Schubert, E., Hurlburt, D., Adib, P., and Oren, S. (2006) "The Texas Energy-Only Resource Adequacy Mechanism," *Electricity Journal*, 19(10): 39–49.

Schweppe, F.C., Caramanis, M.C., Tabor, R.D., and Bohm, R.E. (1988) *Spot Pricing of Electricity*, Boston: The Kluwer Press.

Sener, A. and Kimball, S. (2007) "Reviewing Progress in PJM's Capacity Market Structure via the New Reliability Pricing Model," *Electricity Journal*, 20(10): 40–53.

Shy, O. (2001) *The Economics of Network Industries*, Cambridge: Cambridge University Press.

Simon, H. (1996) *The Sciences of the Artificial*, 3rd edition, Cambridge, MA: MIT Press.

Smith, A. (1776; 1976) *An Enquiry Into the Nature and Causes of the Wealth of Nations*, Indianapolis: Liberty Fund Press.

Smith, V. (2007) *Rationality in Economics: Constructivist and Ecological Forms*, Cambridge: Cambridge University Press.

Smith, V. and Kiesling, L. (2003) "Demand, Not Supply," *Wall Street Journal*, August 20, 2003.

Smith, V. and Kiesling, L. (2005) "A Market-Based Model for ISO-Sponsored Demand Response Programs," *Center for the Advancement of Energy Markets/Distributed Energy Financial Group Examination of Demand Response Programs at the ISO Level*.

Spence, M. (1975) "Monopoly, Quality and Regulation," *Bell Journal of Economics*, 6(2): 417–429.

Standard & Poor's "Electric Utilities," in Bossong-Martines, E.M. (ed.) (2006) *Standard & Poor's Industry Surveys*, New York: McGraw-Hill.

Steiner, P. (1957) "Peak Loads and Efficient Pricing," *Quarterly Journal of Economics*, 71: 585–610.

Stigler, G. (1971) "The Theory of Economic Regulation," *Bell Journal of Economics and Management Science*, 3: 3–21.

Stoft, S. (2002) *Power System Economics*, New Jersey: IEEE Press.

Summit Blue ESPP 2003 Review Report (2004), Available at www.energycooperative. org/pdf/ESPP-Final-Report.pdf (accessed September 6, 2007).

Summit Blue ESPP 2004 Review Report (2005), Available at www.energycooperative. org/pdf/ESPP-2004-Evaluation-Final-Report.pdf (accessed September 6, 2007).

Summit Blue ESPP 2005 Review Report (2006), Available at www.energycooperative. org/pdf/ESPP-Evaluation-Final-Report-2005.pdf (accessed September 6, 2007).

Sutherland, R. and Treadway, N. (2005) *Resource Adequacy and the Cost of Reliability: The Impact of Alternative Policy Approaches on Customers and Electric Market Participants*. CAEM-DEFG Resource Adequacy Project Final Report.

Sweeney, J. (2002) *The California Electricity Crisis*, Palo Alto: Hoover Institution Press.

Thisse, J.F. and Norman, G. (eds) (1994) *The Economics of Product Differentiation. Volume 1. Elgar Reference Collection. International Library of Critical Writings in Economics, No. 37*, Aldershot, U.K.: Elgar.

Tirole, J. (1988) *The Theory of Industrial Organization*, Cambridge: MIT Press.

U.S.–Canada Power System Outage Task Force (2004) *Final Report*, Online. Available at https://reports.energy.gov (accessed September 6, 2007).

Vogelsang, I. and Finsinger, J. (1979) "A Regulatory Adjustment Process for Optimal Pricing by Multiproduct Monopoly Firms," *Bell Journal of Economics*, 10(1): 157–171.

Walter, B., Fulton, F. and Mahnovski, S. (2004) *Estimating the Benefits of the GridWise Initiative: Phase I Report*, Rand Science and Technology for the Pacific Northwest National Laboratory.

Westfield, F. (1970) "Innovation and Natural Monopoly Regulation," in William Capron (ed.) *Technological Change in Regulated Industries*, Washington, DC: The Brookings Institution.

Williamson, O. (1975) *Markets and Hierarchies: Analysis and Antitrust Implications*, New York: Free Press.

Williamson, O. (1976) "Franchise Bidding for Natural Monopolies – In General and with Respect to CATV," *Bell Journal of Economics*, 7(1): 73–104.

Williamson, O. (1985) *The Economic Institutions of Capitalism*, New York: Free Press.

Wilson, R. (2002) "Architecture of Power Markets," *Econometrica*, 70(4): 1299–1340.

Winston, C. (ed.) (2000) *Deregulation of Network Industries: What's Next?* Washington, DC: American Enterprise Institute Press.

Woodley, J. (2003) "Volatility, Capacity and Reliability," presented to the Harvard Electricity Policy Group, 21 May 2003. Online. Available at www.ksg.harvard.edu/hepg/Papers/Woodley_capacity.reliability_5–21–03.pdf.

Index